MW01617925

WASHINGTON

PORTRAIT OF A CITY

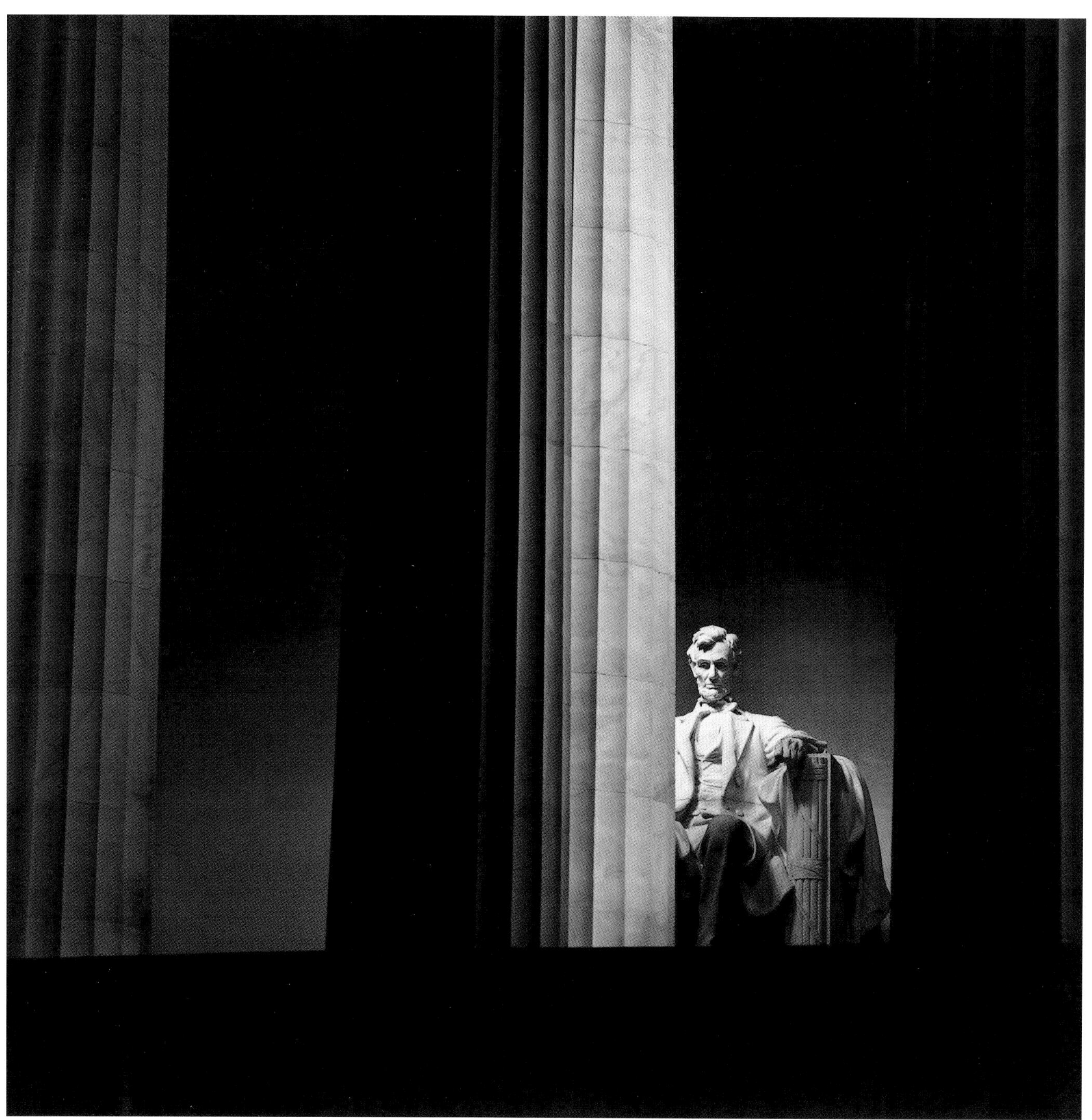

WASHINGTON

PORTRAIT OF A CITY

Photography by George Kousoulas

Introduction by Daniel Patrick Moynihan

NORFLEET PRESS
New York

Published by
NORFLEET PRESS INC.
1133 Broadway
New York, N.Y. 10010
212 633-2940
jgtnor@aol.com

FIRST EDITION

LIBRARY OF CONGRESS CATALOGING-IN-PUBLICATION DATA
Kousoulas, George W.
Washington : portrait of a city / photography by George Kousoulas ; introduction by Daniel Patrick Moynihan.
p. cm.
Includes bibliographical references.
ISBN 0-9649934-2-2
1. Architectural photography—Washington (D.C.) 2. Washington (D.C.)—Buildings, structures, etc.—Pictorial works. 3. Washington (D.C.)—Pictorial works. I. Moynihan, Daniel P. (Daniel Patrick), 1927– II. Title.
TR659 .K68 2001
779'.4753'092—dc21 2001030643

Editorial consultant and author of this book's "Washington Reference": Christopher Weeks

Director & Publisher: John Graham Tucker
Designer: Bruce Campbell
Copy editor: Maya Khazarian Lea

Printed and bound in Italy

Frontispiece: Lincoln Memorial

CONTENTS

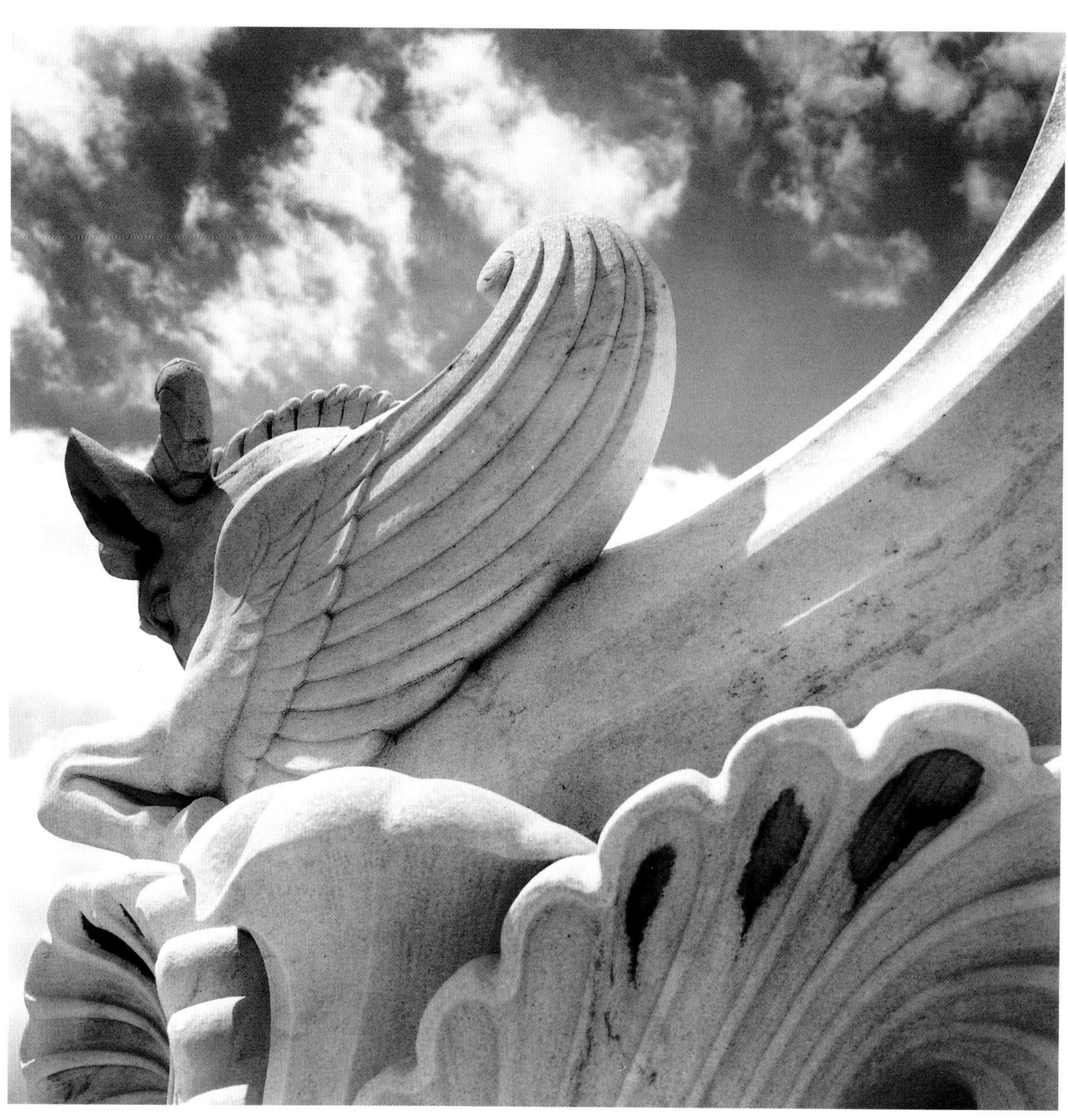

INTRODUCTION

An intriguing paradox of the American experiment, as we persist in calling it, is our insistence that our government is based on those of the classical republics, and equal insistence that ours is a wholly "New Order of the Ages," as proclaimed in Latin on the Great Seal of the United States. The Founders of this Nation had few illusions about the ancient governments of Greece and Rome. Reliance on the virtue of man, wrote James Madison, had produced a "fugitive and turbulent existence." Yet one cannot doubt the dream of those who began anew in this land that the mind of man might yet devise a republican government that would endure.

The experiment goes on, not least in Washington, our Nation's capital, a wholly new city designed to facilitate and celebrate this republic and whose character is illustrated with Greek and Roman architectural forms. In this regard there have been good times and, well, less good, but rarely has a conception of urban design held such power for so long.

The location of the capital was settled on or about the evening of June 20, 1790. Thomas Jefferson, the Secretary of State, and Alexander Hamilton, the Secretary of the Treasury, met over dinner in New York City and reached one of the momentous agreements of American political history. The Federal government would assume the debt incurred by the (mostly northern) States during the Revolutionary War. In return, the capital would move south to the banks of the Potomac River.

The Compromise of 1790, as historians refer to the Jefferson-Hamilton deal, moved the seat of government from the otherwise natural choice, New York, the soon-to-be largest city in the country, the center of trade and commerce, to a swamp which turned malarial in April. This was a separation of powers; a check upon regional influence, similar in its way to that between the executive and the legislature in the Constitution. That, after all, had been the means by which the Founders would disassociate this modern Republic from the ancient ones. It is what marks the American Constitution as a signal event in human history.

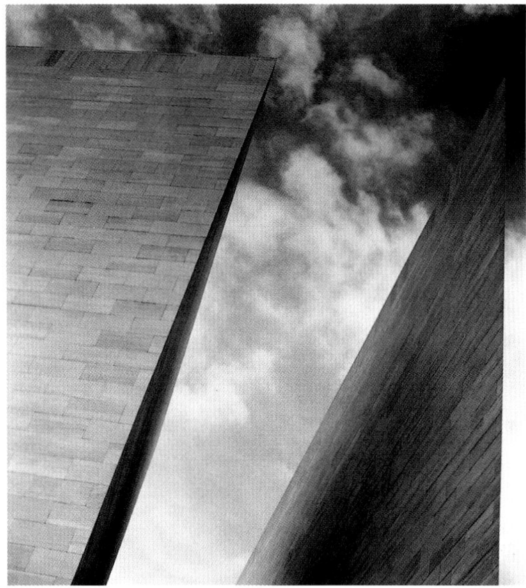

This "new science of politics," as the Founders called it, would be represented in the capital. Major Charles Pierre L'Enfant—engineer, artist, soldier—was awarded the commission for the city's design. His Baroque plan of 1791, with its Versailles-inspired vistas, was borrowed from the capitals of Europe, but was also a kind of diagram of the Constitution. The legislative branch (assumed to be dominant) was given the area's highest elevation, Jenkins Hill, described by L'Enfant as a "pedestal waiting for a monument." Soon, construction began there on the Capitol, the first architectural expression by the new government.

Another, smaller hill, just over a mile from the Capitol, was chosen to represent the executive. There would sit not a monarch's palace, but a "President's House," simple in ornamentation, befitting the office of one elected by the citizenry to serve the republic. Irish architect James Hoban's modest design made a great home; with the addition of Benjamin Latrobe's south portico in 1824, the White House, as it would be called, became a splendid symbol of the Presidency.

Joining the Capitol and the White House was a ceremonial avenue named for Pennsylvania, the state in which independence had been first declared. This symbolized the separate but unified branches of the American government. L'Enfant had wanted academies, playhouses, and rooms for assembly here. In 1800, however, when the Federal government formally arrived in the city, Pennsylvania Avenue was just a marsh. Gradually, it was transformed into the lively thoroughfare envisioned by L'Enfant. Jefferson planted Lombardy poplars which grew and gave it form.

Just south of Pennsylvania Avenue, extending due west from the Capitol toward the Potomac, was a great tree-lined promenade, four hundred feet in width. Jefferson called this a "public walk"; later it would be "the Mall." Diplomatic residences were to line its sides. For its eastern end, L'Enfant proposed a sculpture, "Liberty Hailing Nature Out of its Slumber"; for the other end, on axis with the White House and the Capitol, was to be a bronze equestrian statue of George Washington.

Pennsylvania Avenue and the Mall were the core of the L'Enfant plan. The aspirations of the new age and the new Nation were reflected here in the rational geometry, bold scale, and in the buildings—classically derived yet distinct; their ancient heritage was combined with the best of the innovation and energy of the New World and thus became American.

Throughout the rest of the city, avenues named for the other States radiated from the Capitol and the White House (in an expression of the Federal-State balance) to intersect circles and squares around which would form neighborhoods reflecting the differing tastes and styles of the Union. A conventional street grid was superimposed, creating the city's ubiquitous triangular-shaped city blocks.

All would not be completed right away. Like most cities, Washington grew in fits and starts. But as with the new government, the city was founded on a plan, based upon reason, from which it could grow. It was not without inconsistency (the judicial branch, for instance, was not included), nor was it always closely followed. Indeed, often during the nineteenth century the L'Enfant plan was ignored.

One who honored its spirit better than most was architect Robert Mills. Arriving in Washington in 1829, Mills reveled in the then-flourishing classical revival. Like his mentors, Jefferson and Latrobe, Mills believed neoclassicism's foundation in natural law was ideal for the expression of American democracy. He built the Post Office (now the Tariff Building) and the Patent Office (now the National Museum of American Art and the National Portrait Gallery), bringing an order and formality to Washington's early streetscape.

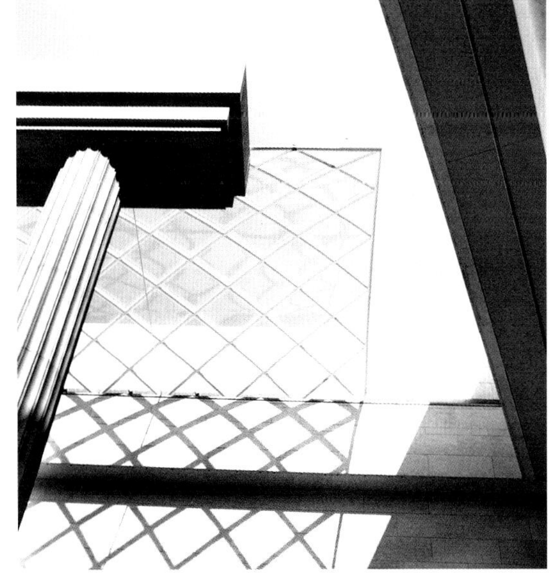

Mills was also awarded the commission to build the monument honoring George Washington. Here, however, he broke from L'Enfant. Rather than the monumental equestrian statue originally proposed, Mills would build an obelisk surrounded by a massive colonnaded

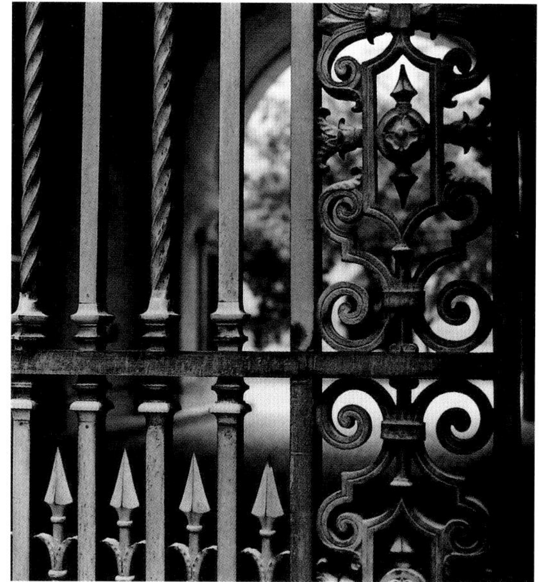

Pantheon—until that is, the sandy clay sediment of the Mall proved an inadequate foundation. Hearings followed. Funds dried up. The Pantheon, it was decided, would be scrapped and the obelisk, now derided by Mills as looking like "a stalk of asparagus," moved off-axis with the Capitol and the White House. Nevertheless, in 1884, the Washington Monument was at last completed and was the tallest structure in the world.

Another building by Mills has caused even more lasting controversy—the Treasury Building. President Andrew Jackson demanded that it be built immediately adjacent to the White House. This had the (presumably) unintended consequence of obstructing direct passage to the Capitol, spoiling the symbolic integrity of L'Enfant's most significant vista. Many have argued, however, that the Treasury's weight and scale provide a needed visual terminus for the Pennsylvania Avenue's western end.

By the time the Treasury Building was completed in 1869, neoclassicism in Washington had fallen out of fashion. The eclectic tastes of the Victorians were emerging as white stone and marble were swapped for red brick and sandstone. Witness James Renwick's turreted castle on the Mall—the Smithsonian Institution—begun in 1849 to the indignation of classicists ever since. Or the original Corcoran Gallery (also by Renwick) designed in the Second Empire style; the Romanesque Old Post Office Building by Willoughby Edbrooke; or Montgomery Meigs' Italian Renaissance Pension Building, which contains perhaps the greatest interior space in town.

Indeed, much of great splendor was built in Washington in the latter half of the nineteenth century but, again, little was done to maintain L'Enfant's original plan. The Civil War had tested the plan's very premise—the Constitution. Indeed, at century's close the core of the plan, the Mall, remained pretty much as it had since 1865. Old soldiers' barracks still littered what had become a rambling, loosely kept

English garden with a noisy, smokey train depot in the middle.

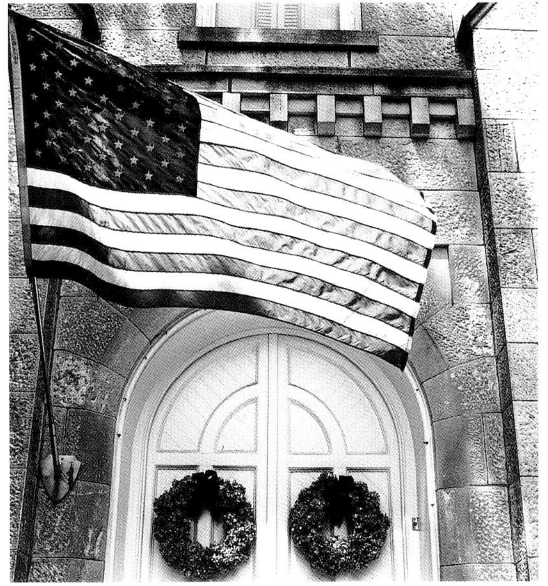

Then, in 1900, inspired by the centennial celebration of the Federal City's establishment, the Columbian Exhibition of 1893 and all the enthusiasm of the Progressive Era, a commission was established by Senator James McMillan, the Chairman of the Senate Committee on the District of Columbia. Its purpose was to correct the half-century of neglect by returning to and expanding L'Enfant's vision. The greatest architects, planners, and sculptors of the Nation were assembled—Charles Follen McKim, Frederick Law Olmstead, Jr., Augustus Saint-Gaudens, and Daniel H. Burnham, who admonished, "Make no little plans; they have no magic to stir men's blood."

Their proposal, known as the McMillan Plan, was anything but little. The critic Benjamin Forgey has written that it was "as ambitious in its reach as L'Enfant's brilliant original." They cleared off the Mall, tore down its train depot and reestablished the Mall's regular geometry with public buildings and rows of elms along the lengths of its sides. Plans were laid for the Lincoln Memorial. Burnham designed a new train depot, Union Station, featuring centurions sculpted by Augustus Saint-Gaudens' brother (Louis Saint-Gaudens) for a site on Columbus Circle, near the Capitol. Olmstead enhanced the Capitol grounds and a statue of General Ulysses S. Grant on horseback went up at the eastern end of the Mall, second only in size to that of *Vittorio Emanuele* in Rome. A great city was again underway.

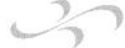

Alas, Pennsylvania Avenue languished. It, too, had encountered little change since the Civil War. Little *good* change, that is. Now it was known as "Murder Bay." In 1925, President Calvin Coolidge proposed the creation of the Federal Triangle, giving the area between the Avenue and the Mall over to municipal building. Congress responded with the Public Buildings Act of 1926. Secretary of the Treasury Andrew W. Mellon took on the job, intent on erecting "buildings of the highest

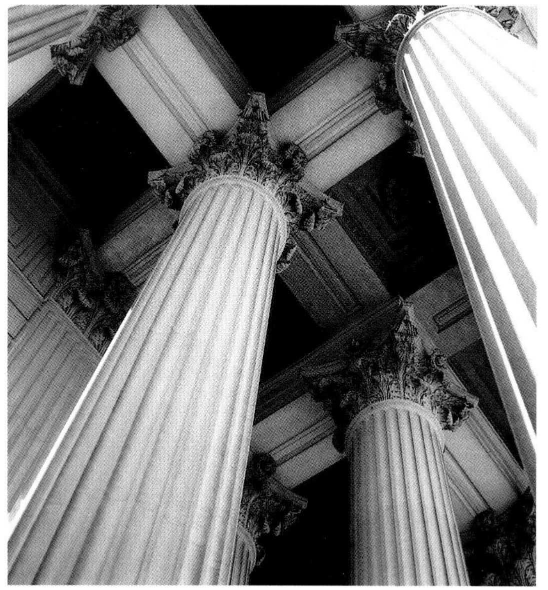

possible character." The south side of Pennsylvania Avenue was cleared, construction began, but then the Great Depression came, and all stopped. A wretched parking lot was left amidst a Beaux-Arts cityscape. The Avenue remained unfinished.

This was all too apparent in January 1961, as the new President, John F. Kennedy, made his way in the inaugural parade from the Capitol to the White House. Actually *looking* at downtown Washington for what was probably the first time in his life, Kennedy saw the state of Pennsylvania Avenue and it bothered him. Later that day he said as much to Arthur J. Goldberg, his Secretary of Labor, who seized the opportunity. In the informal manner of the time, a committee was formed to look into new Federal construction that included the idea of reviving Pennsylvania Avenue. Goldberg was named Chairman; I was asked to draft the recommendations.

We proposed in our report of June 1, 1962, that Pennsylvania Avenue should be "lively, friendly and inviting, as well as dignified and impressive." In short order, the President's Council on Pennsylvania Avenue, led by yet another great architect, Nathaniel Alexander Owings, was underway. Owings decided that there would be no new government buildings on the Avenue. He wanted hotels, restaurants, opera, trees, people—a "living downtown," as the term became. In a year and a half, a plan was developed and presented to the President.

Kennedy loved it. One of his last instructions before leaving for Dallas in November 1963 was to schedule a coffee with Congressional leaders to go over the plan. With his death, it became something that had to be done.

In the years that followed there came also a greater awareness of the city that sought to keep much of the old while adding much that was new. The Old Post Office is an example. Another, Union Station, once nearly lost, is again a grand gateway to the capital. Today, the barrel-vaulted and coffered stations of Washington's modern subway system recall Mills or Latrobe. And there's the new Thurgood Marshall Judiciary Building by Edward Larabee Barnes, described by Forgey as "an abstract variation of classicism."

We are beyond Greek and Roman now, yet the antiphony persists. As President Kennedy put it, recalling Pericles' evocation to the Athenians: "We do not imitate—for we are a model to others." Thus our committee's report to the President established "Guiding Principles for Federal Architecture." Among these was the recommendation that America's public buildings ought embody no official style but, rather, should represent "the finest contemporary architectural thought." This, too, endures.

On Pennsylvania Avenue, it endures in I.M. Pei's sculptural East Wing of the National Gallery; in Conklin & Rossant's Navy Memorial, which graces another of L'Enfant's vistas, this one down Eighth Street, between the National Archives and the Portrait Gallery; and in the last piece of the Federal Triangle, the Ronald Reagan Building and International Trade Center, by the partnership of Pei, Cobb & Freed. Its completion in 1998 brings, in a sense, a century of urban planning to a close.

In a larger sense, however, it goes on. That is to say, Washington goes on, in those who live and visit here, in those drawn to its building and monuments, drawn to the past, then going forward again, beginning anew.

Daniel Patrick Moynihan
Washington, D.C.

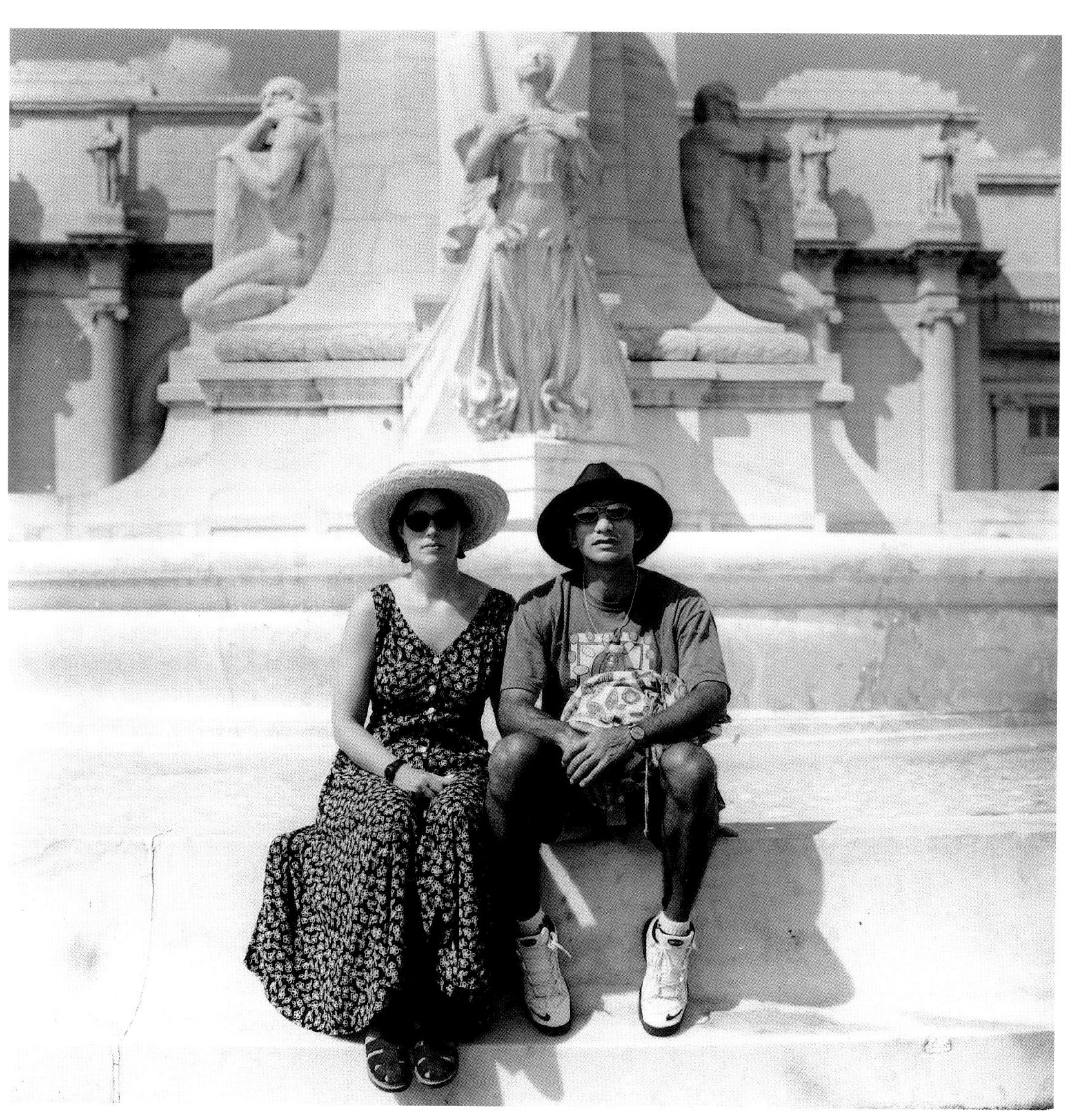

WASHINGTON

PORTRAIT OF A CITY

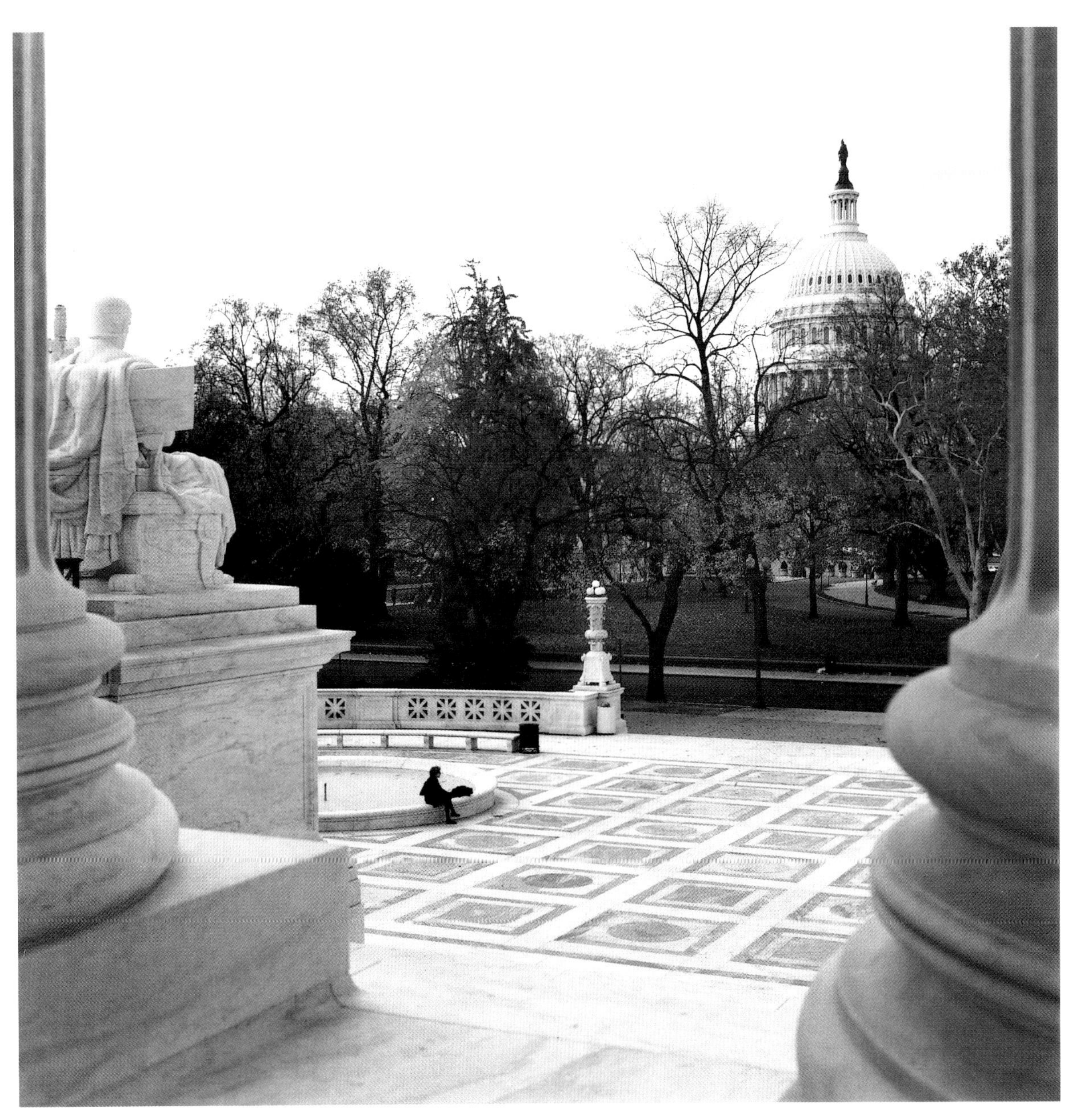

Plaza, Supreme Court Building

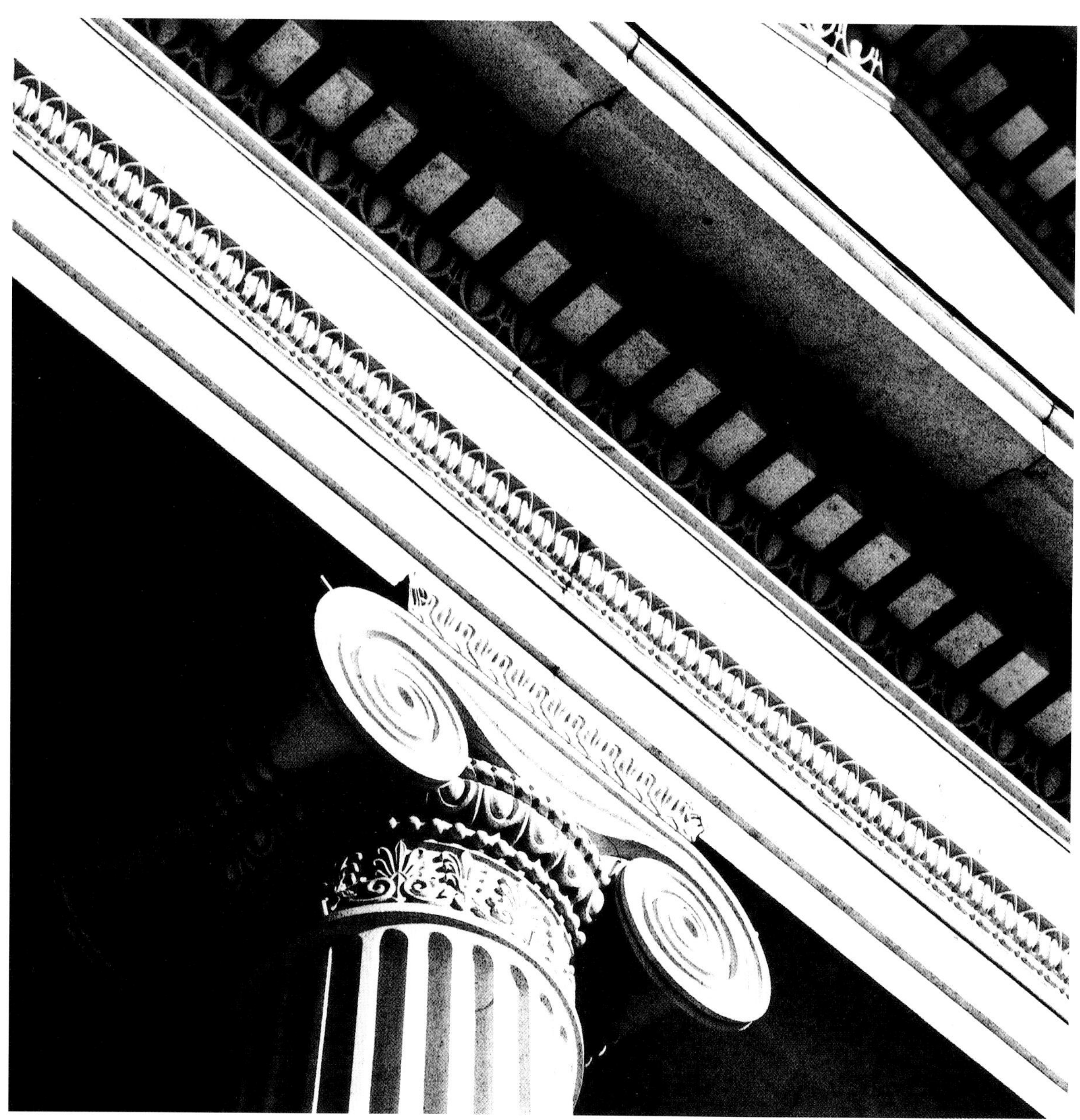

Detail, Treasury Building

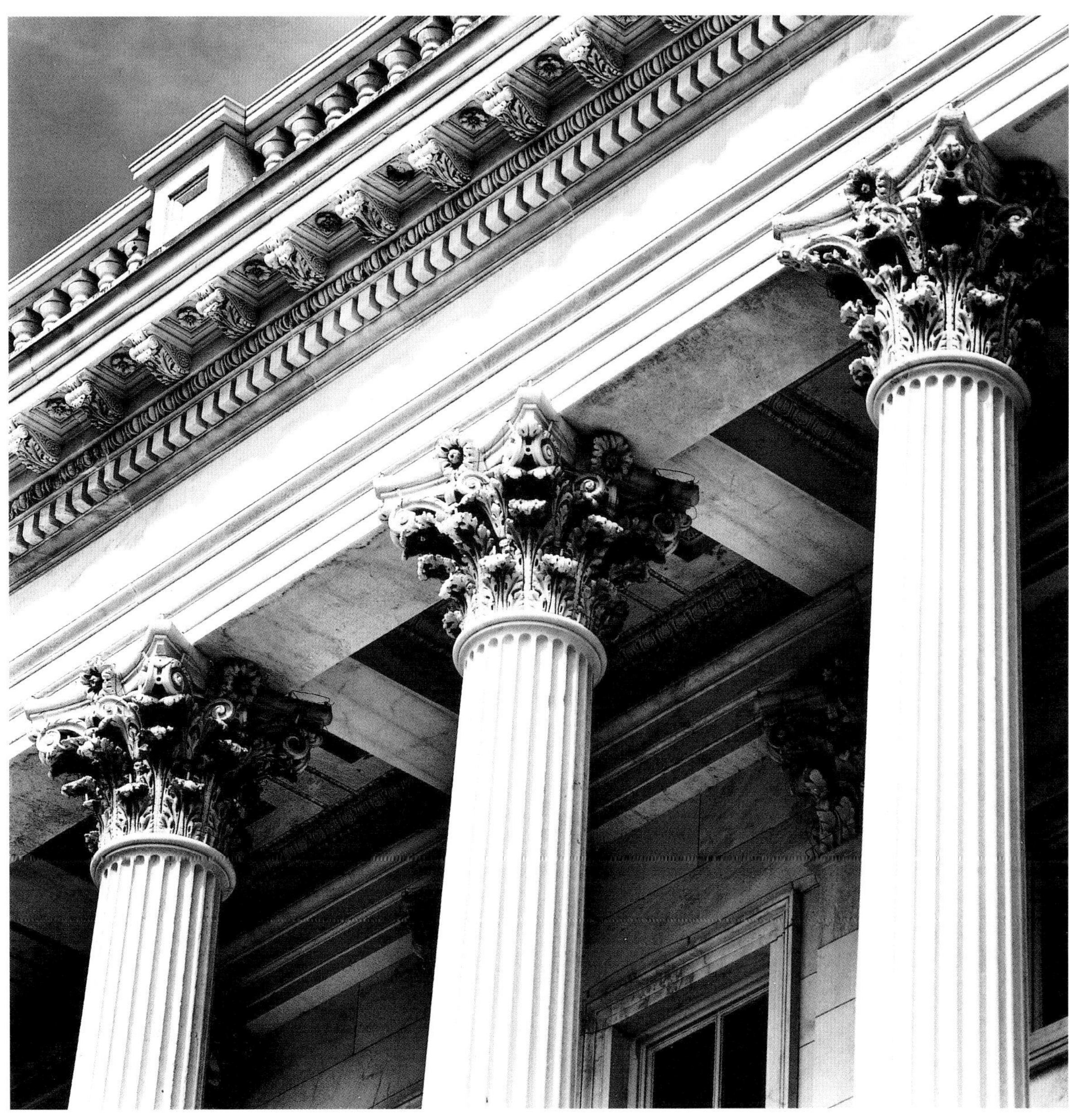

Senate wing, The Capitol

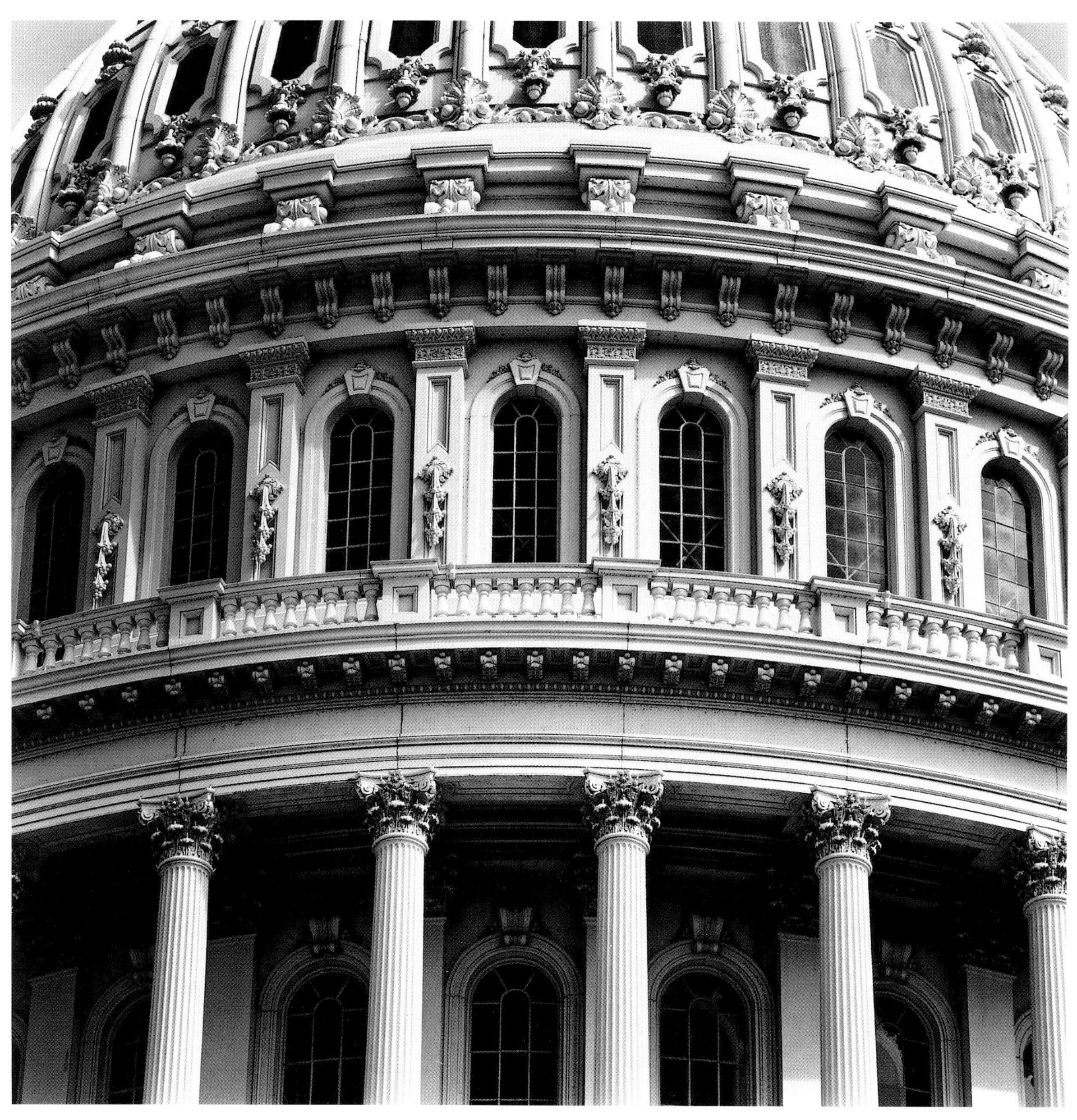

Capitol Dome

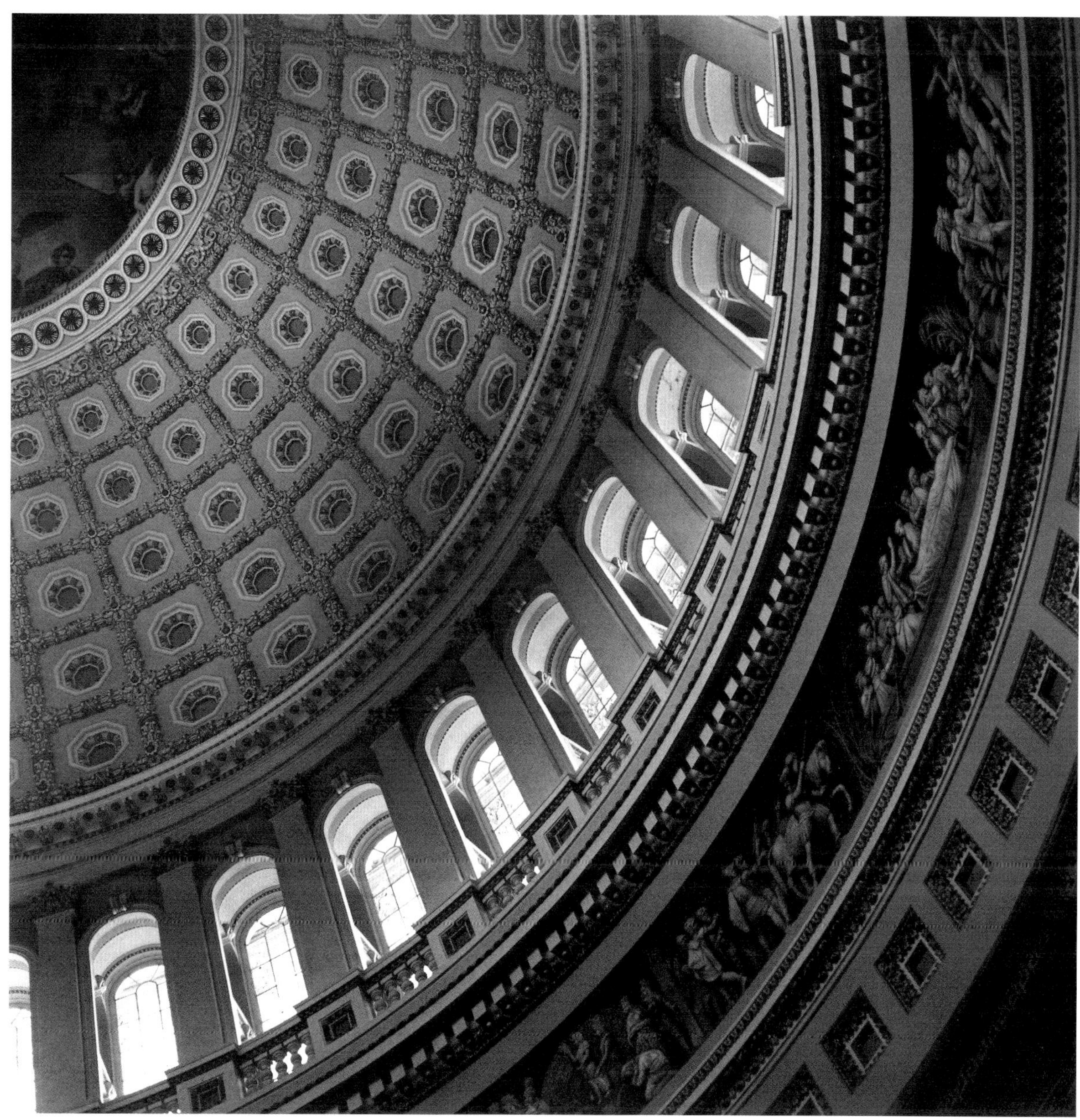

Capitol Dome

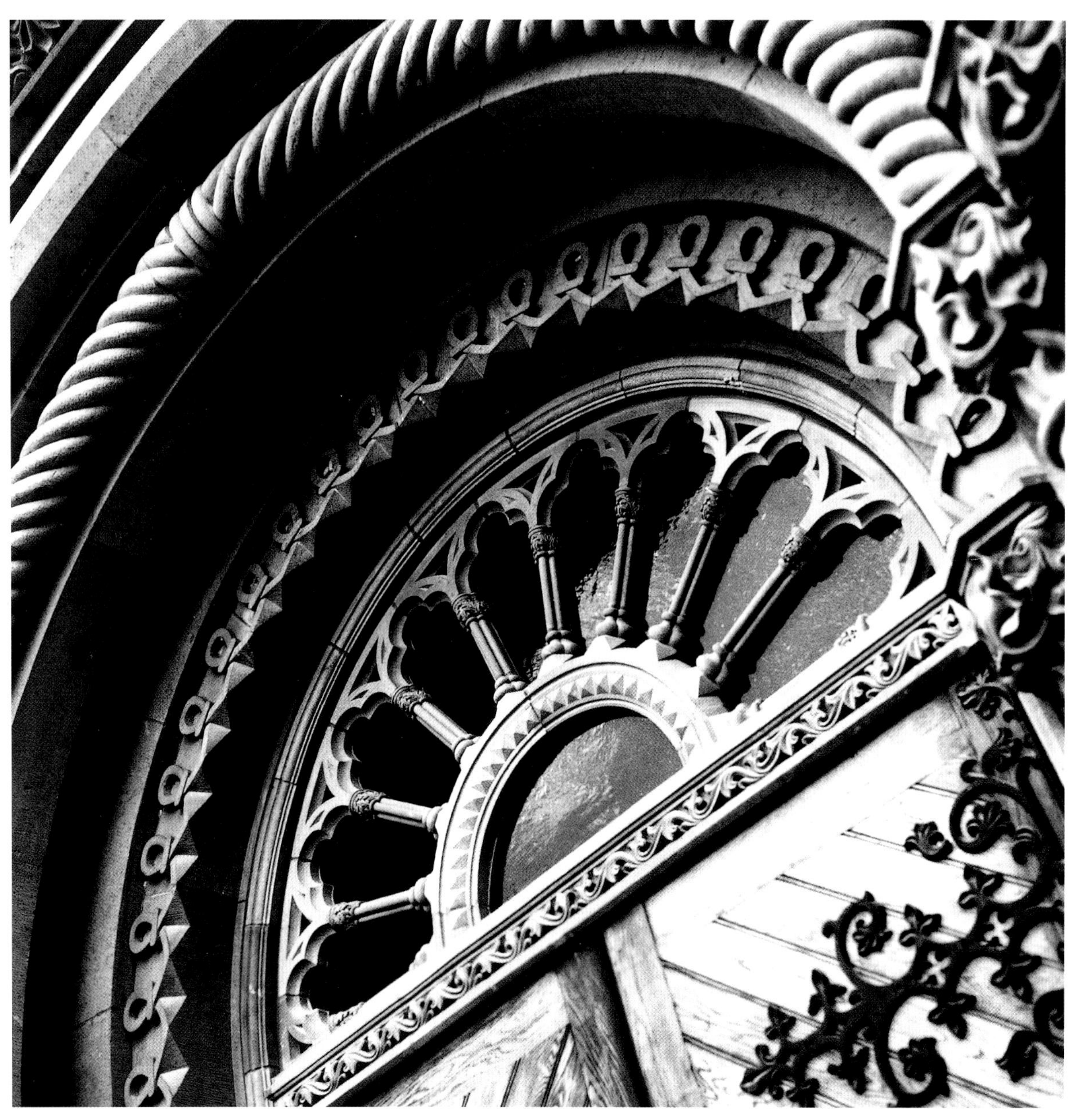

Smithsonian Building

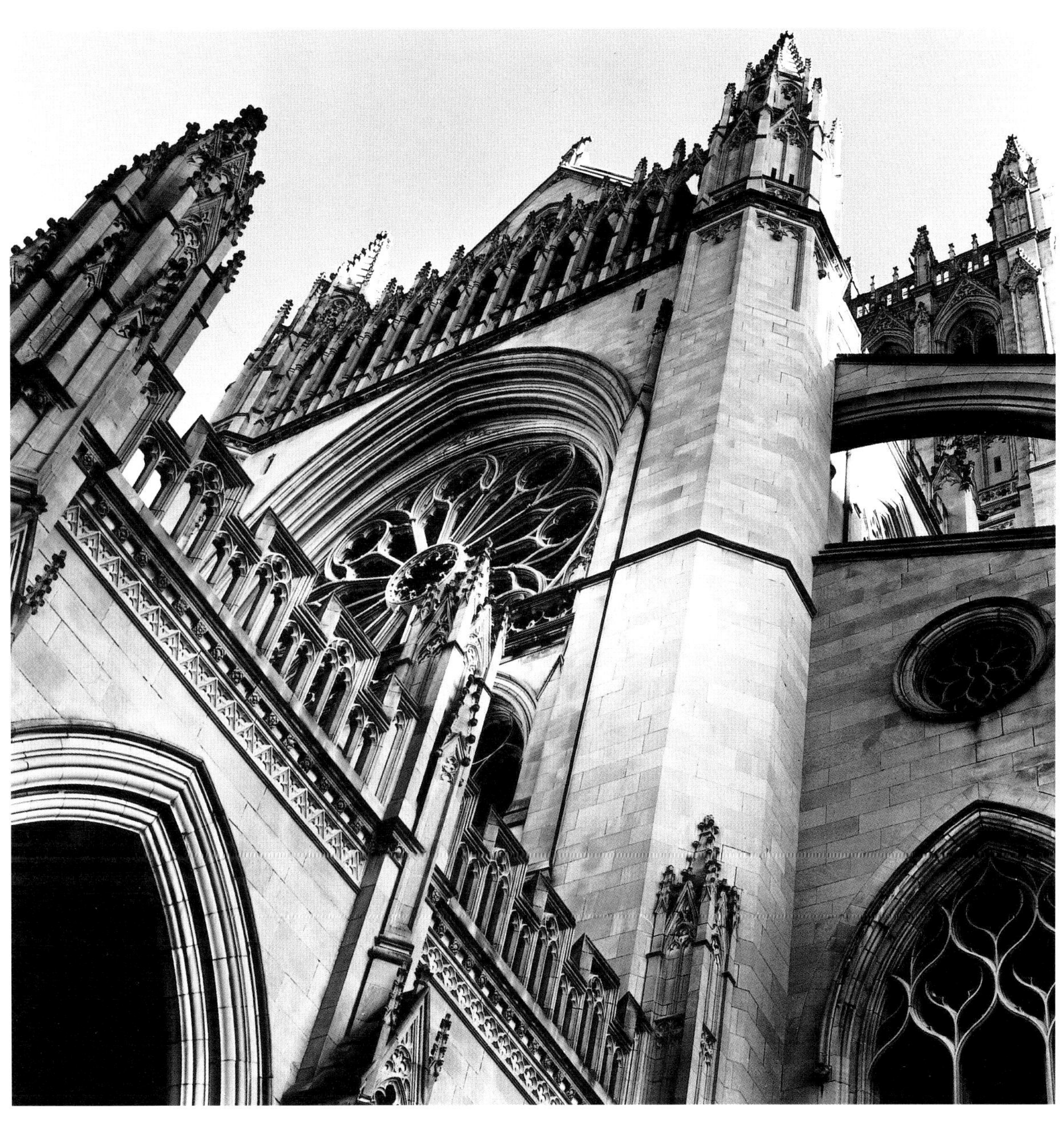

Washington National Cathedral

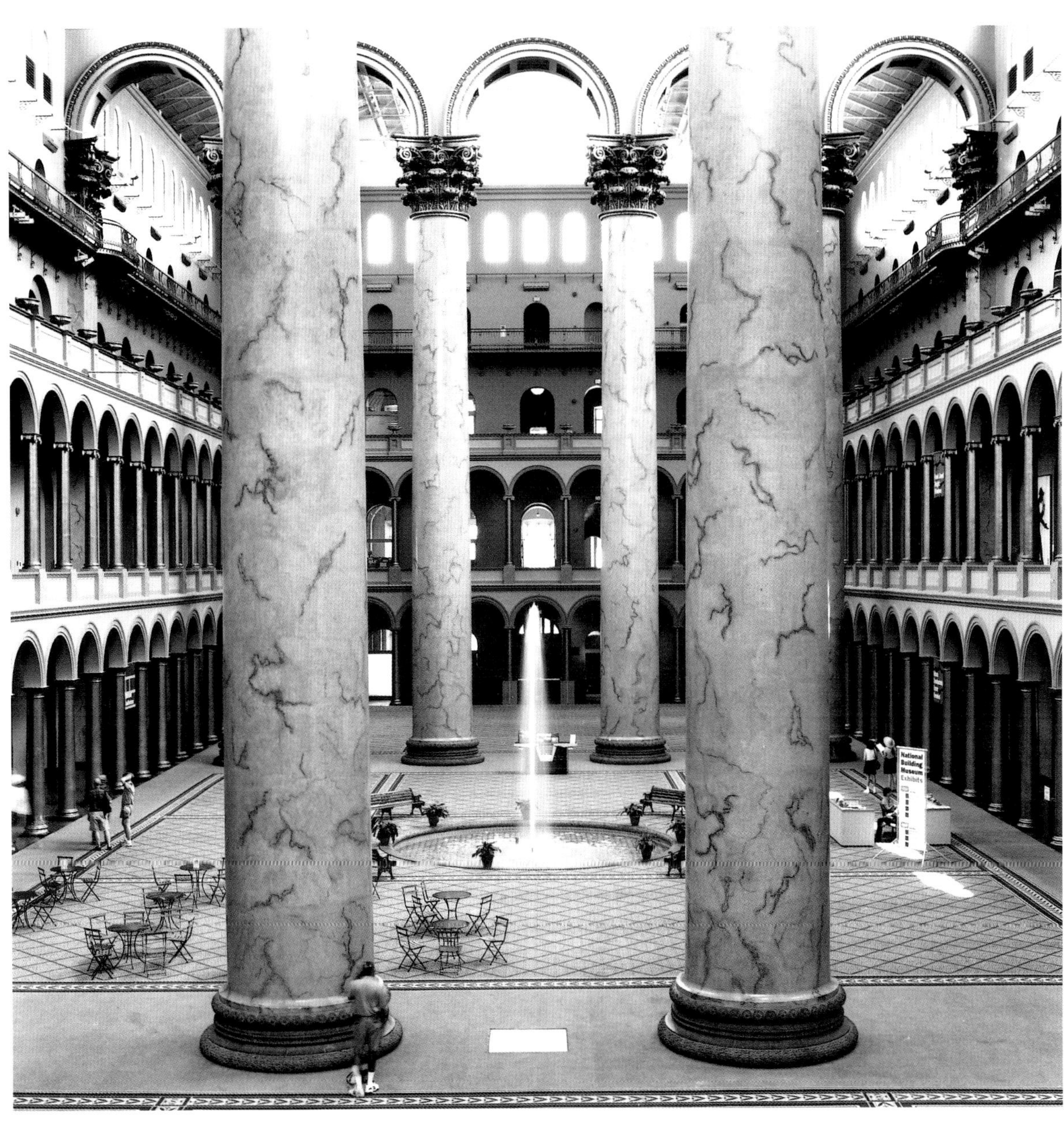

National Building Museum

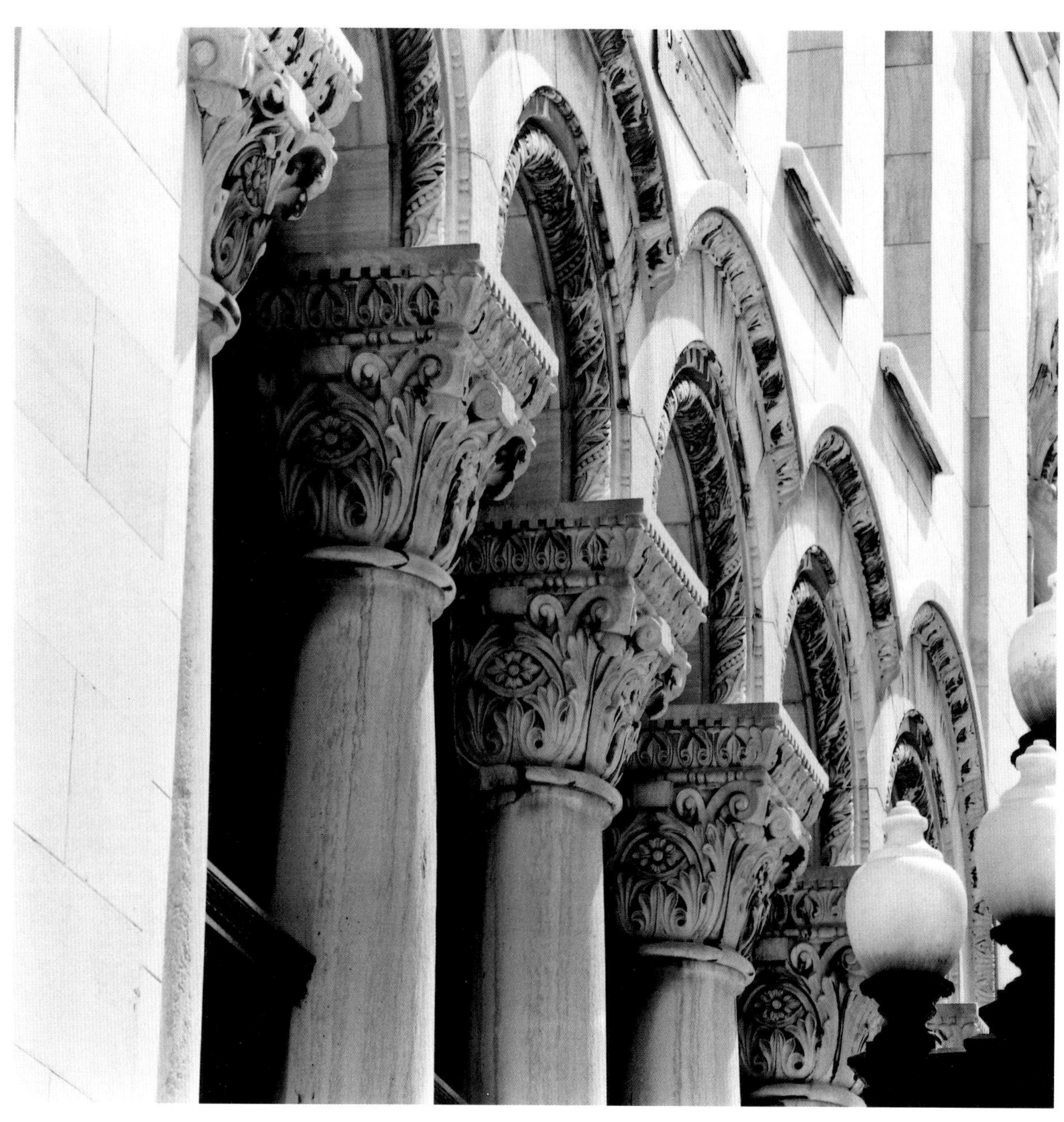

U.S. Soldiers' and Airmen's Home

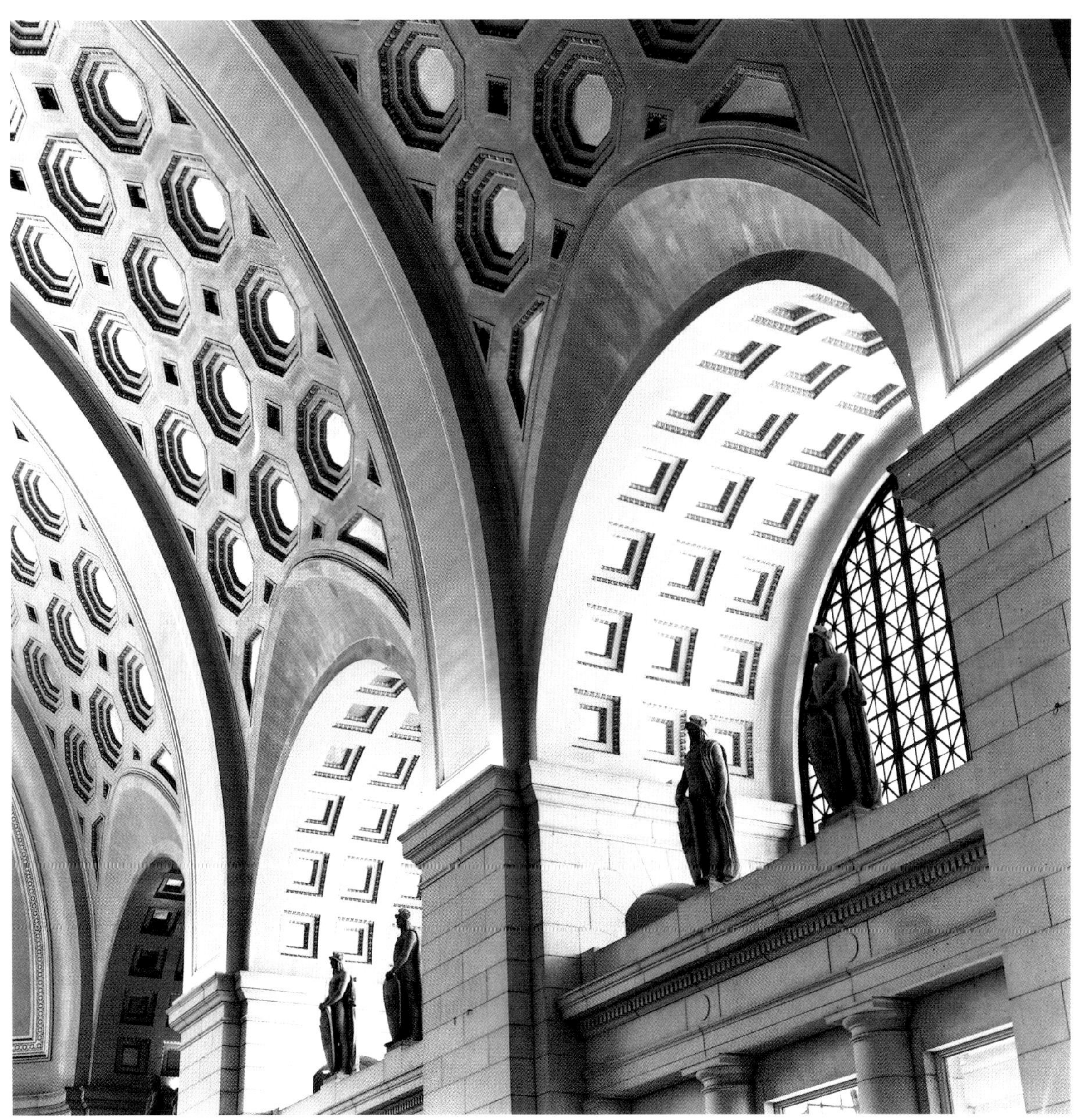

Union Station

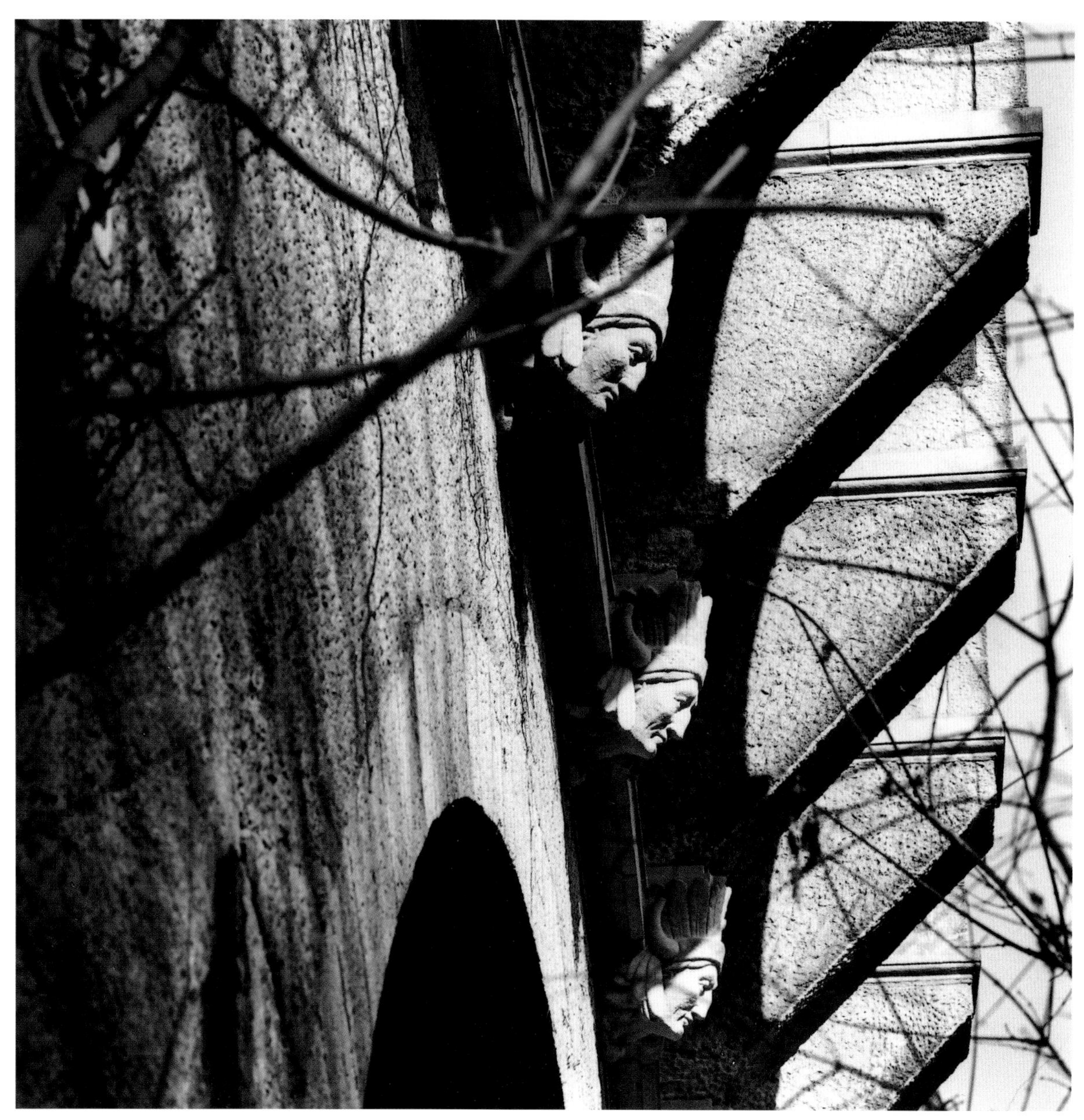

Buffalo Bridge

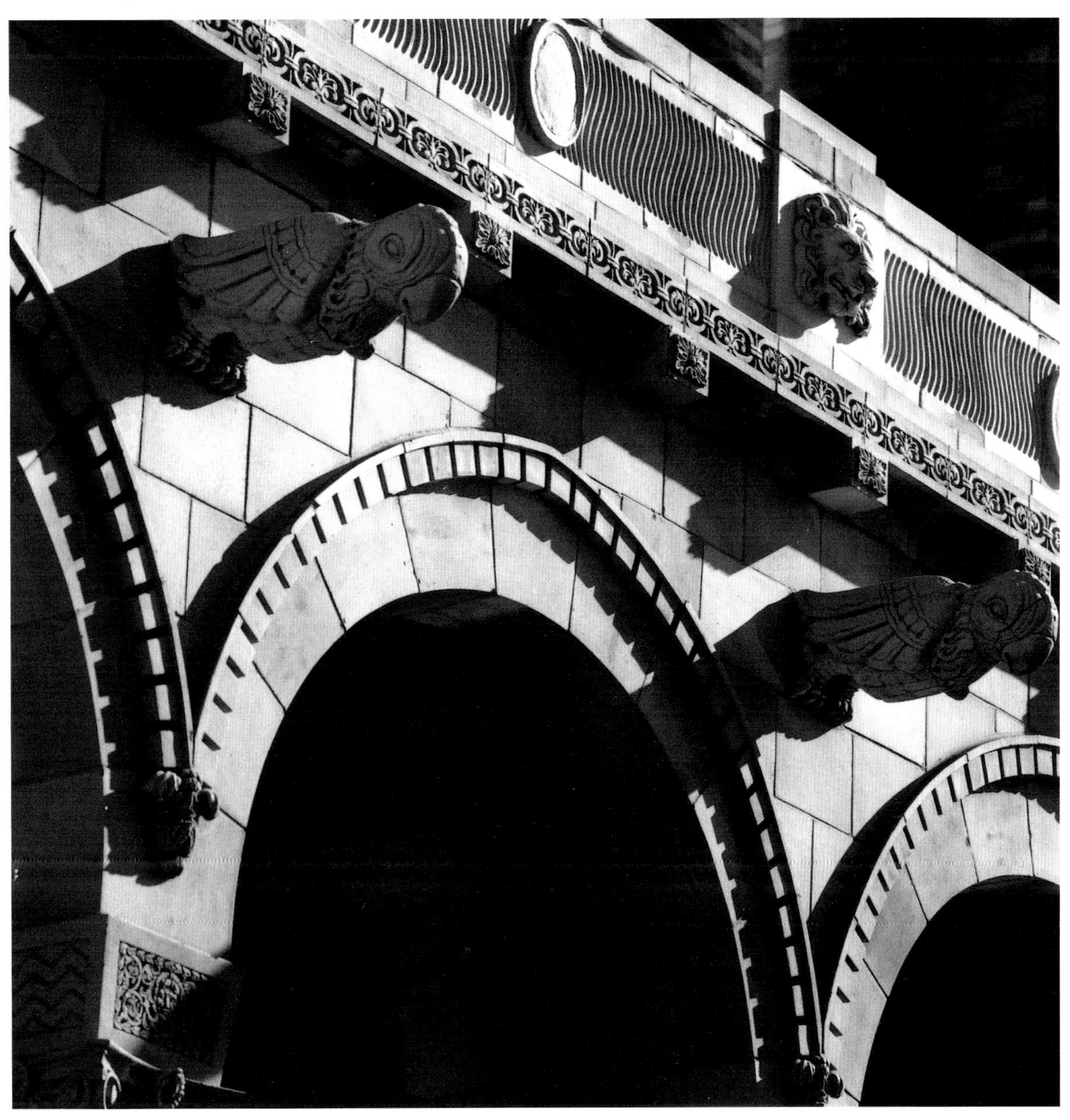

Apartment building, Connecticut Avenue

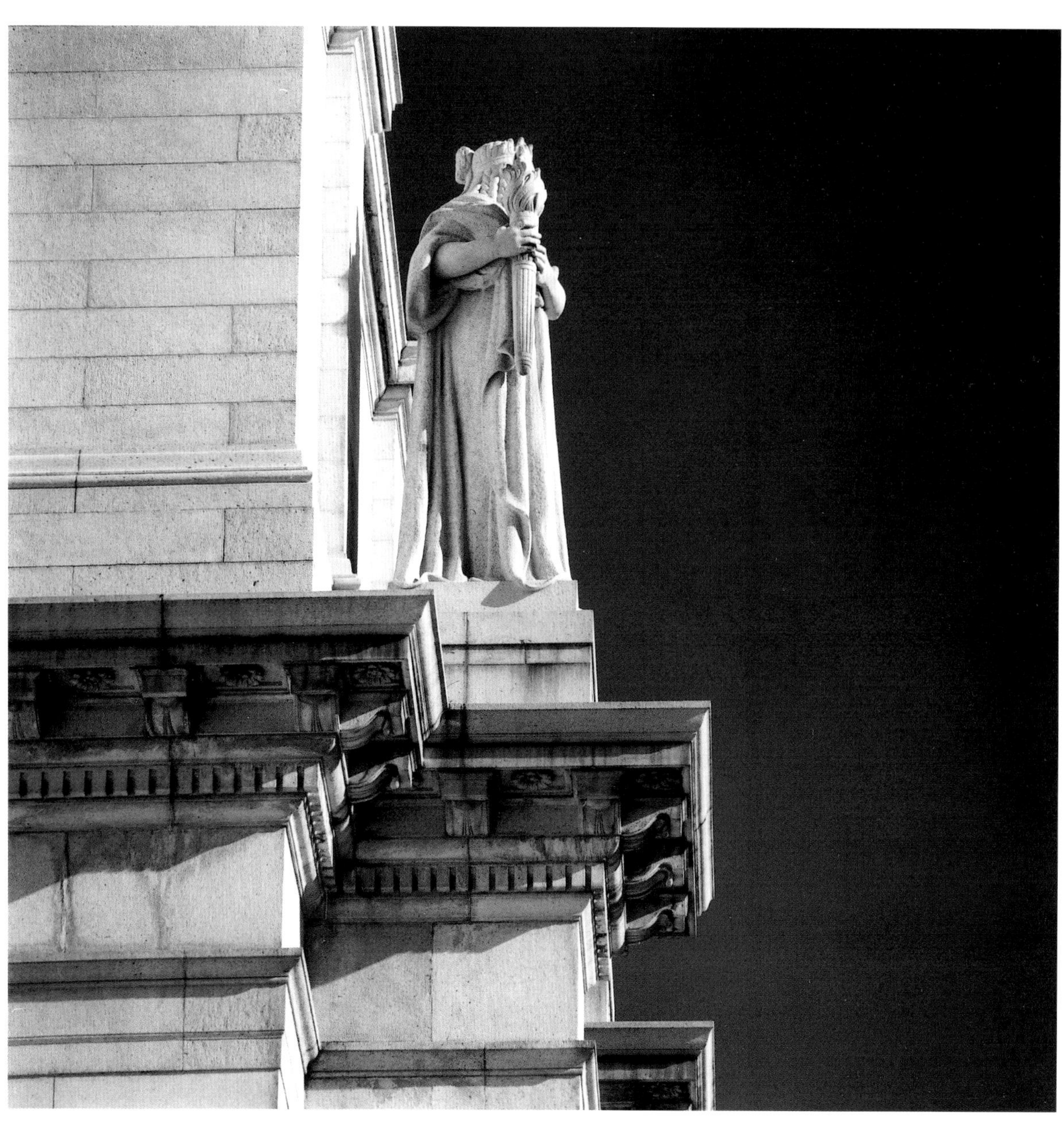

Union Station

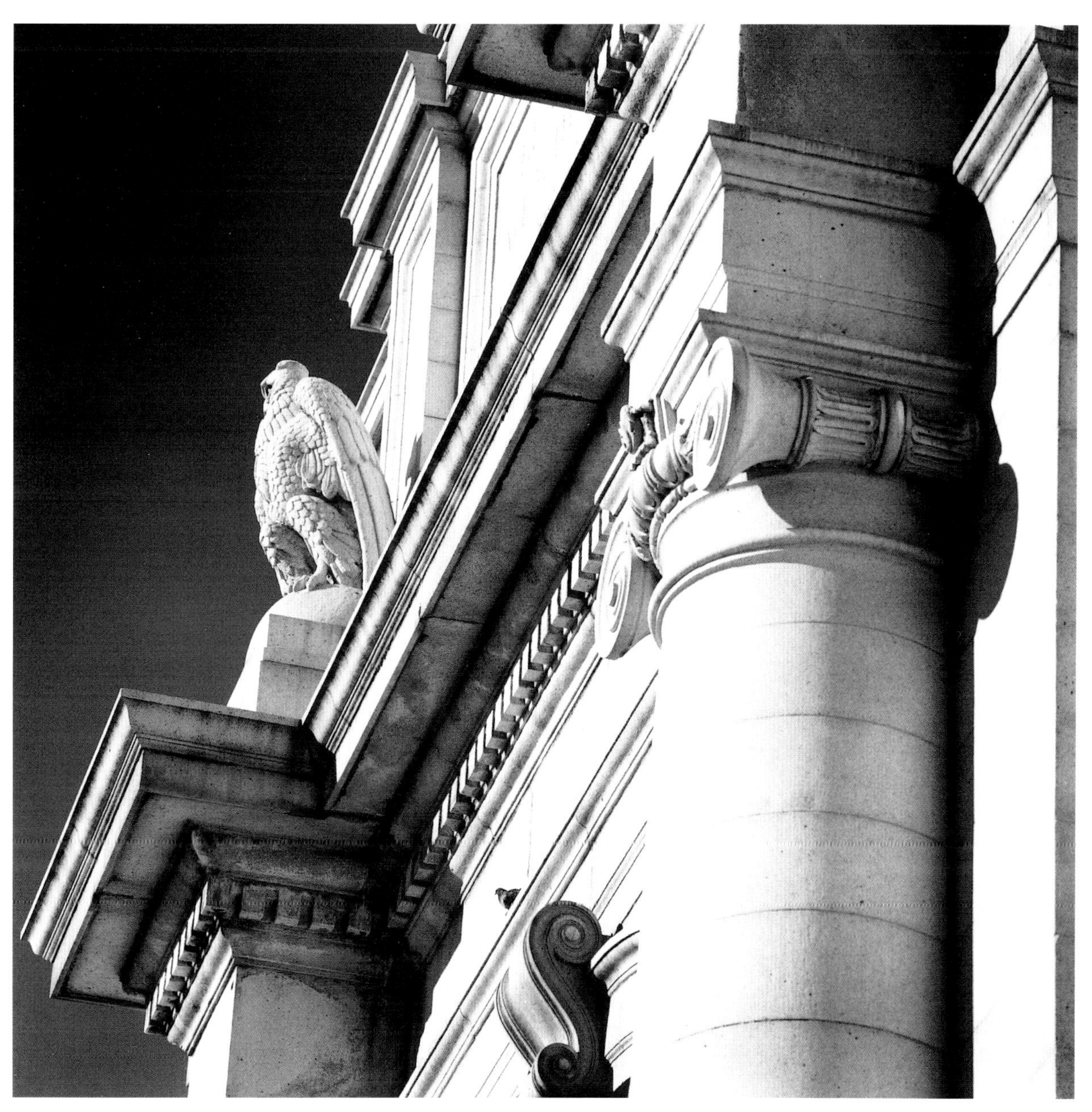

Union Station

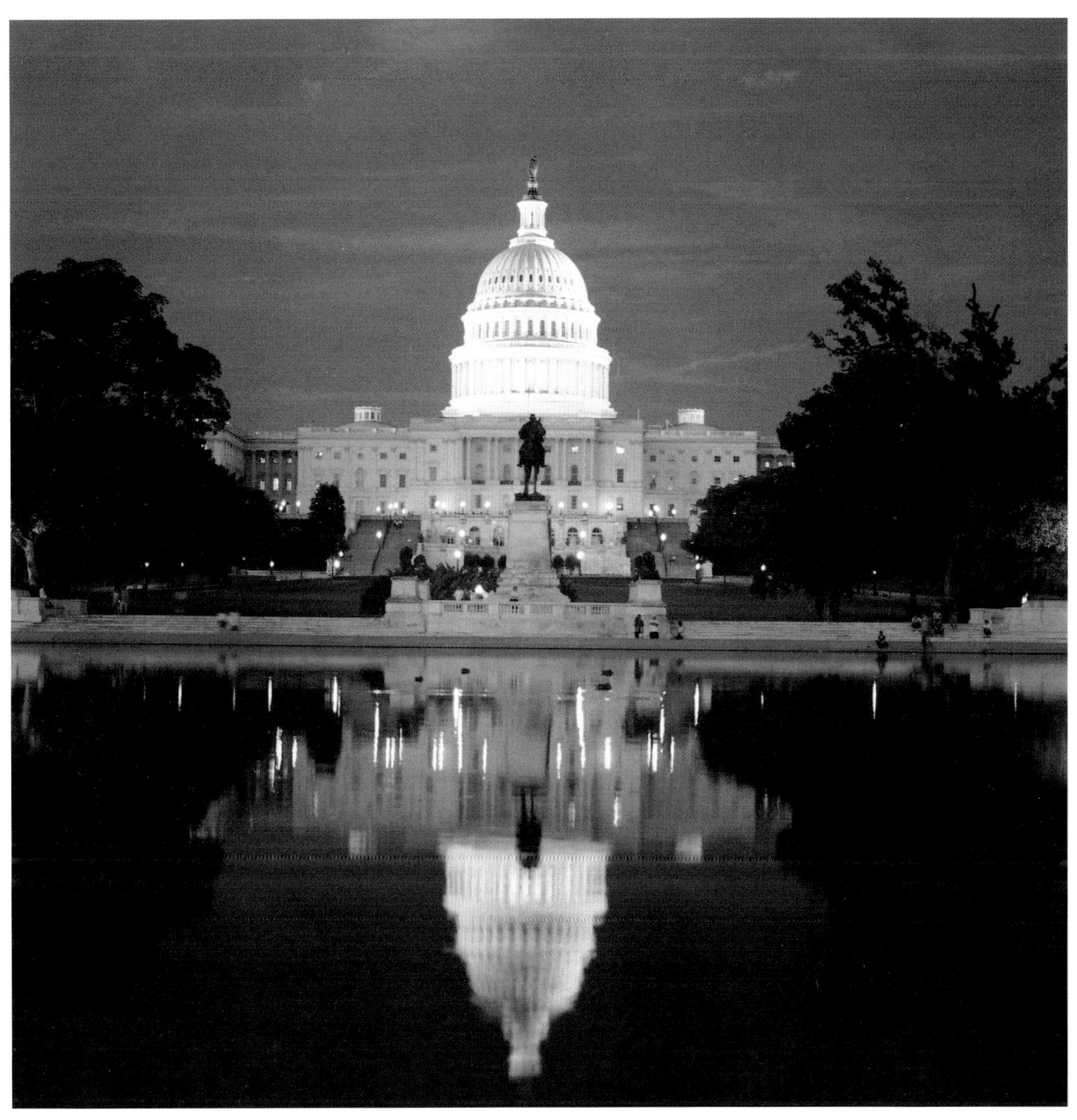

The Capitol

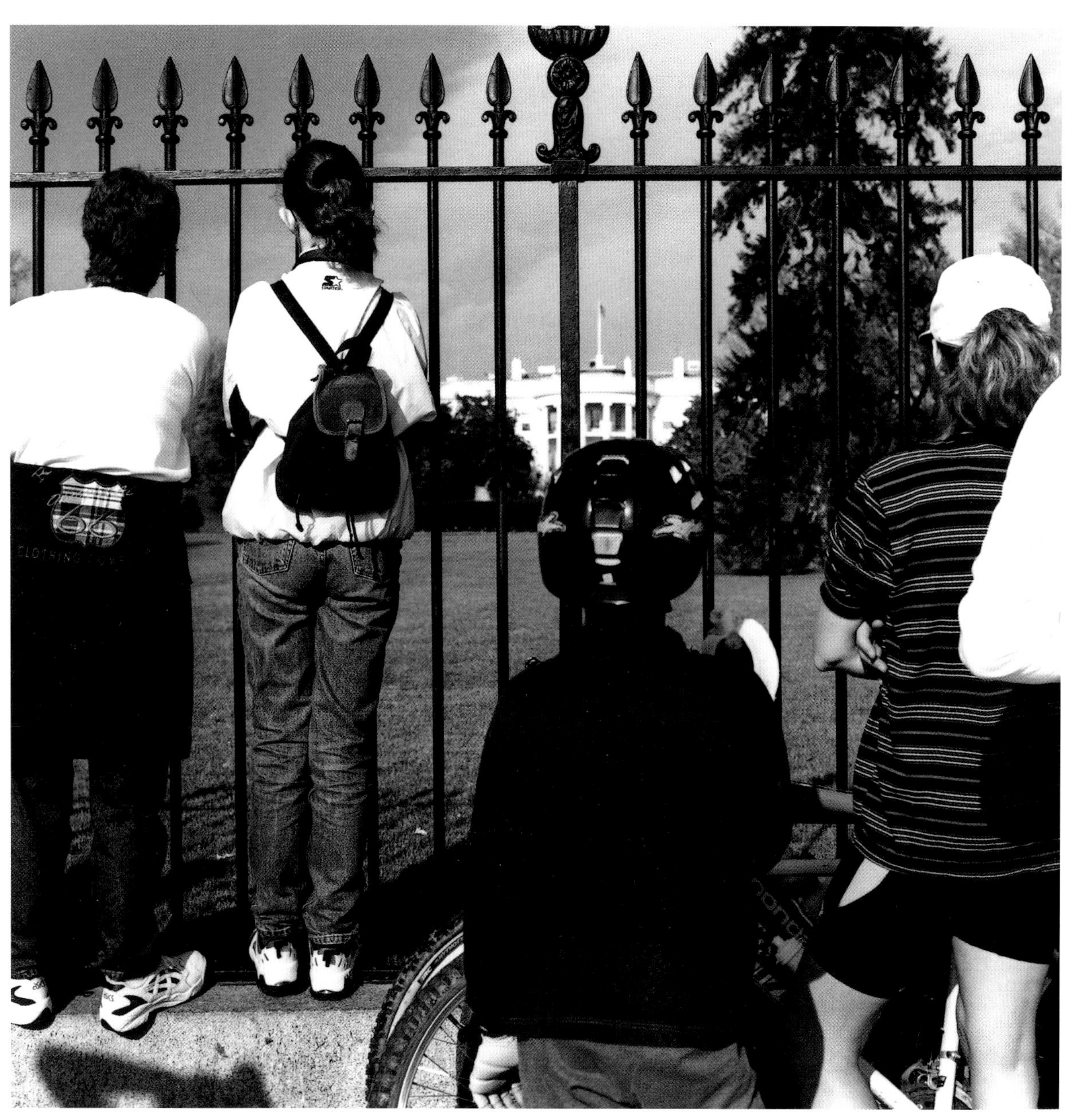

South lawn, The White House

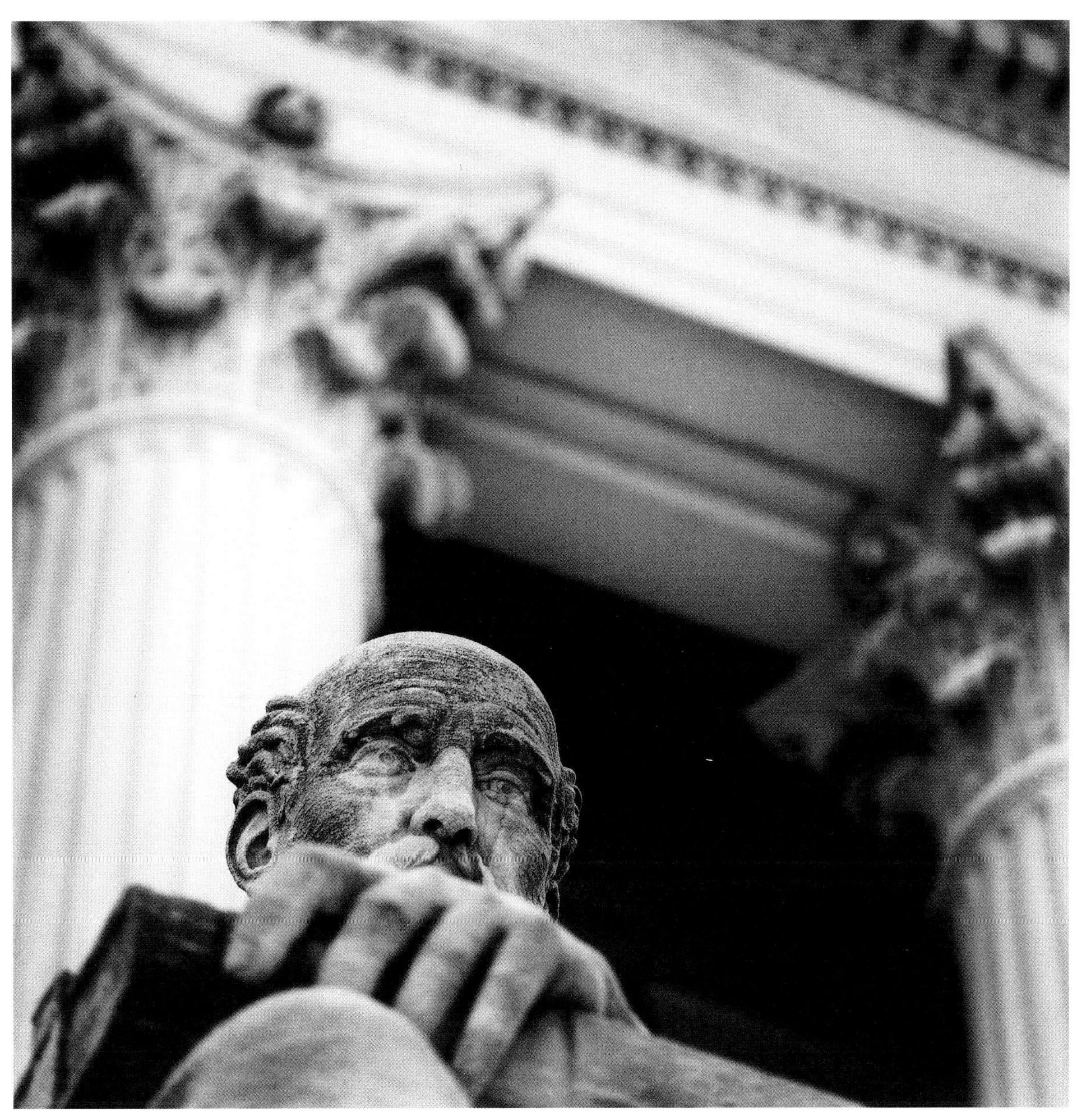

National Archives

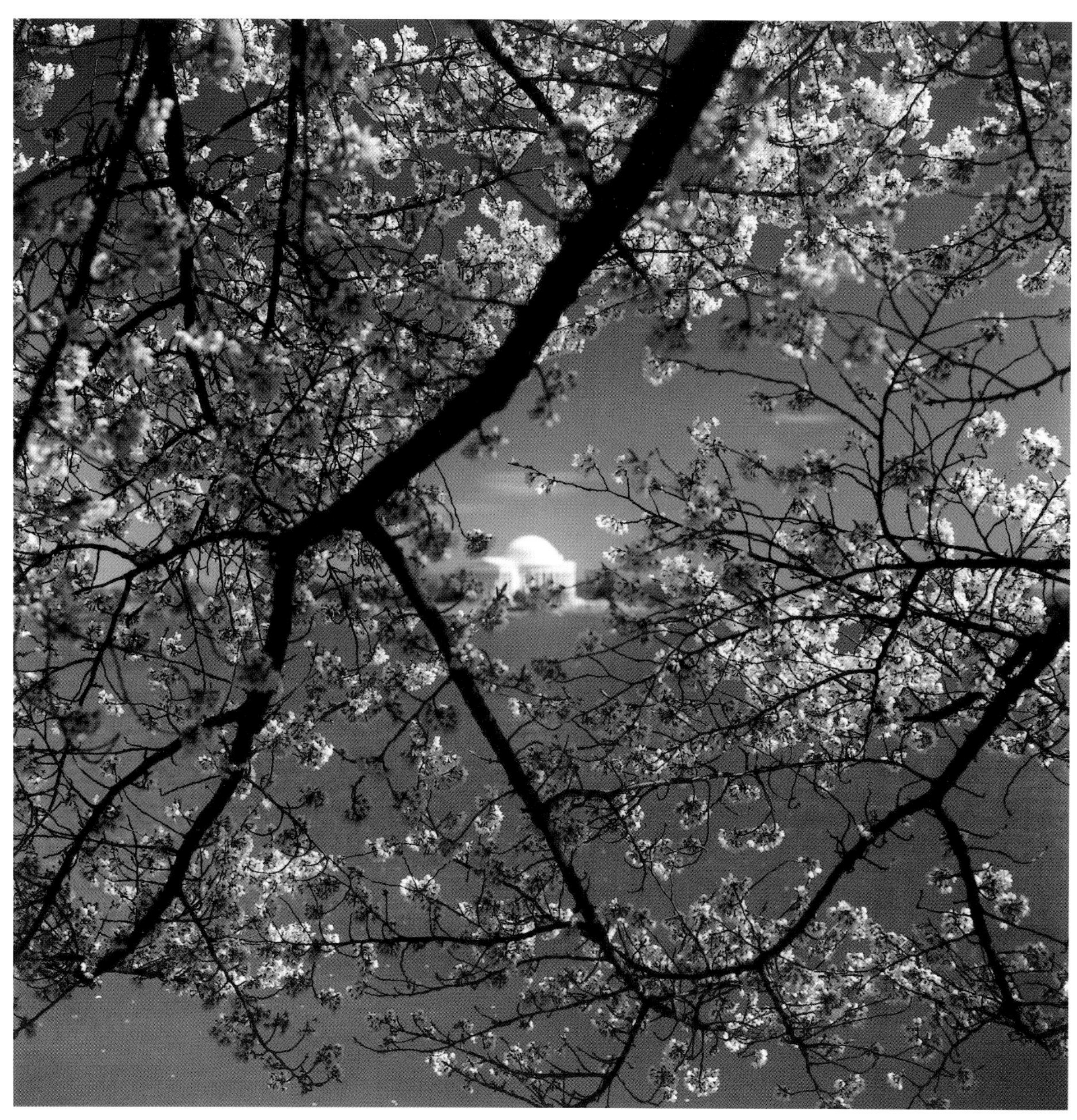

Cherry blossoms, Jefferson Memorial

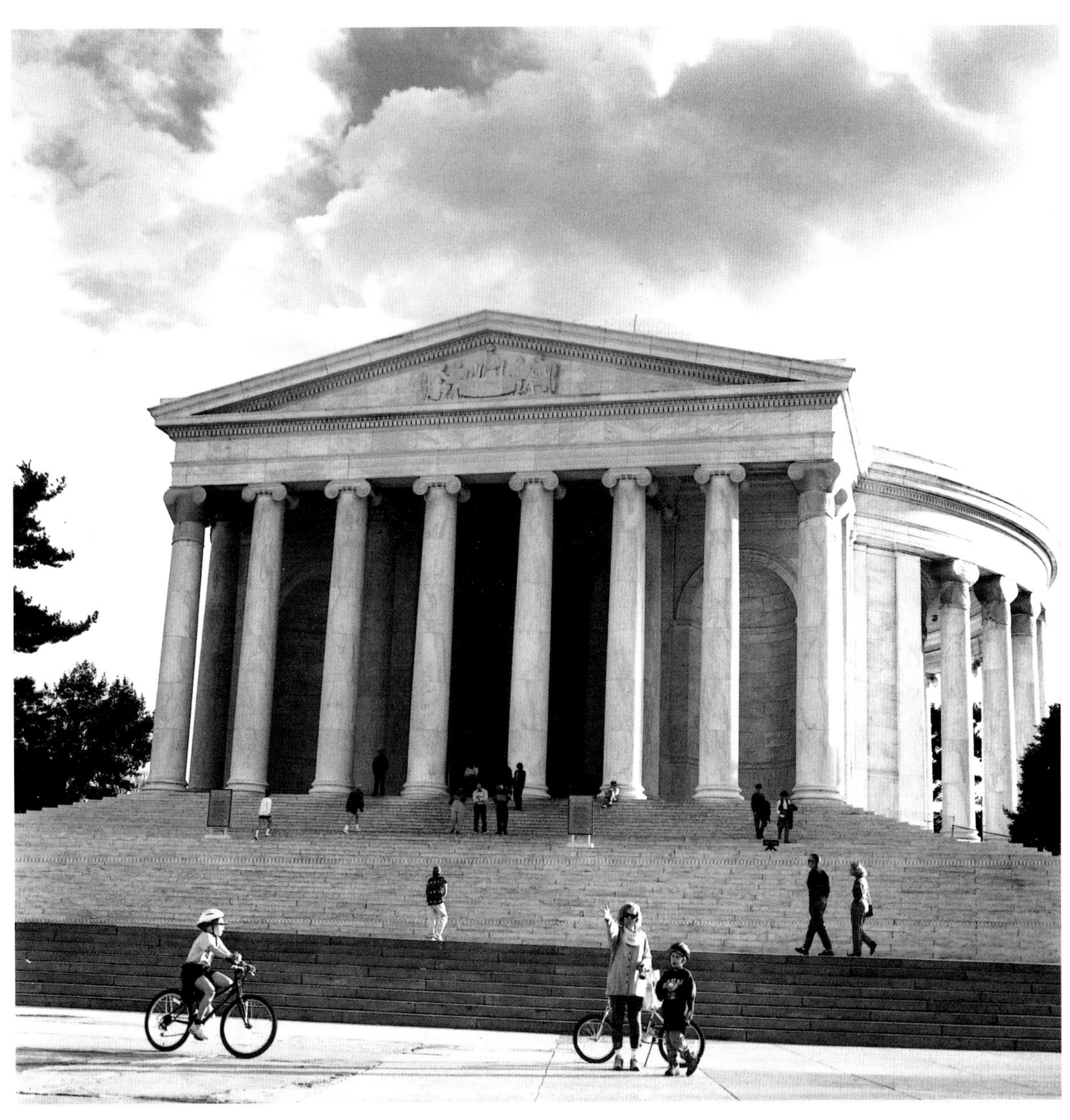

Jefferson Memorial

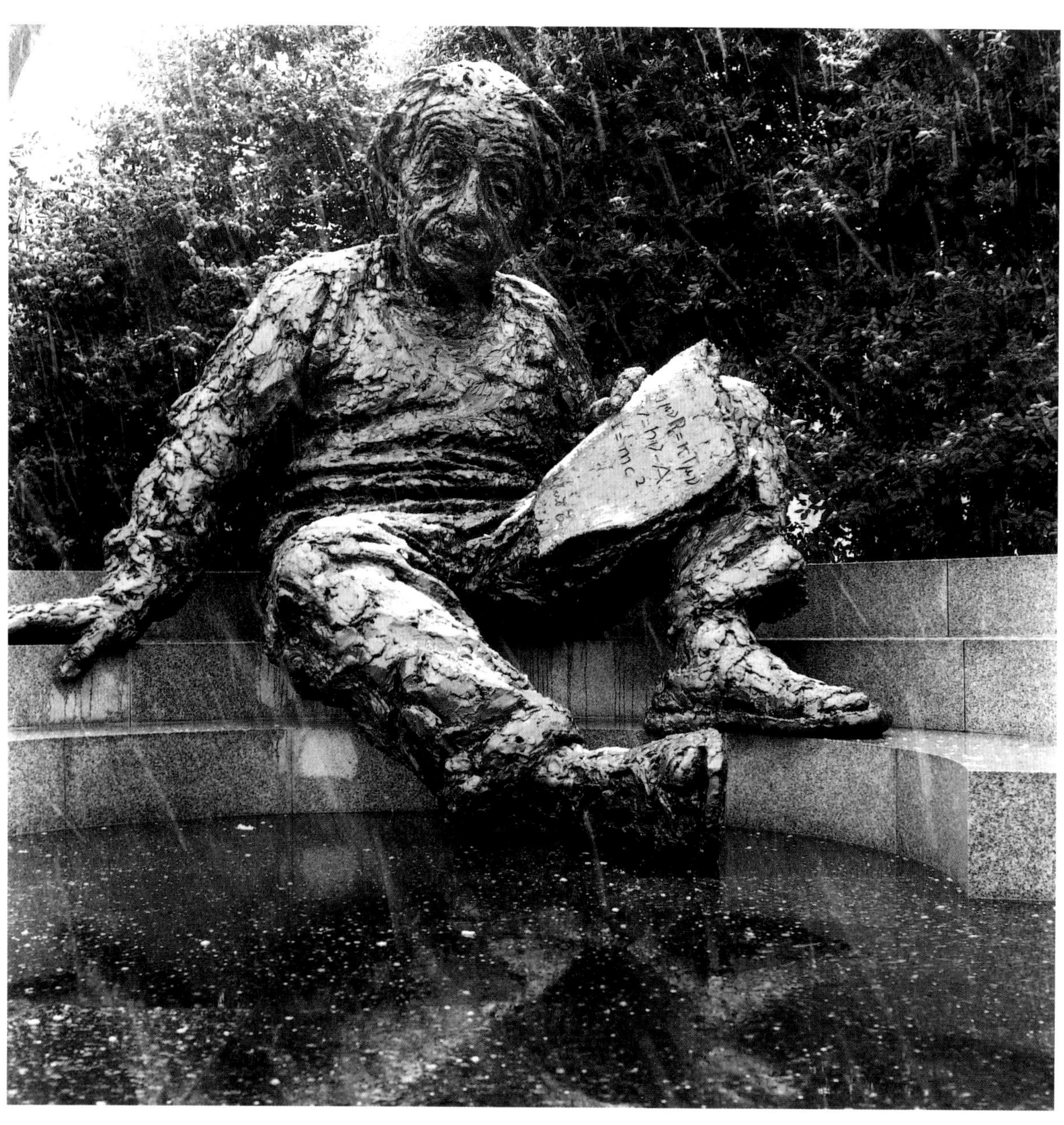

Einstein Memorial, National Academy of Sciences

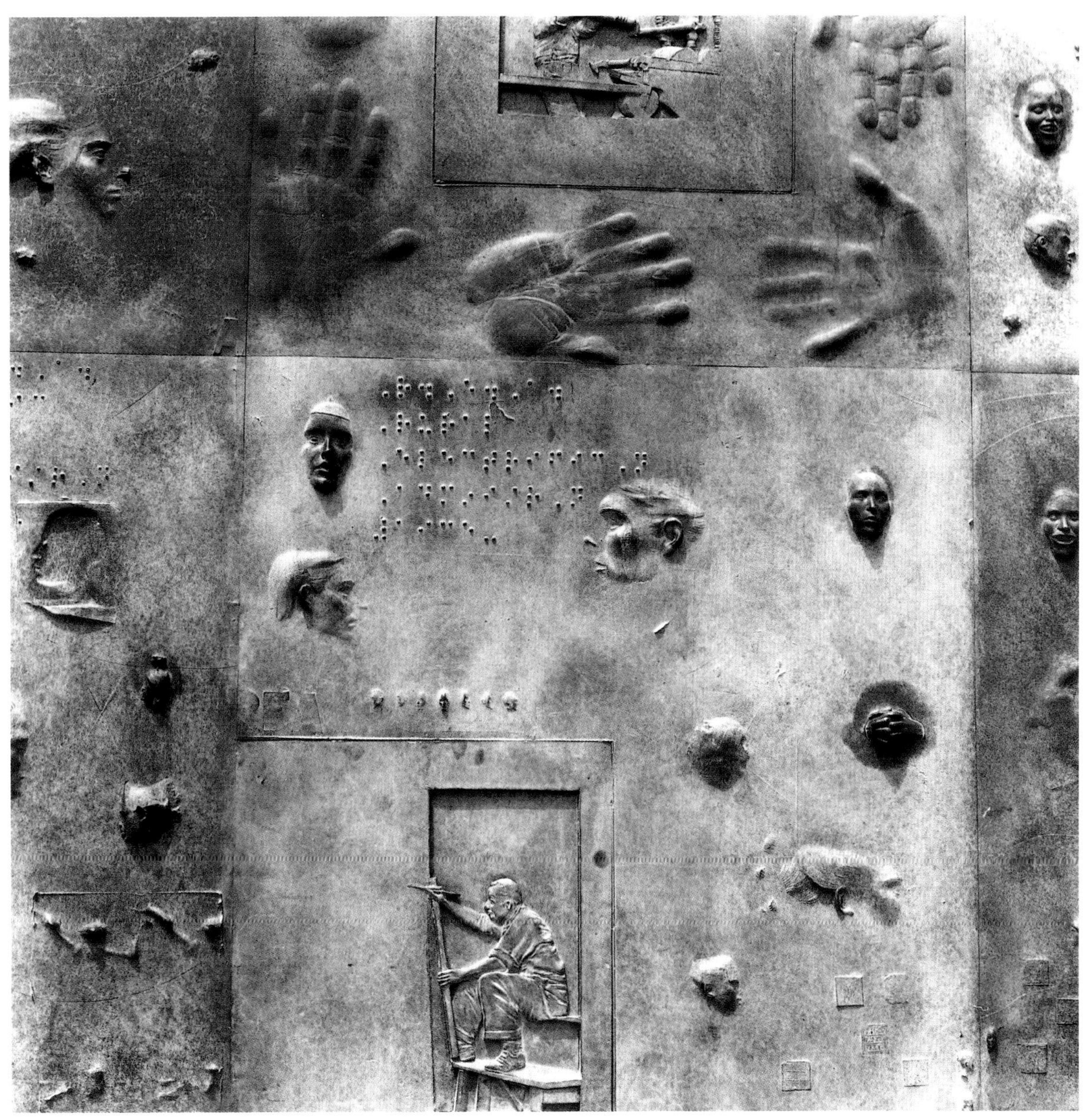

F.D.R. Memorial

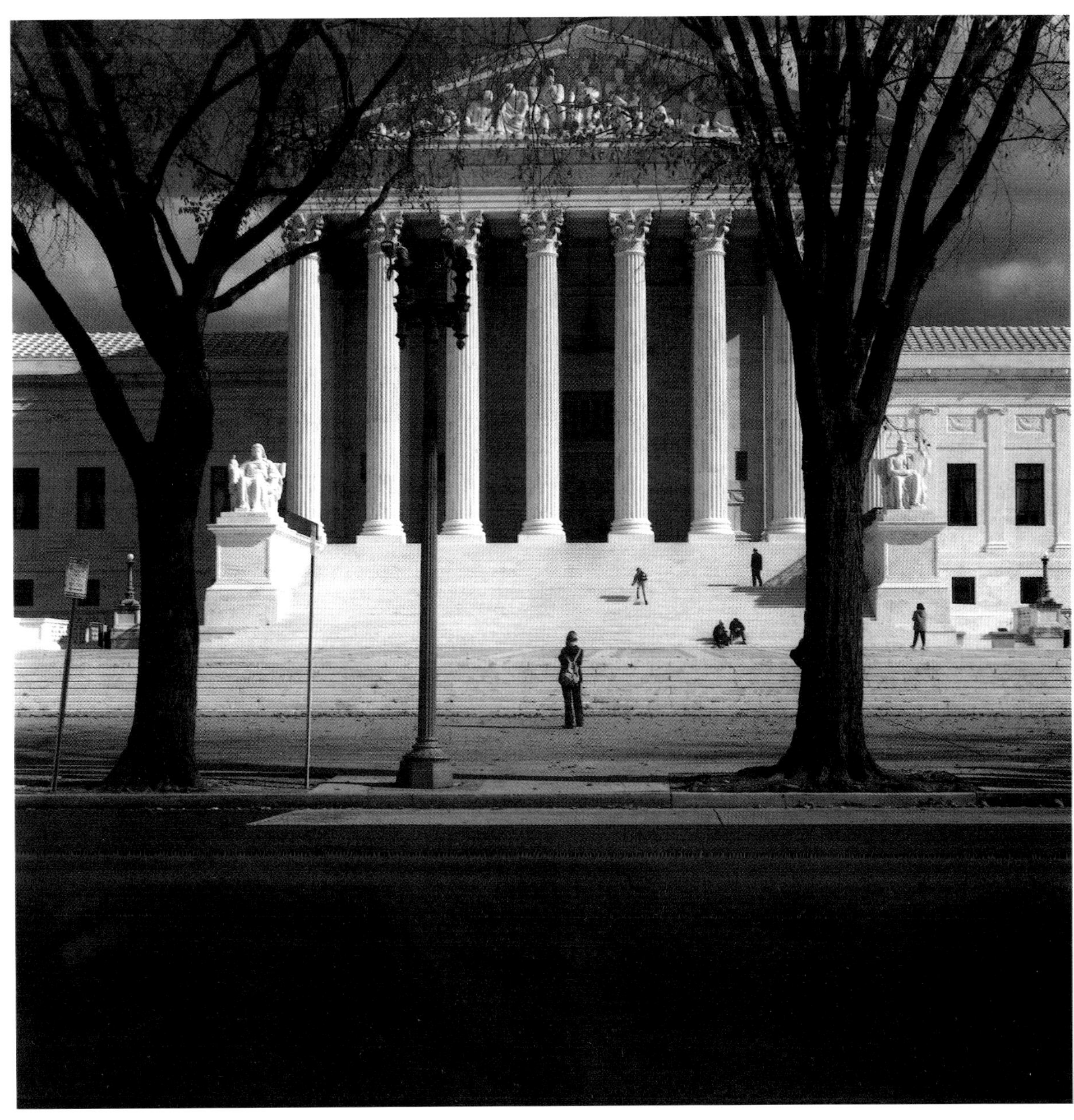

Supreme Court Building

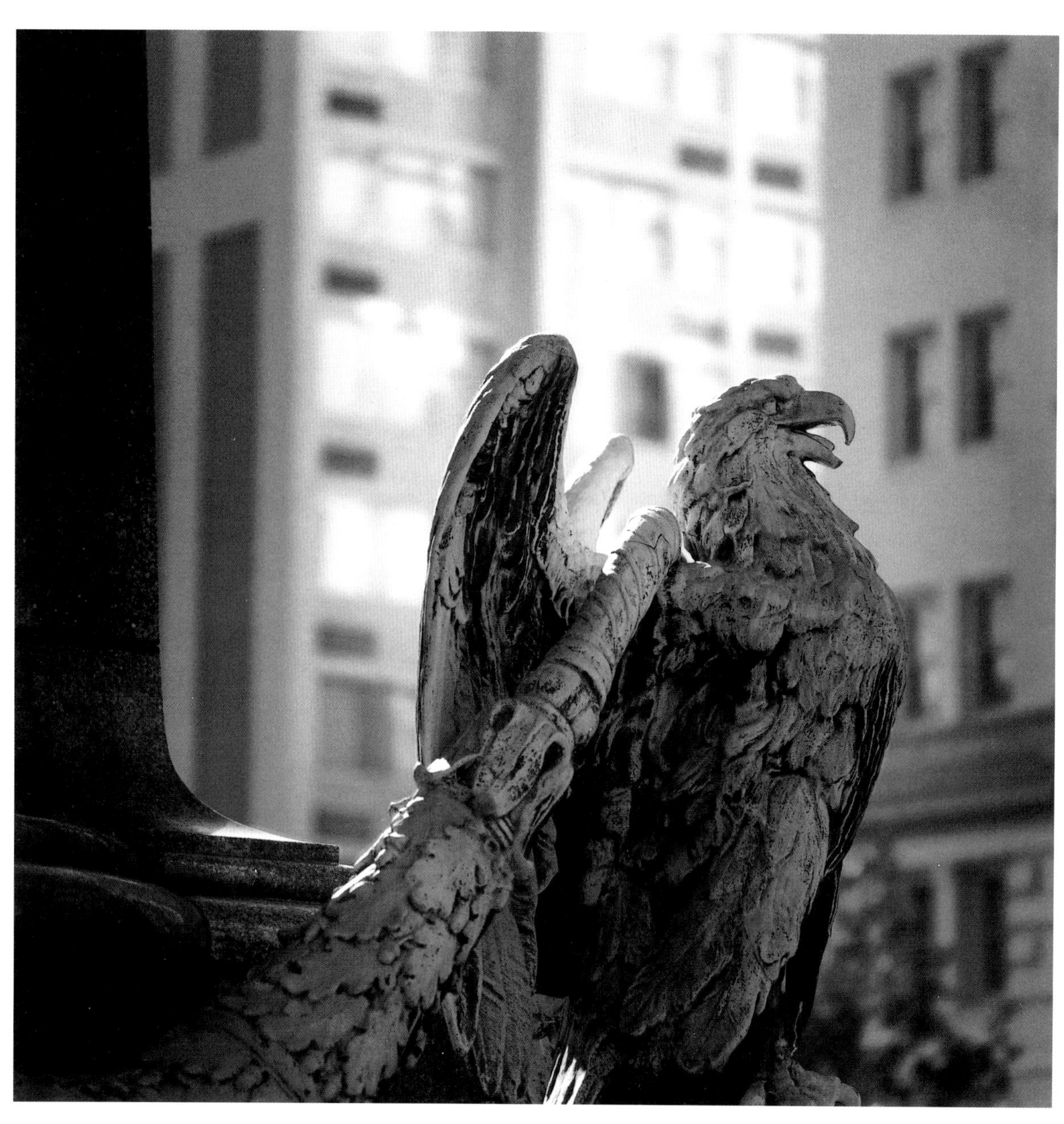

Pedestal detail, statue of General George B. McClellan

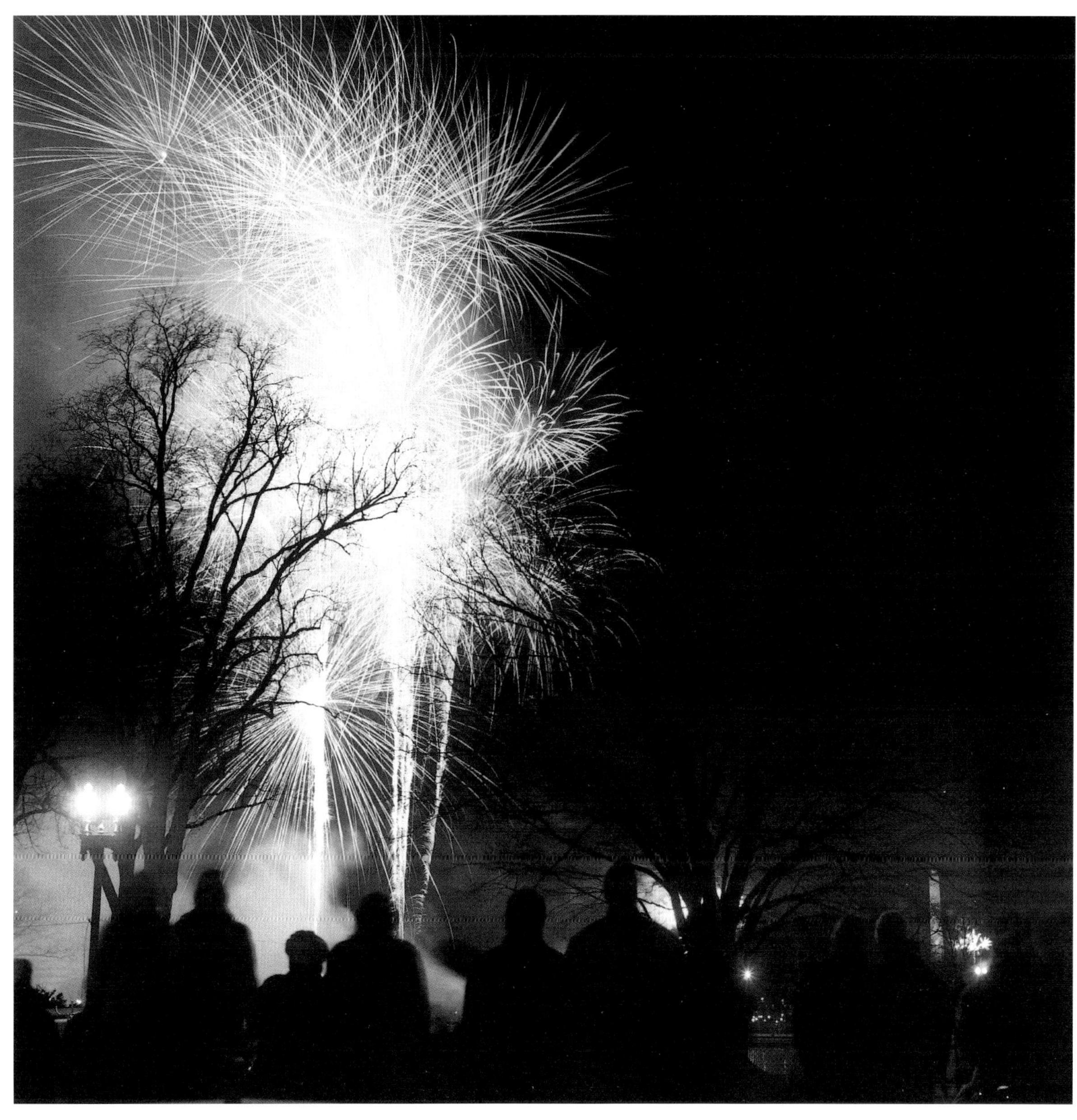

Fireworks, Capitol grounds

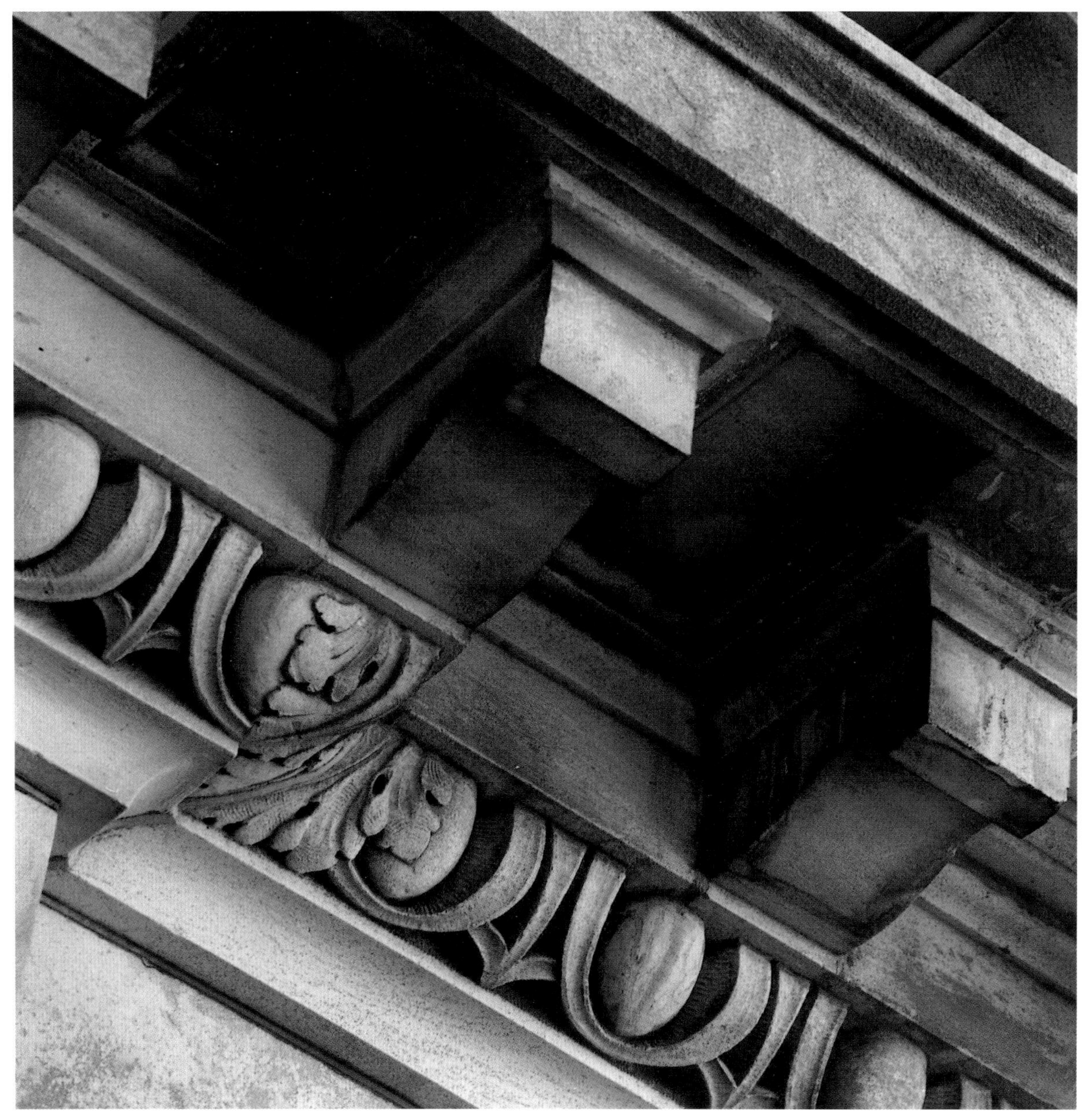

Detail, Anderson House

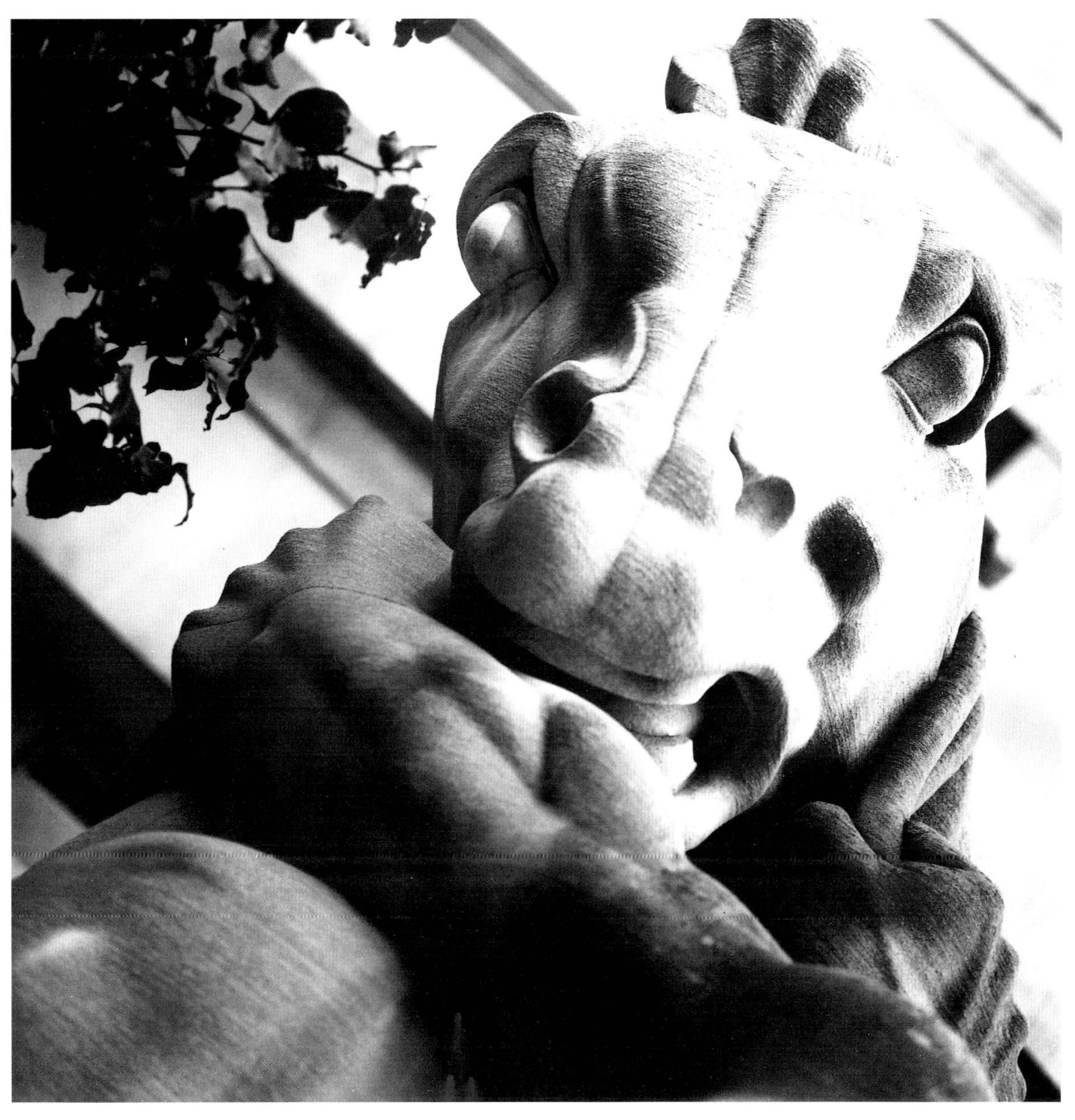

Detail, Federal Trade Commission

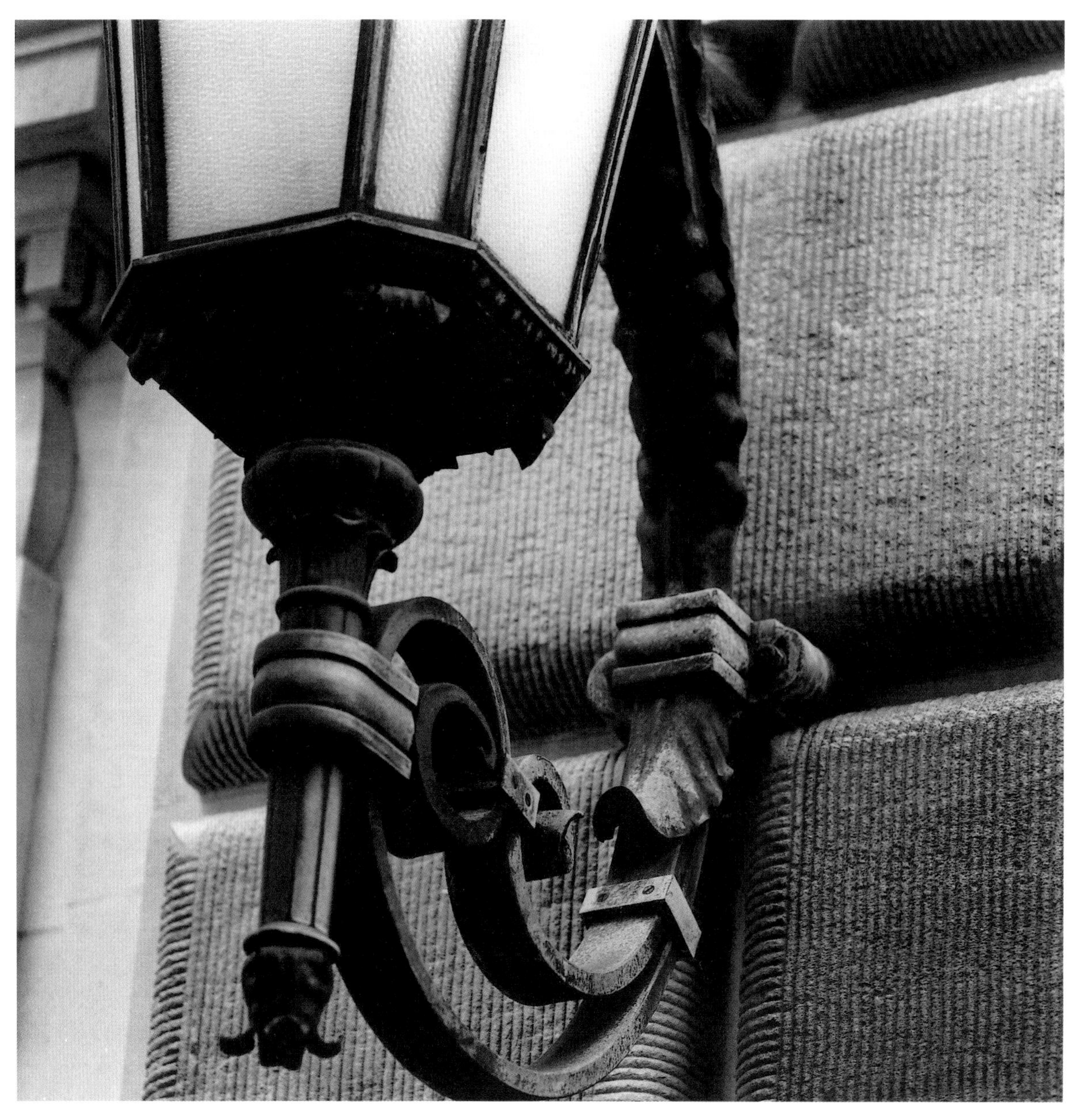

Detail, Department of Commerce

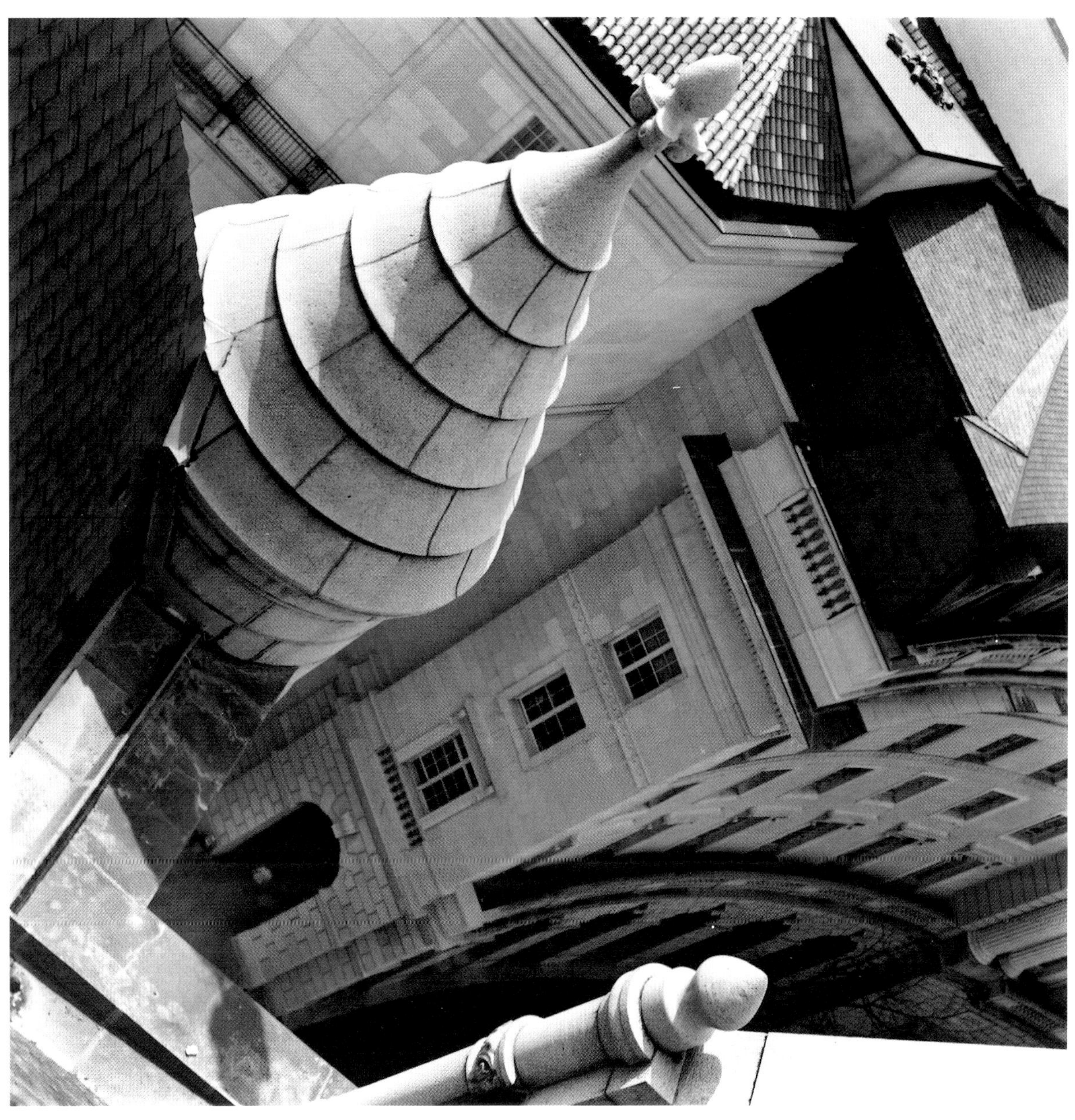

Rooftop, Old Post Office

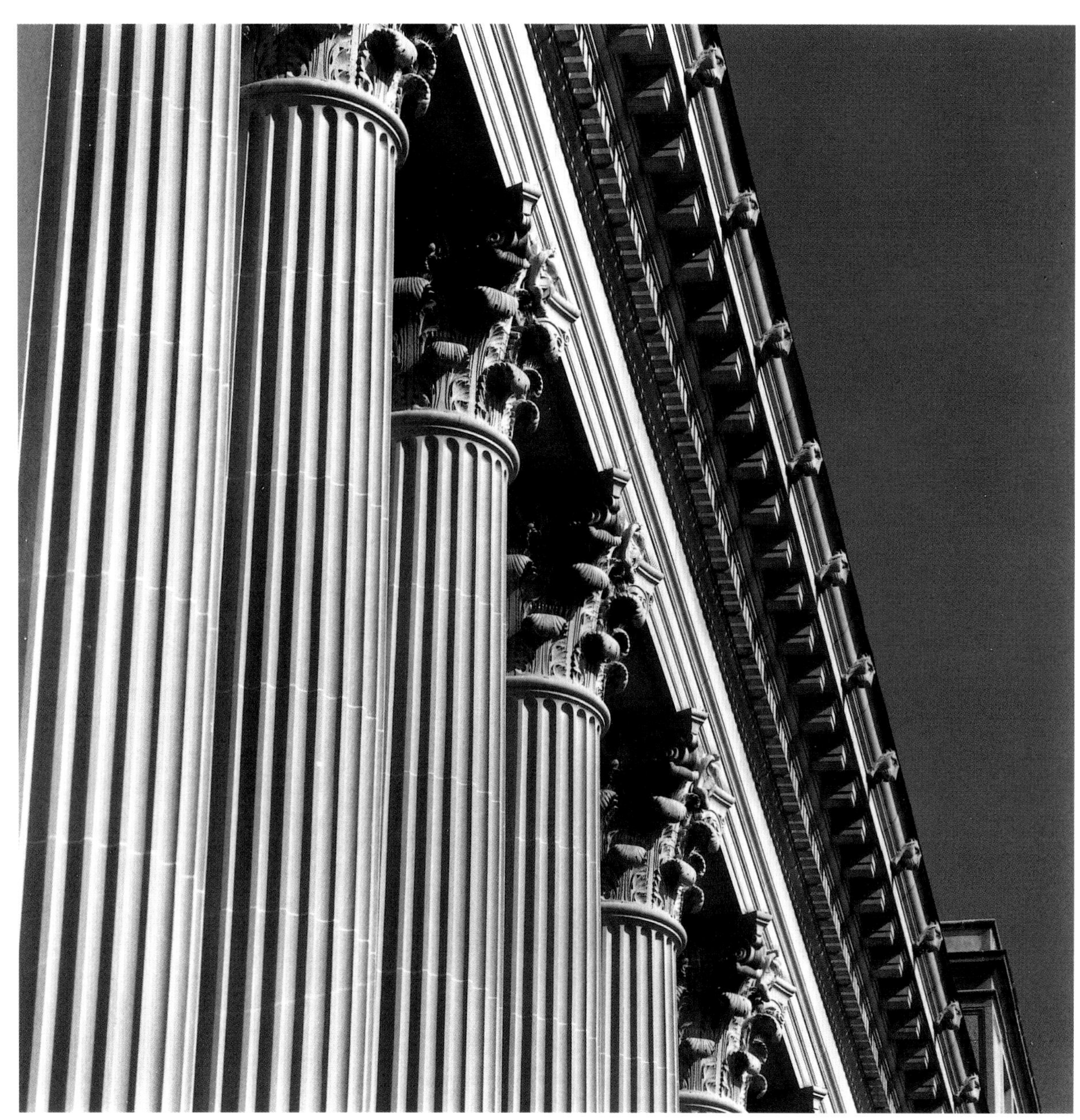

Veterans Administration Building

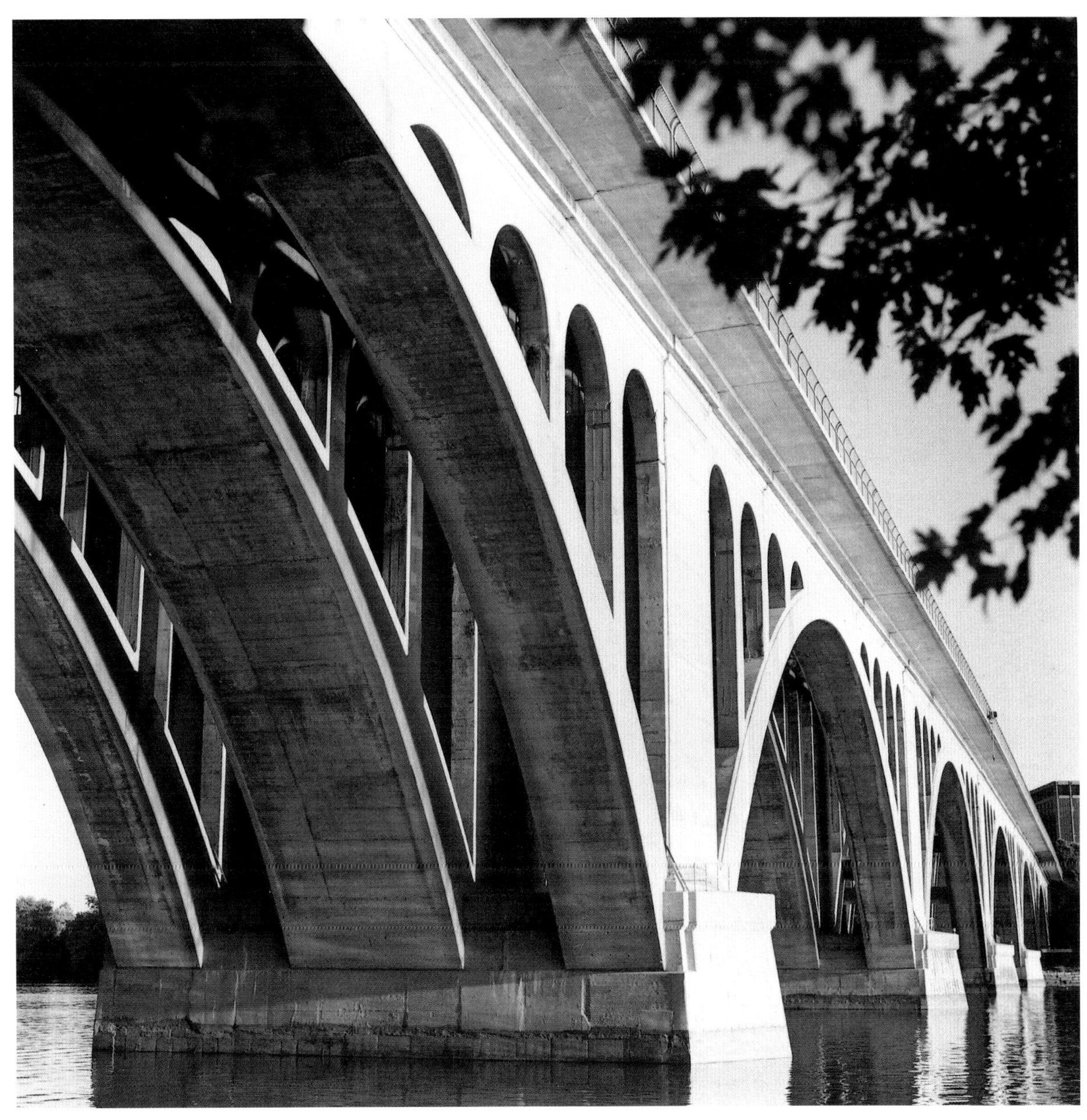

Key Bridge

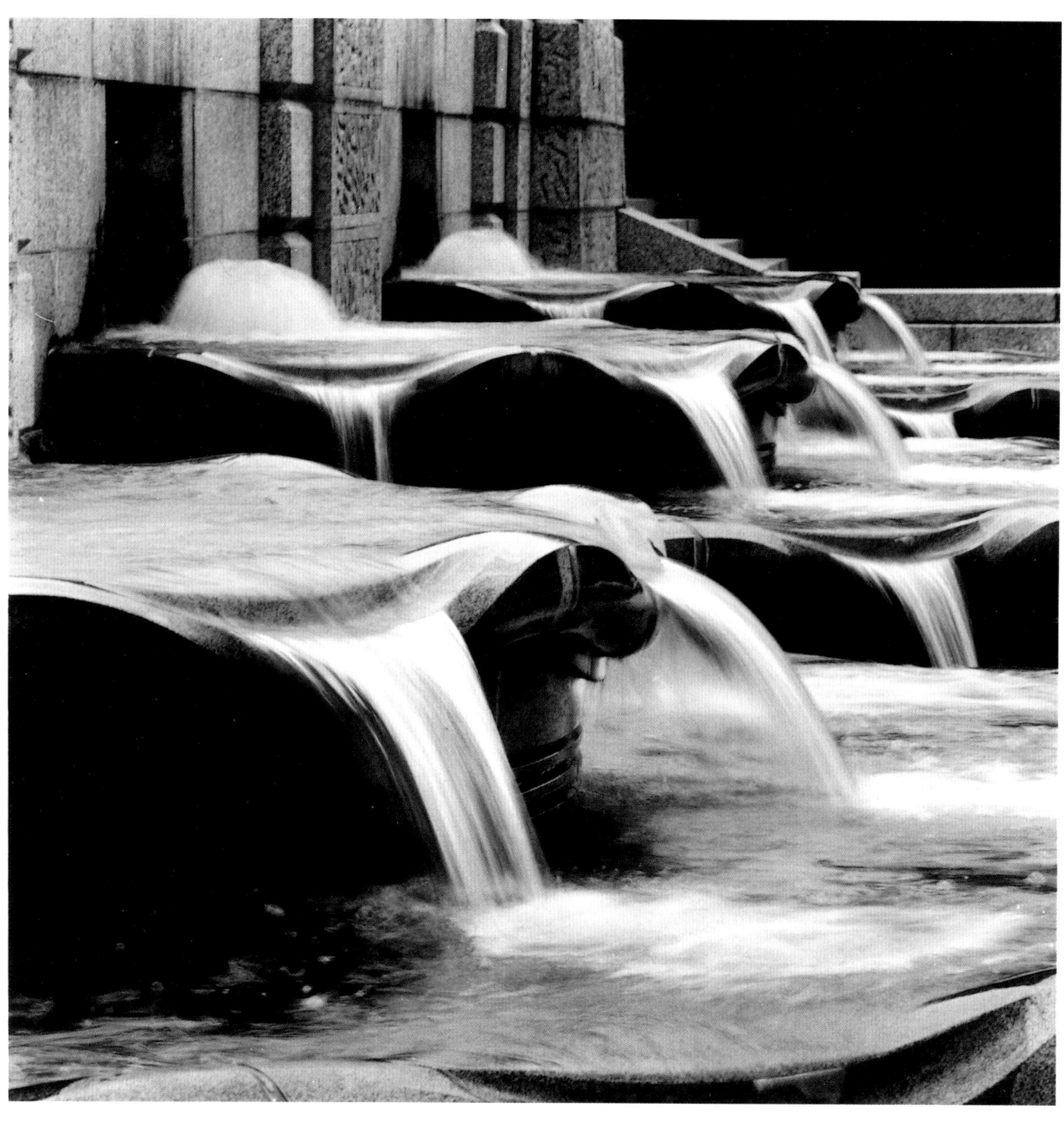

Fountain, Capitol grounds

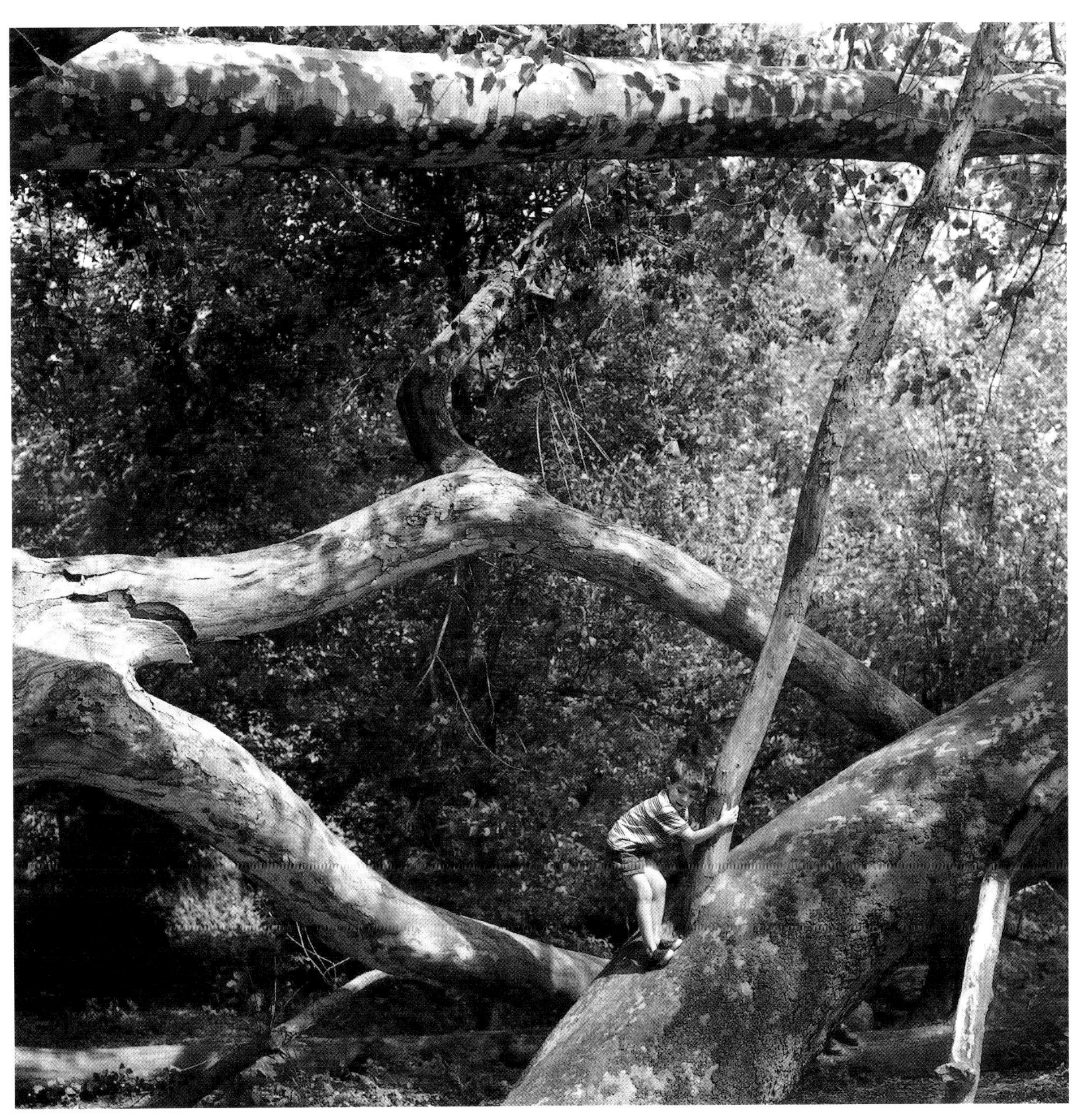

Matthew, Chesapeake and Ohio Canal

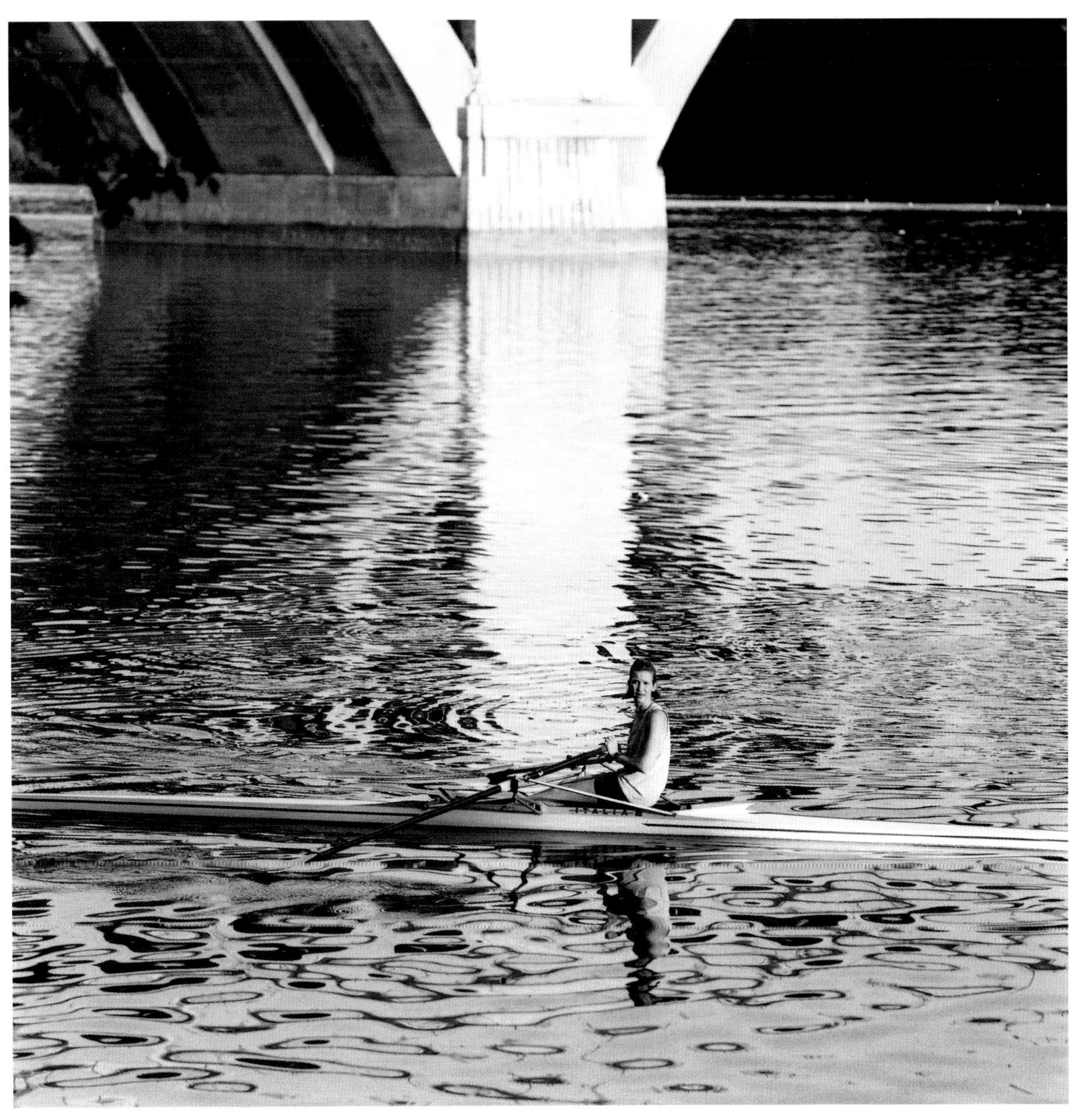

Potomac River

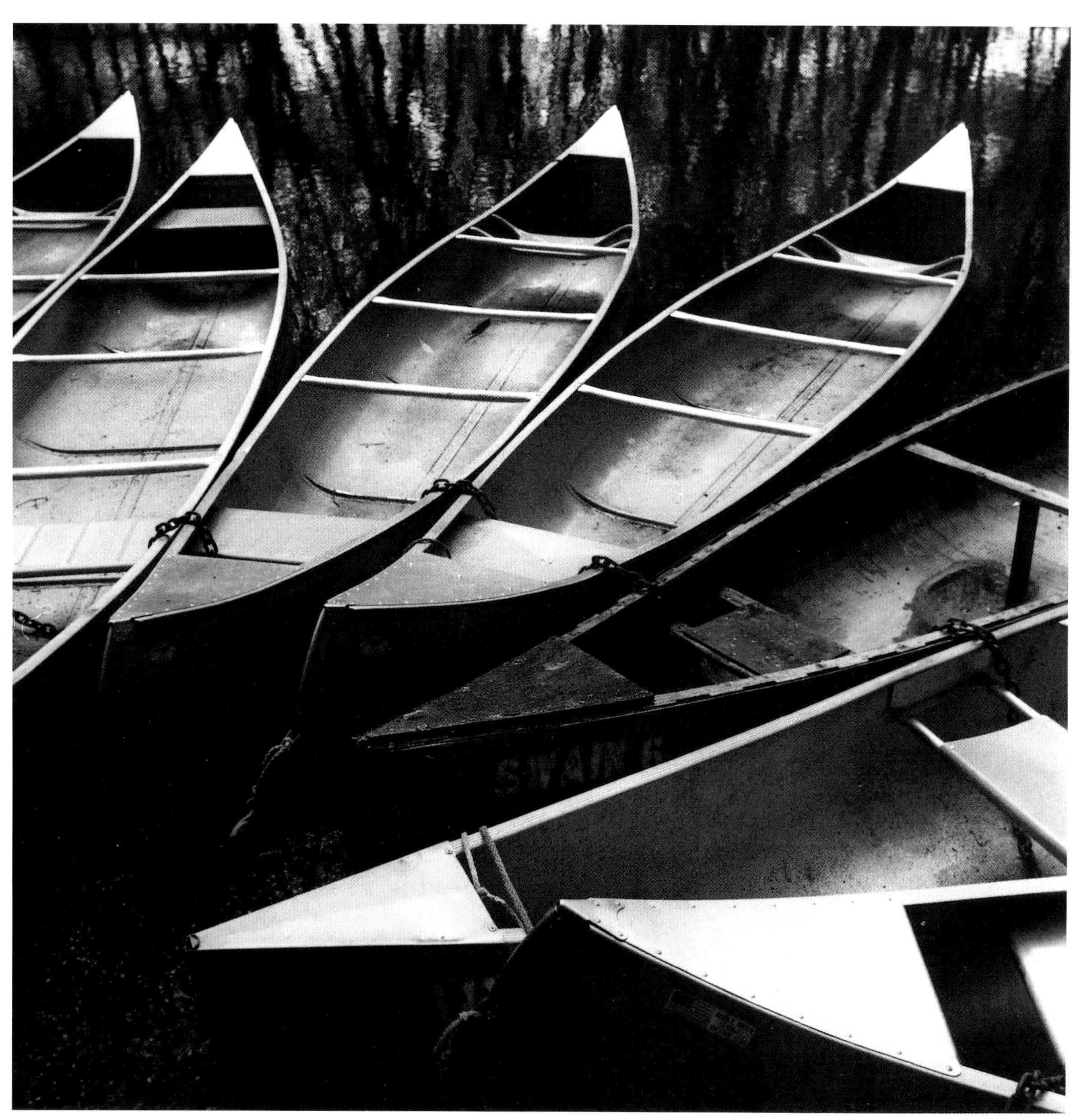

Chesapeake and Ohio Canal

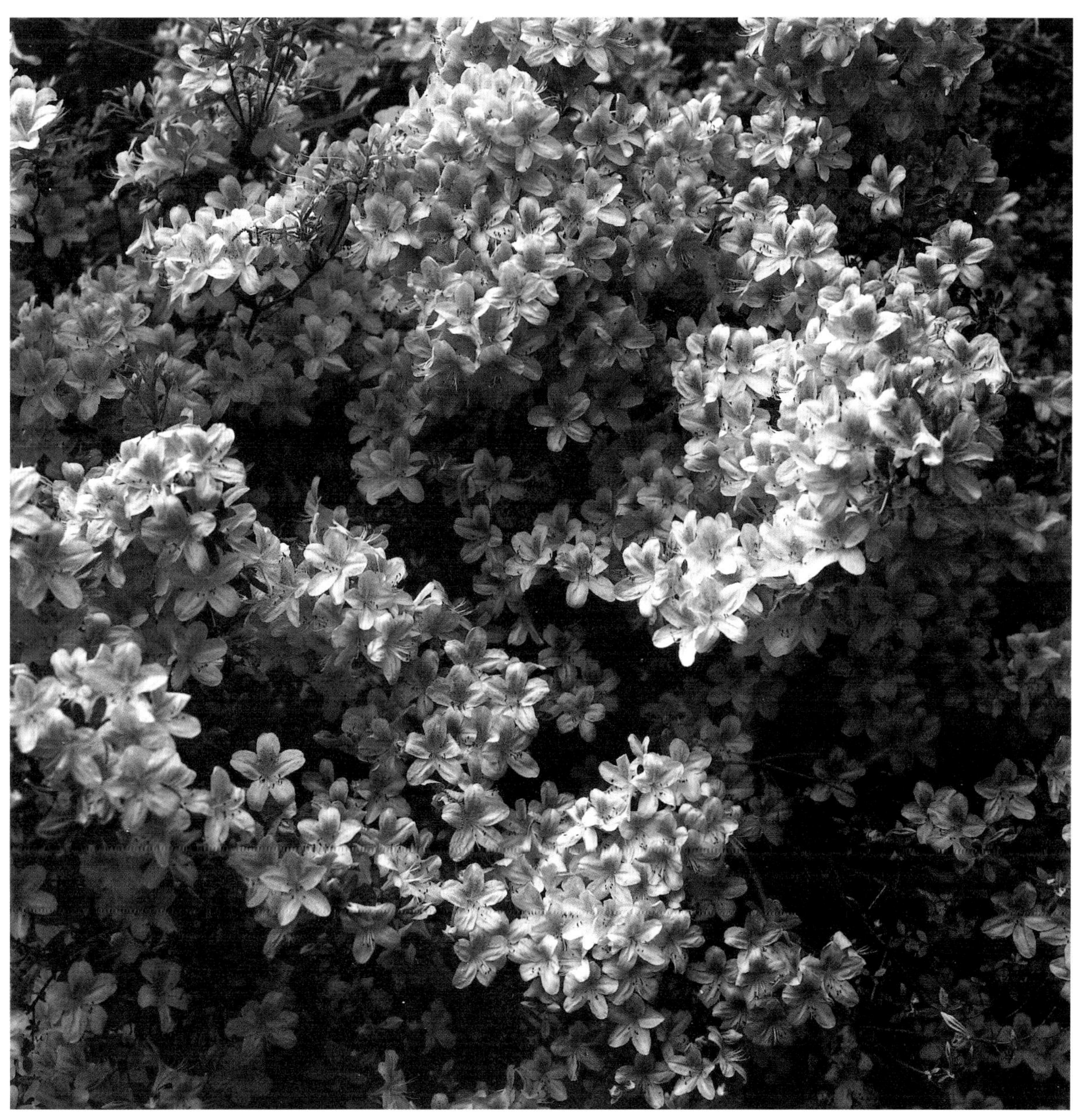

Azaleas, Federal Reserve garden

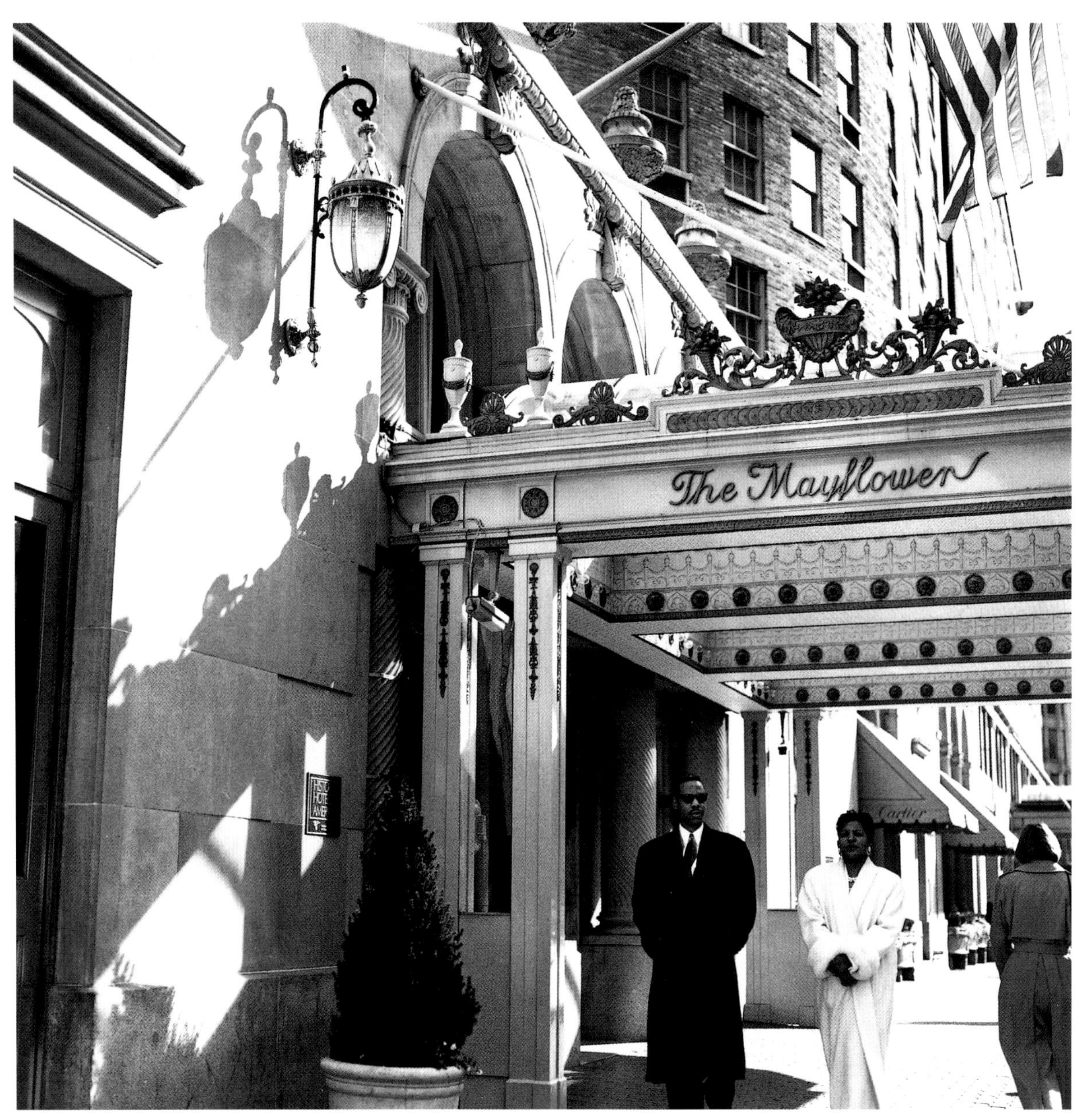

Mayflower Hotel

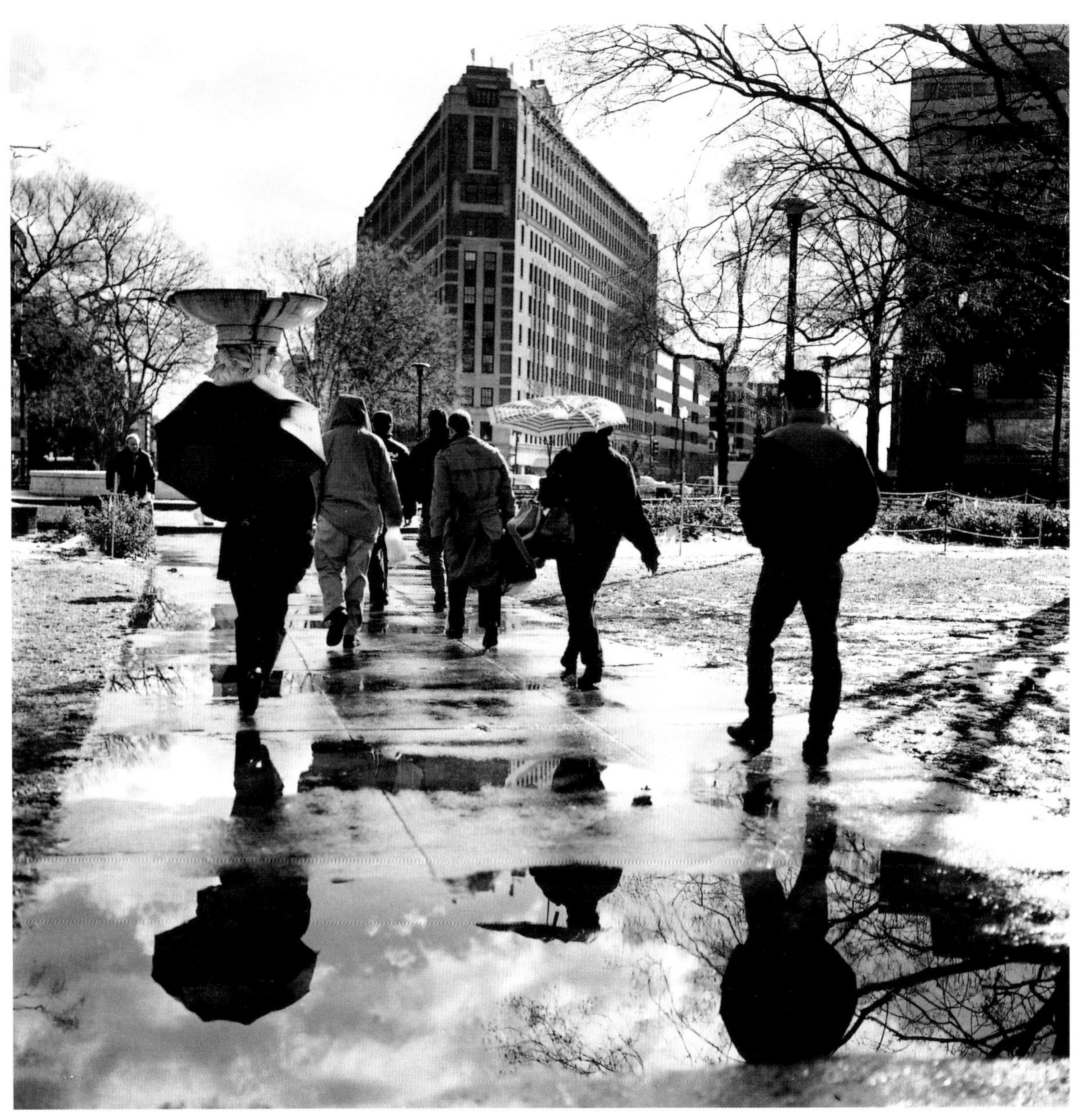

Dupont Circle

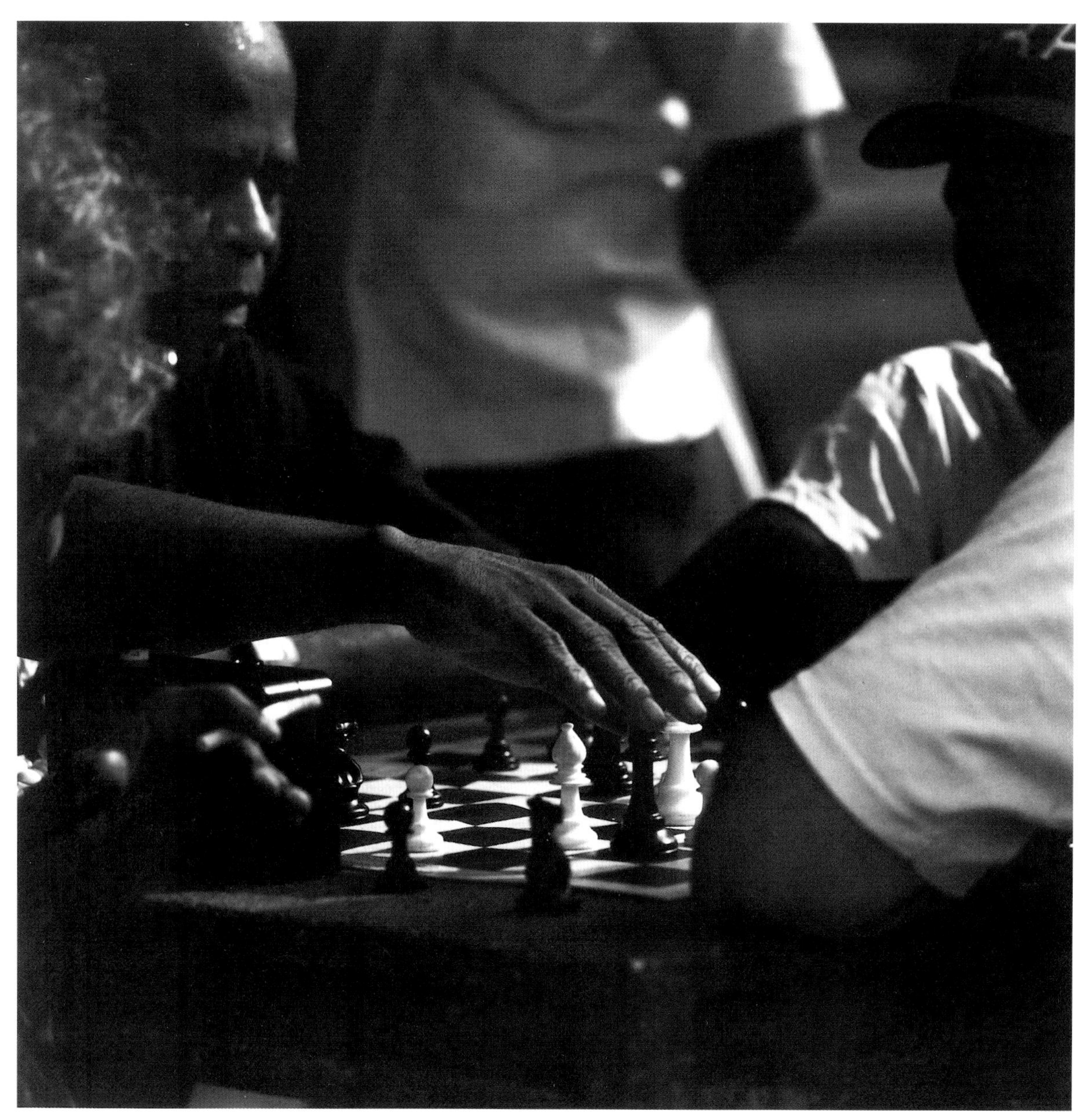

Dupont Circle

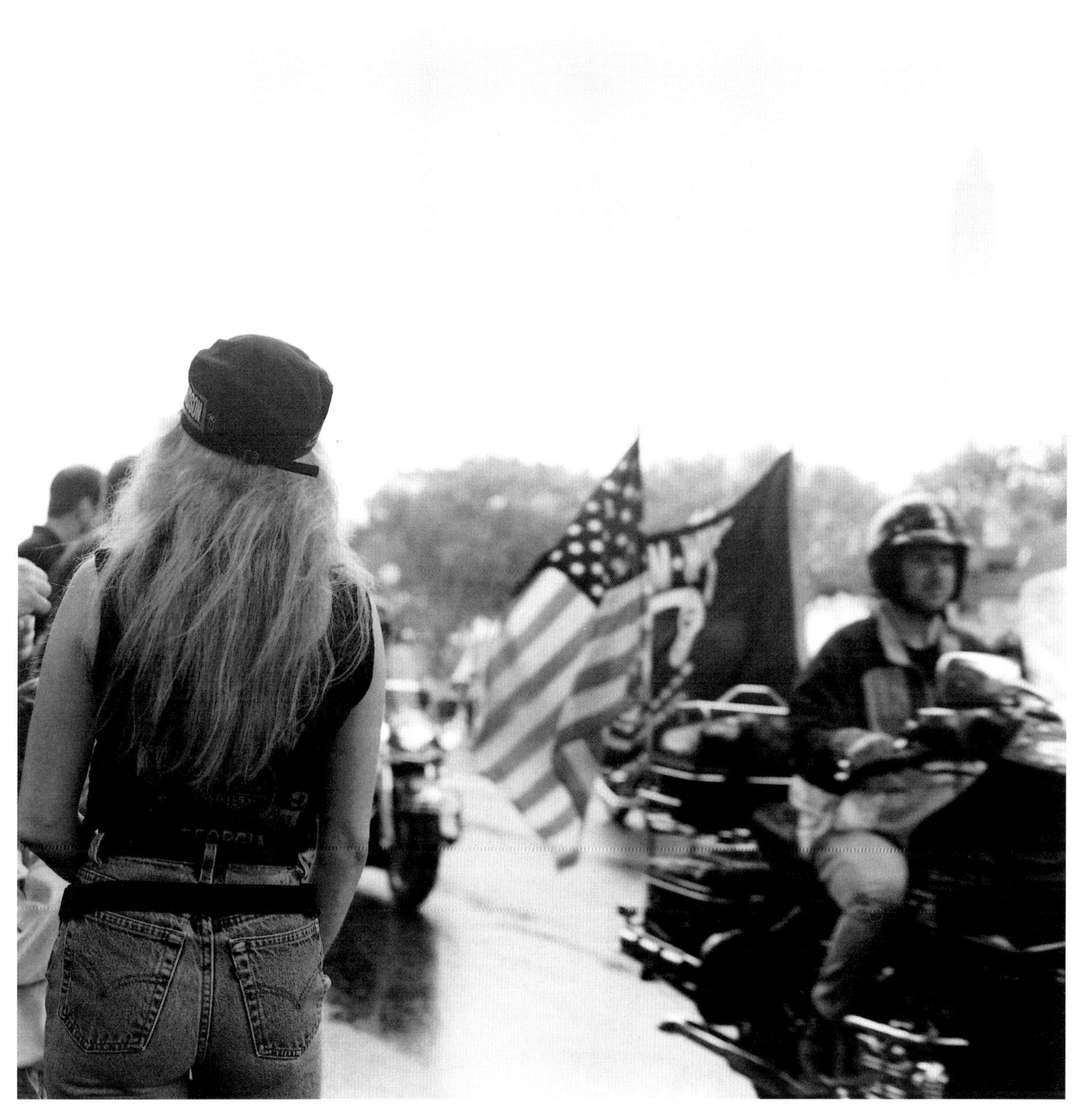

Memorial Day, Constitution Avenue

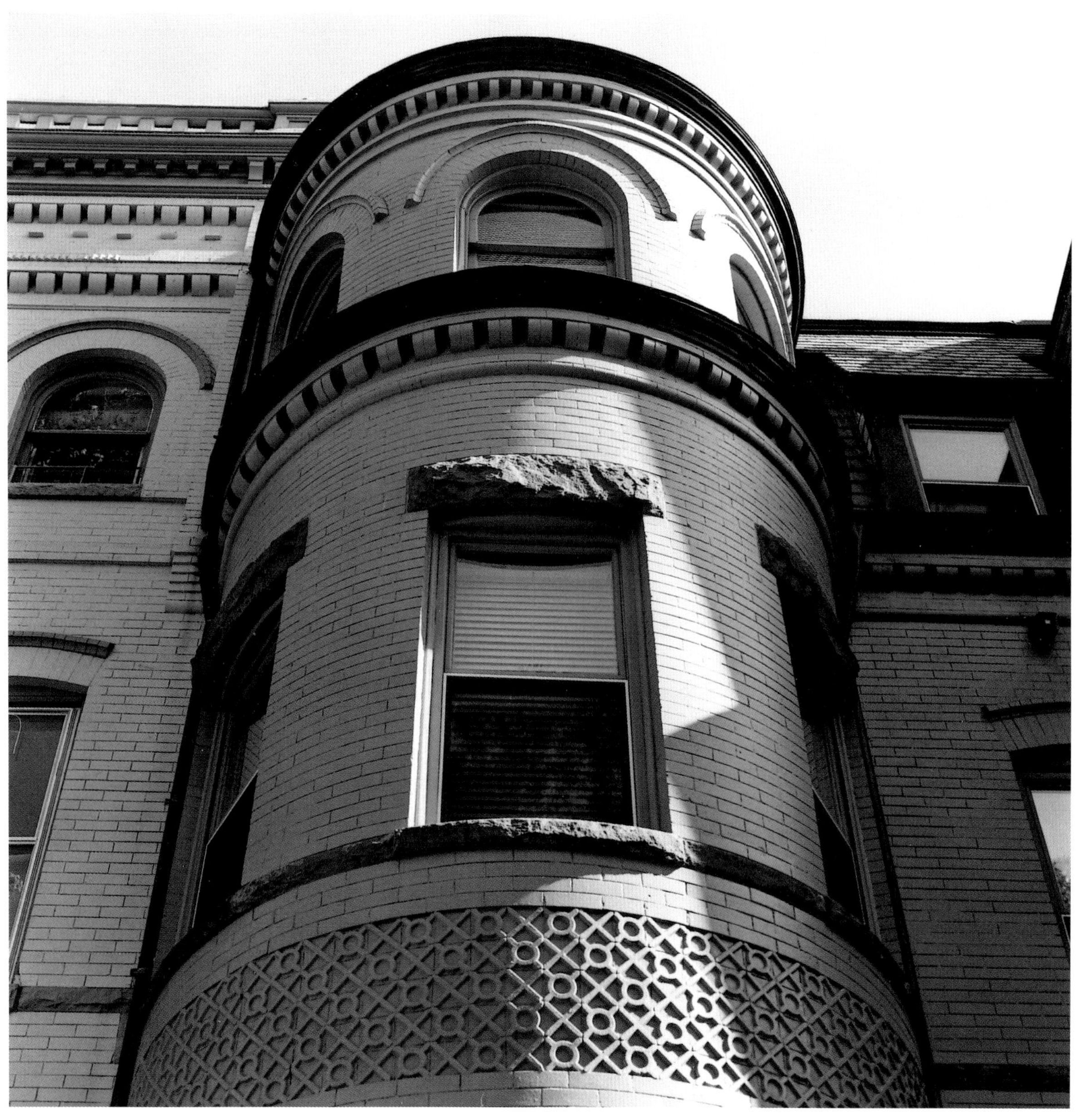

Queen Anne rowhouse, Georgetown

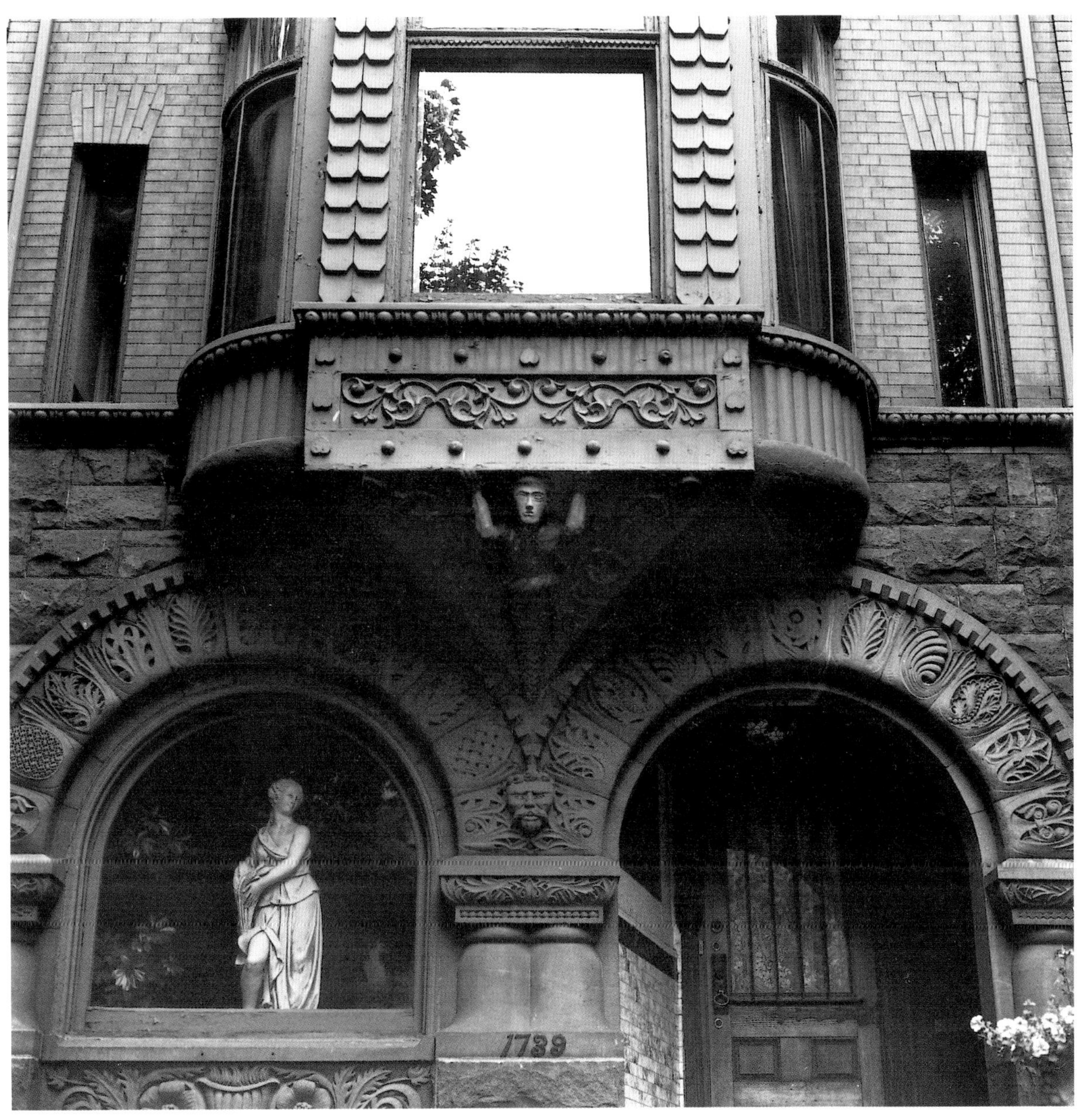

Romanesque townhouse, Dupont Circle

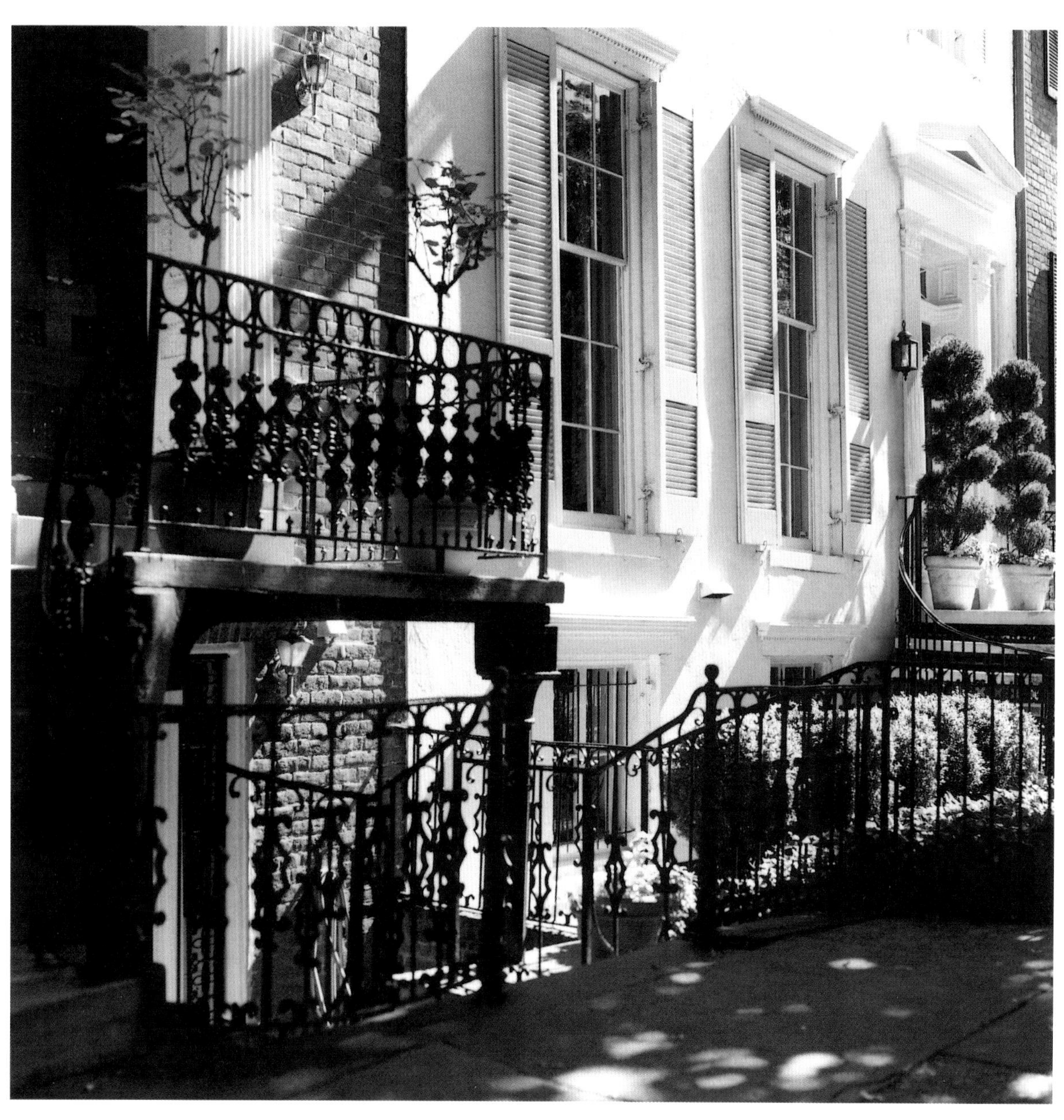

N Street, Georgetown

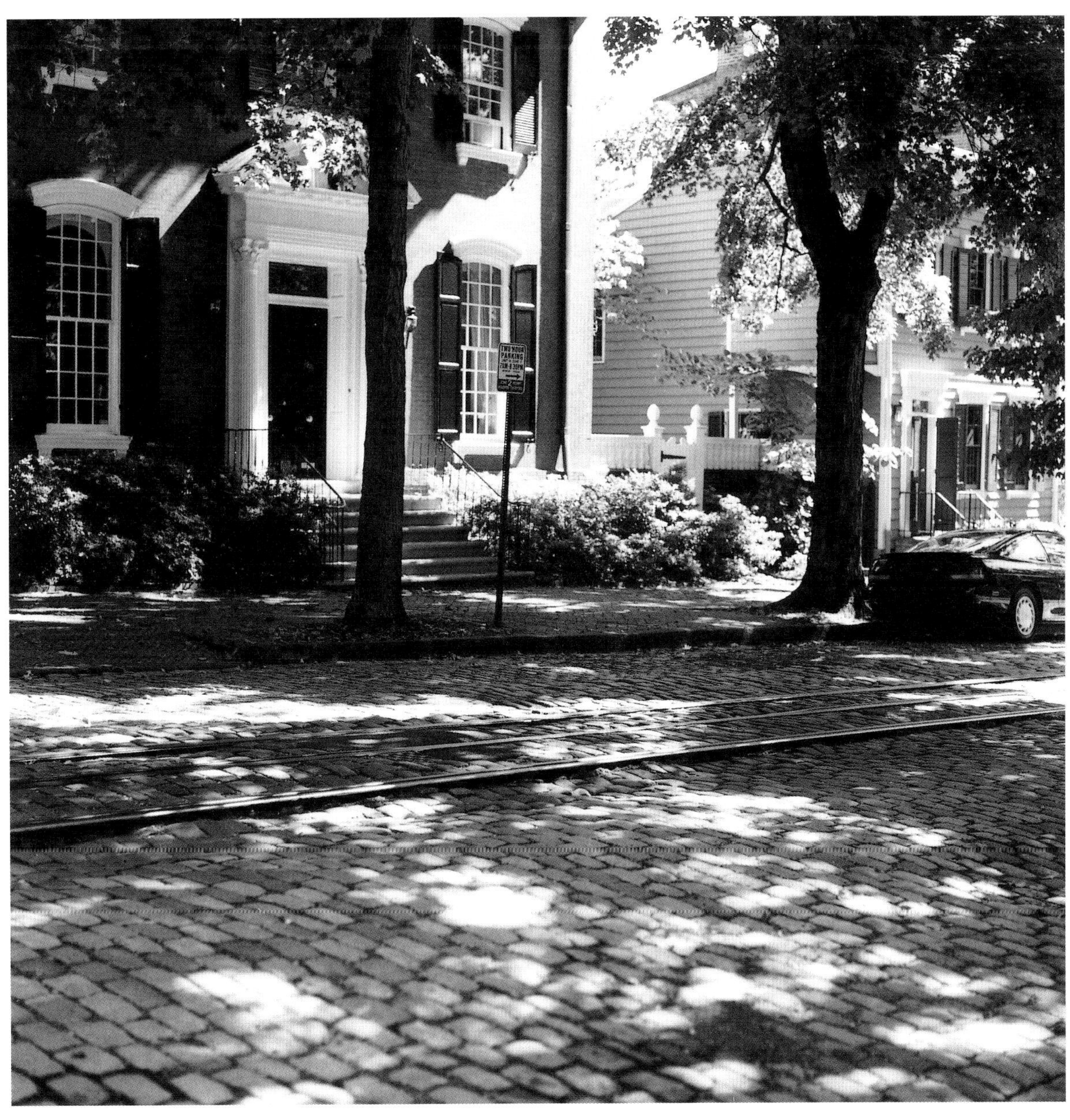

O Street, Georgetown

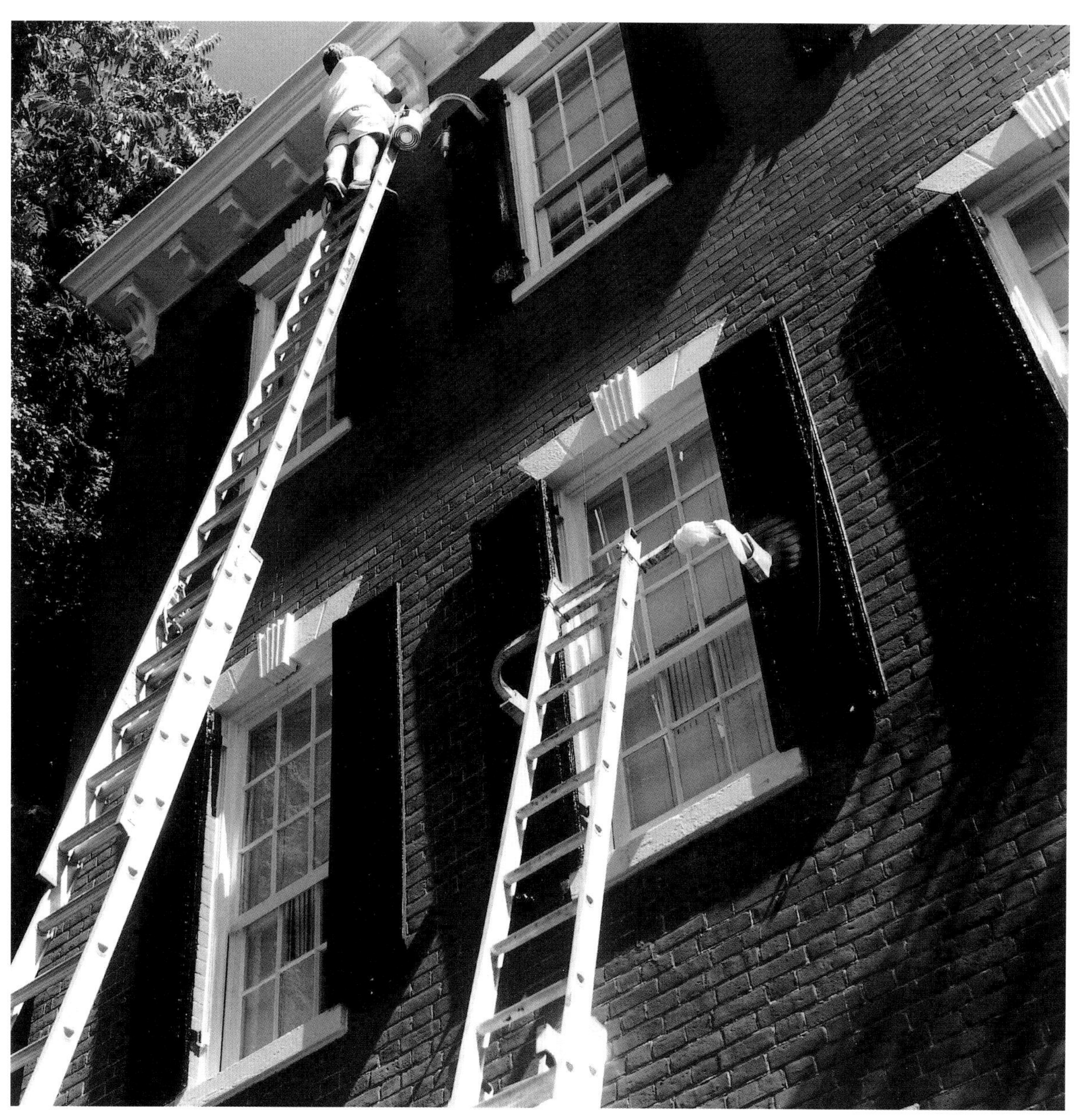

Neo-Federal house, Georgetown

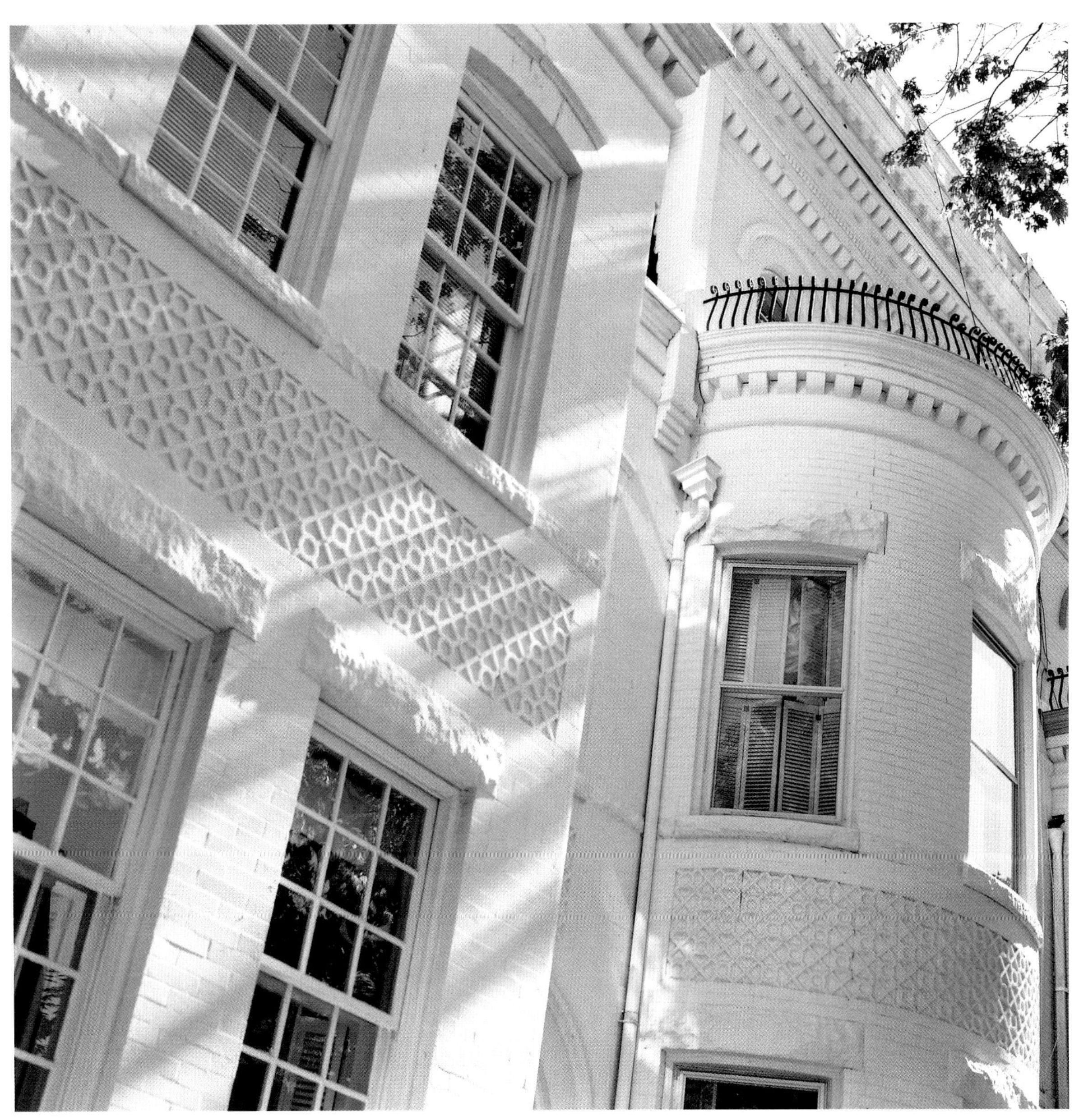

Queen Anne townhouses, Thirty-third Street

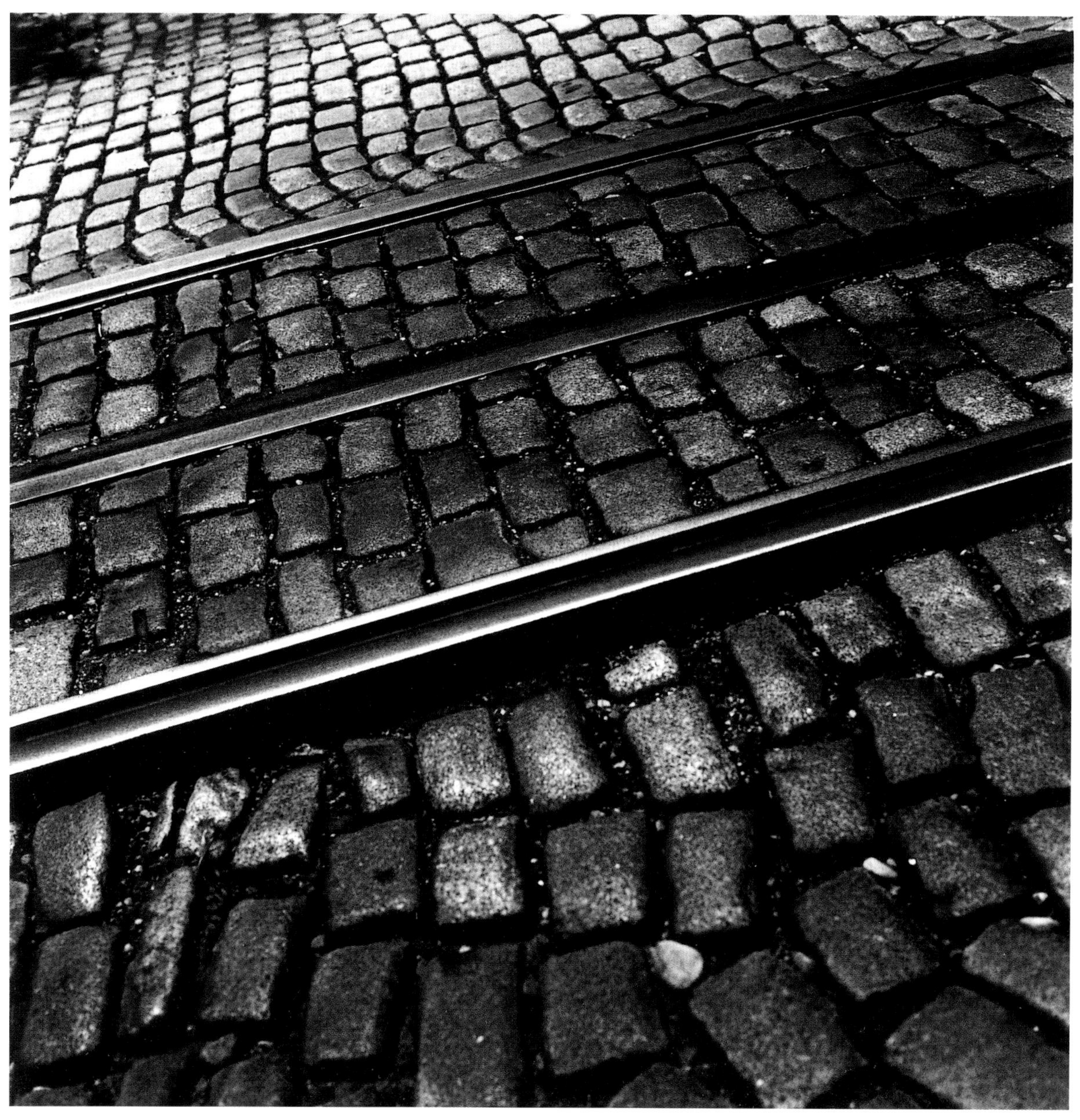

P Street, Georgetown

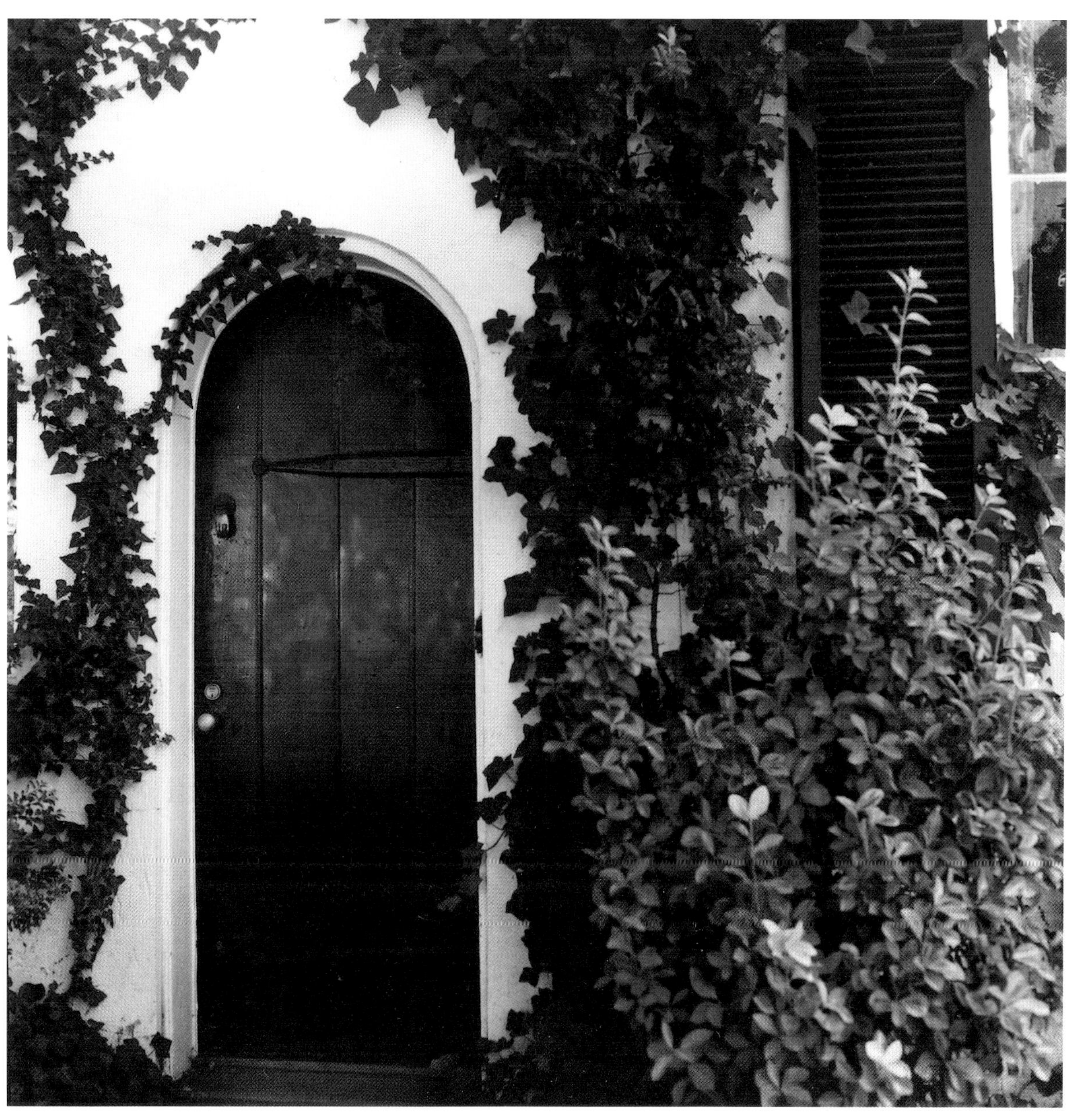

Passageway, Georgetown

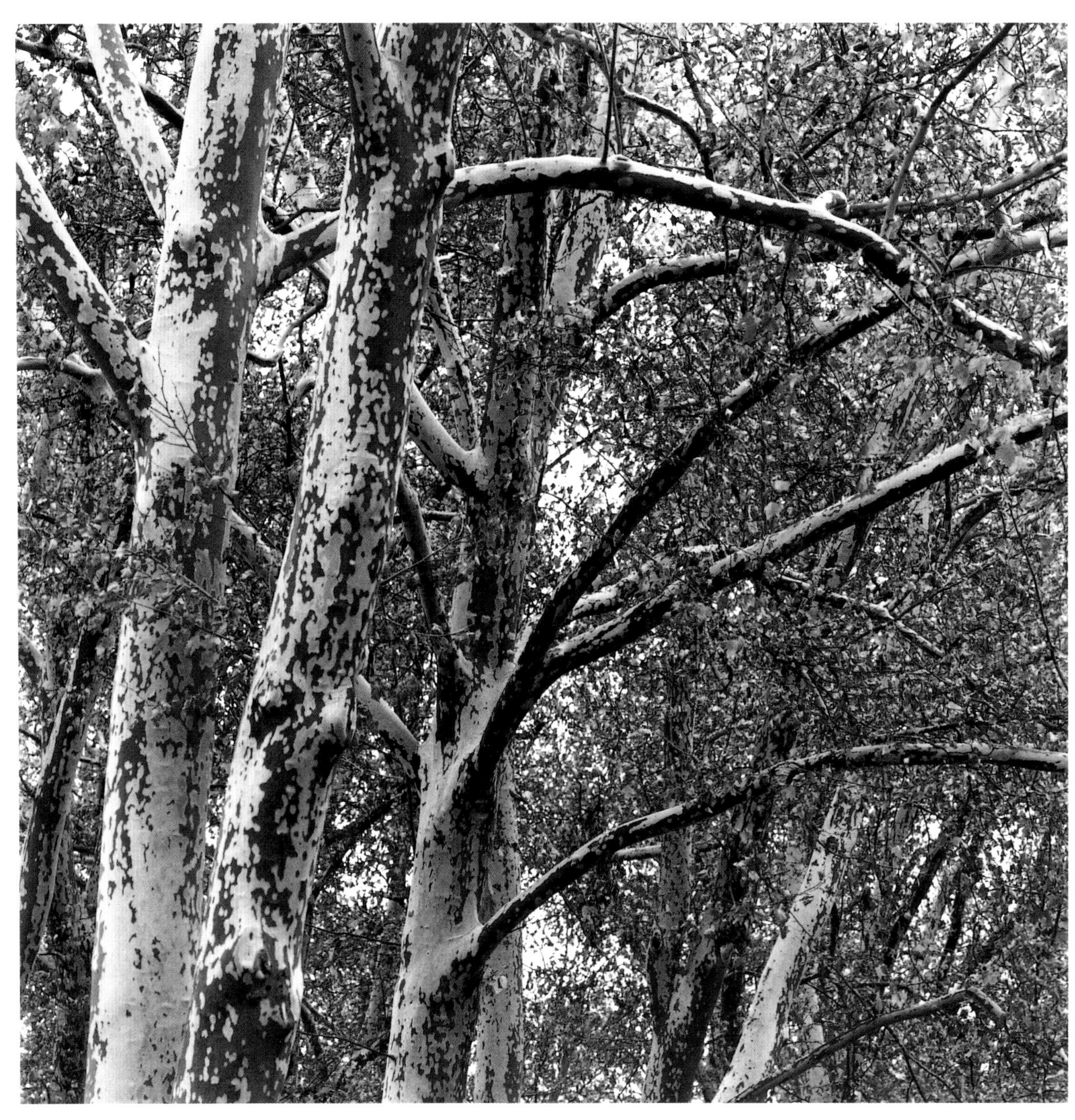

Sycamores, West Potomac Park

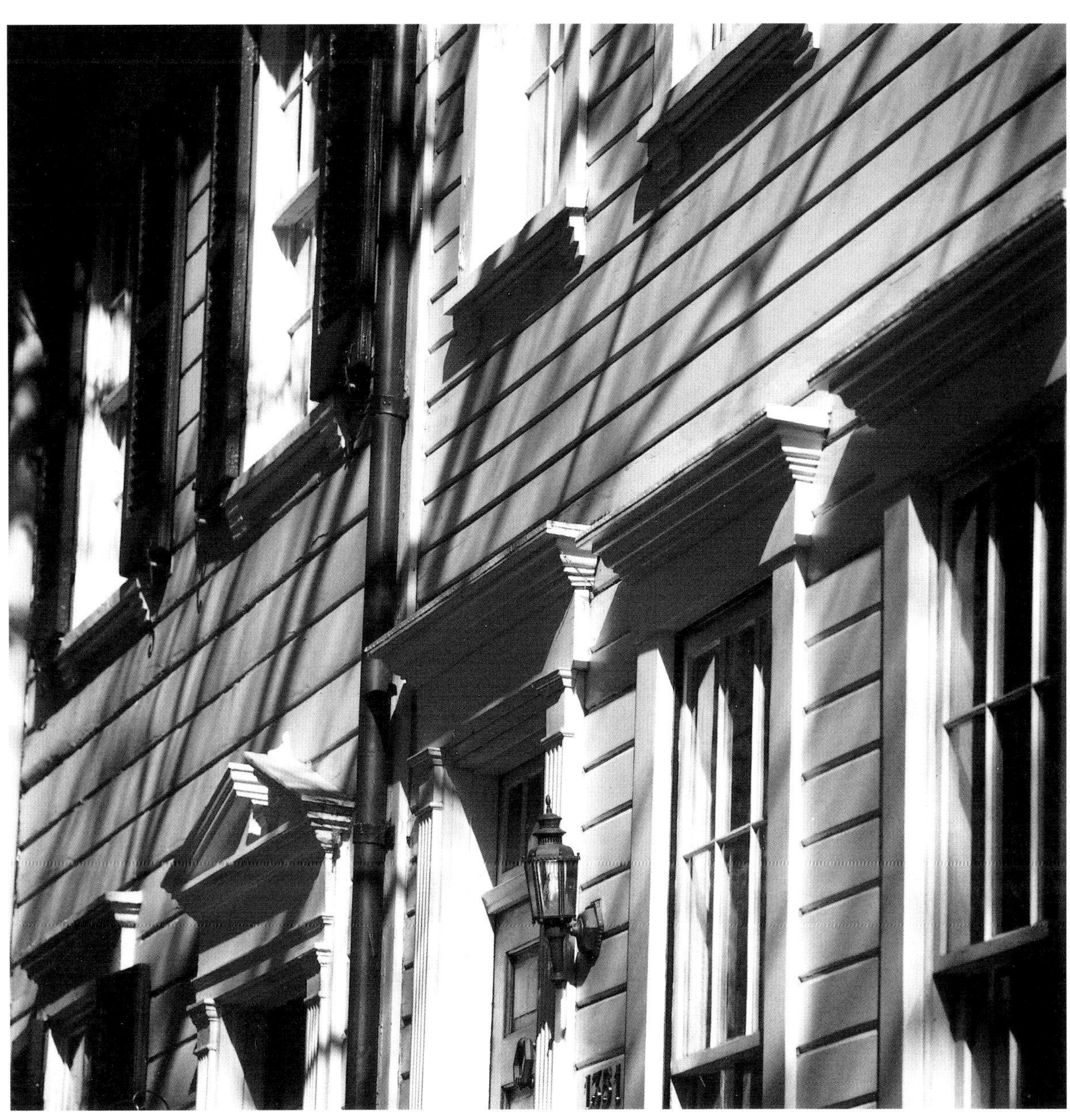

Federal rowhouses, Thirtieth Street

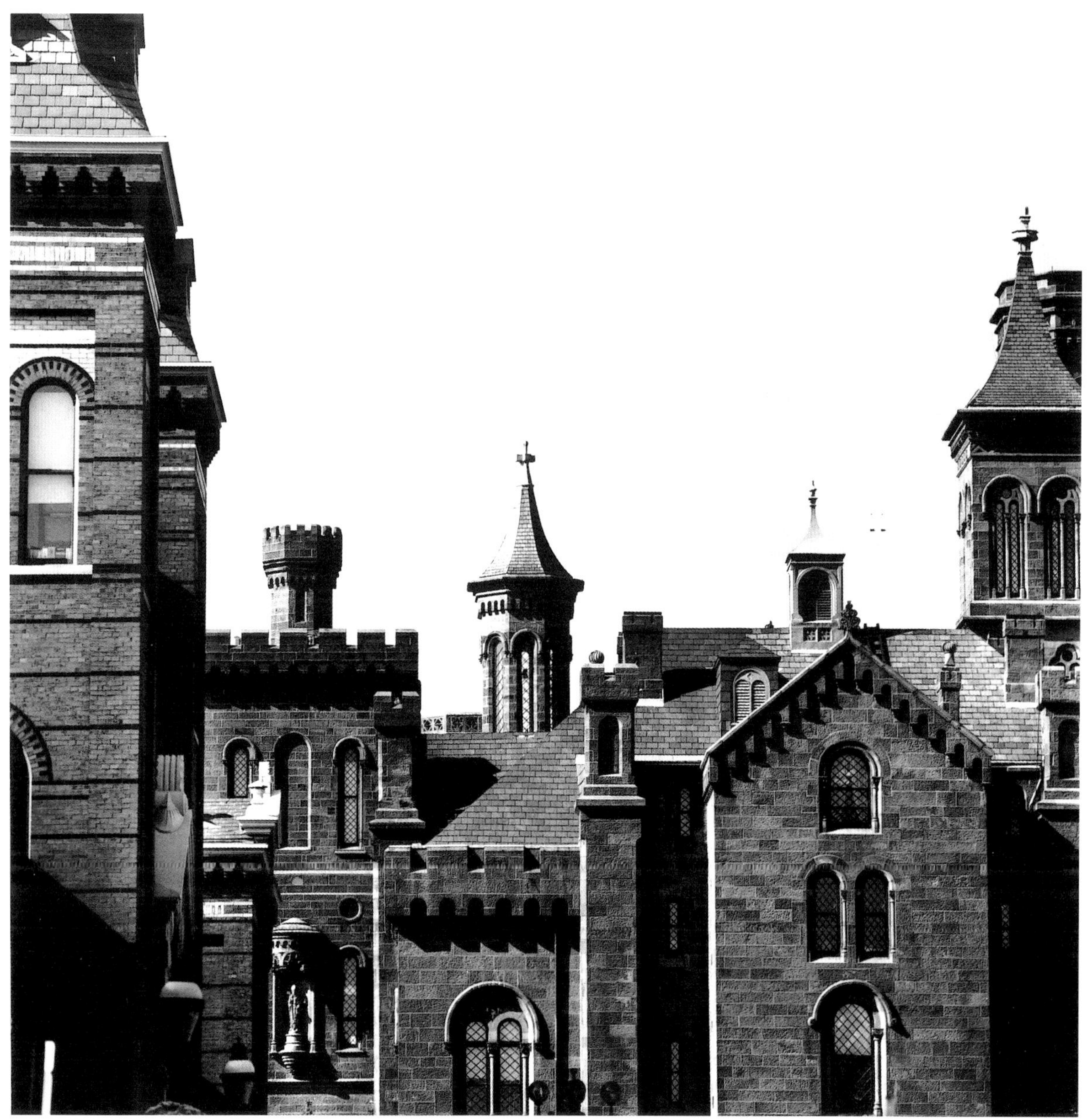

Smithsonian Building

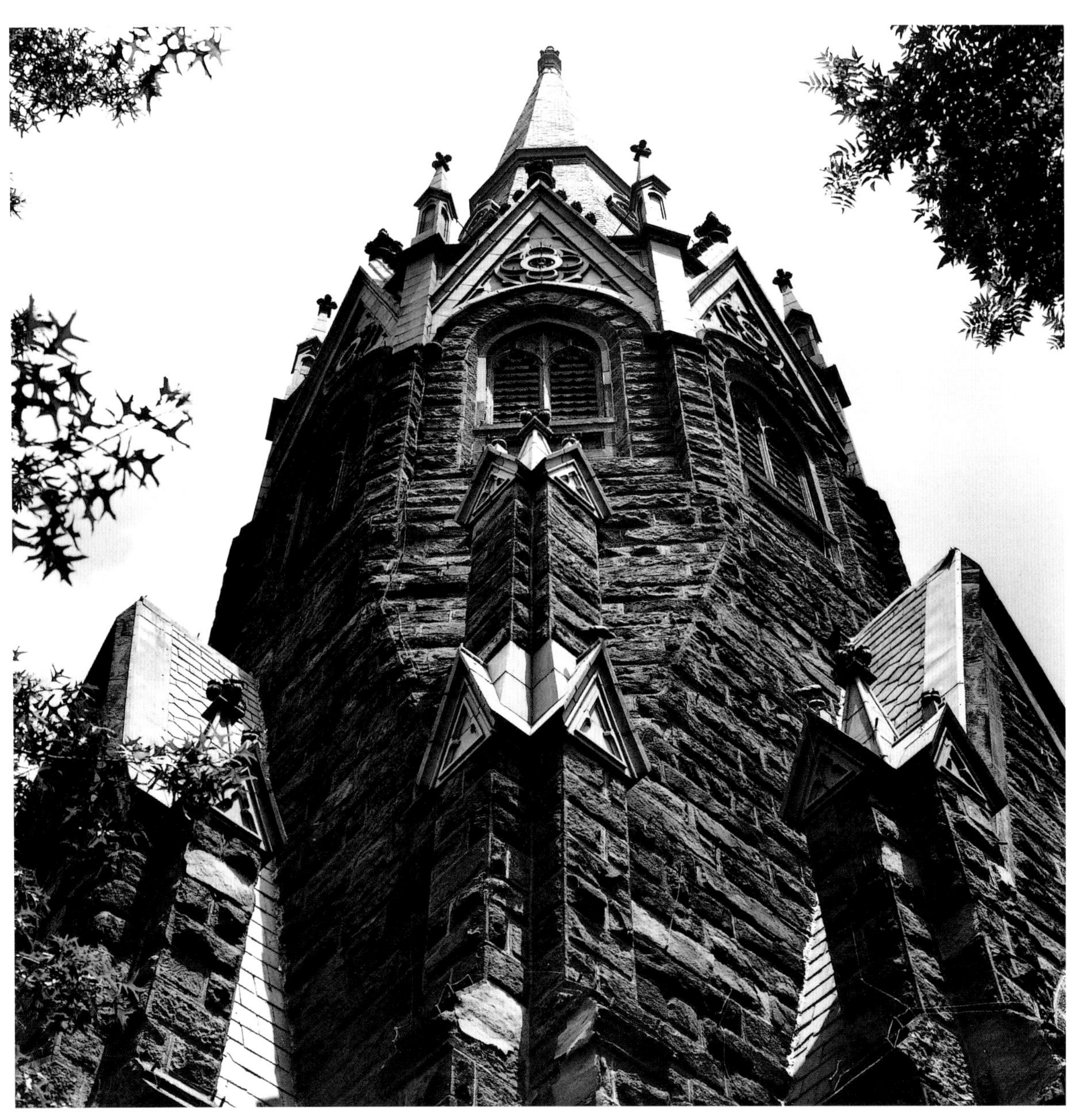

Luther Place Memorial Church

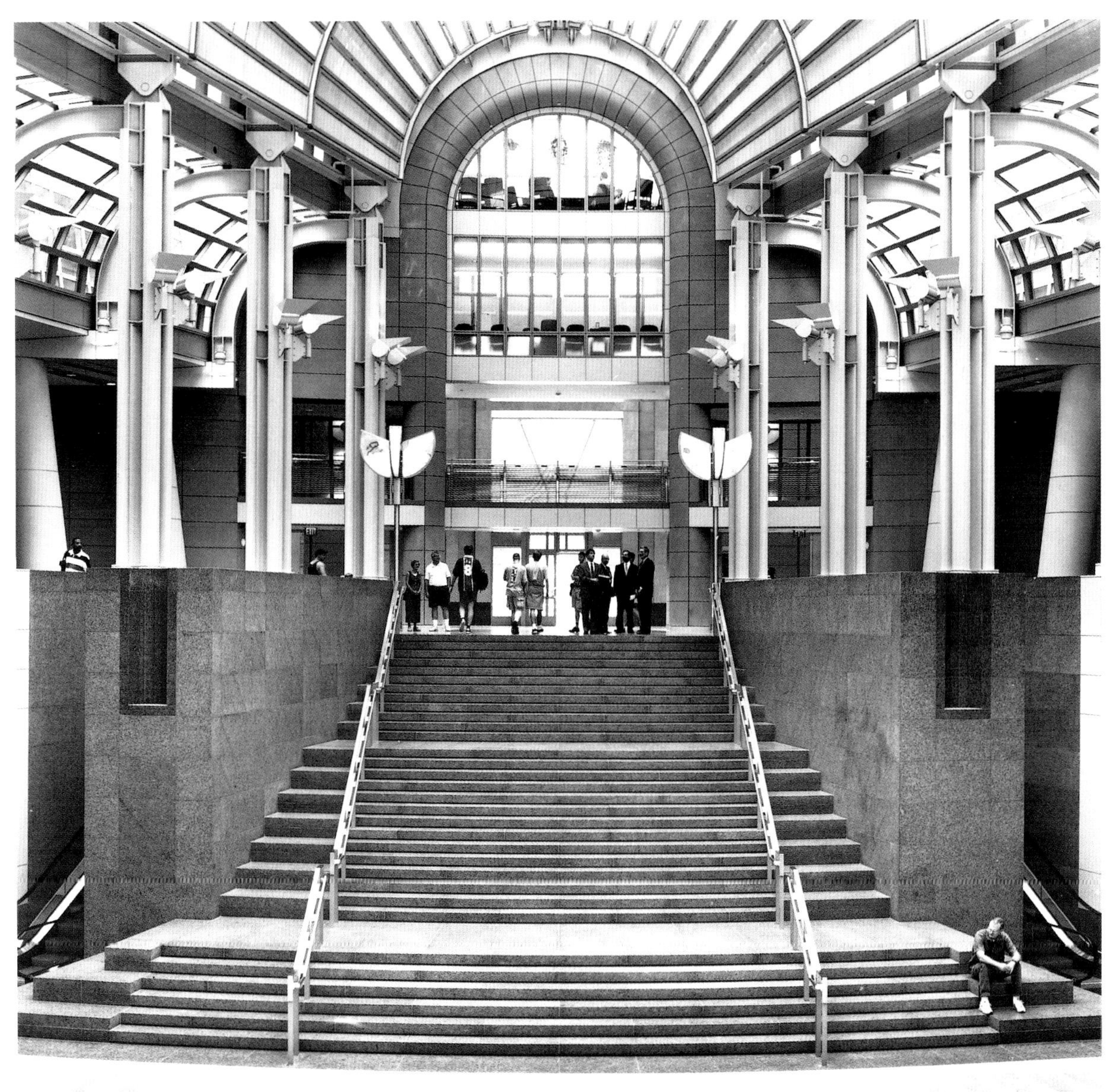

Ronald Reagan Building

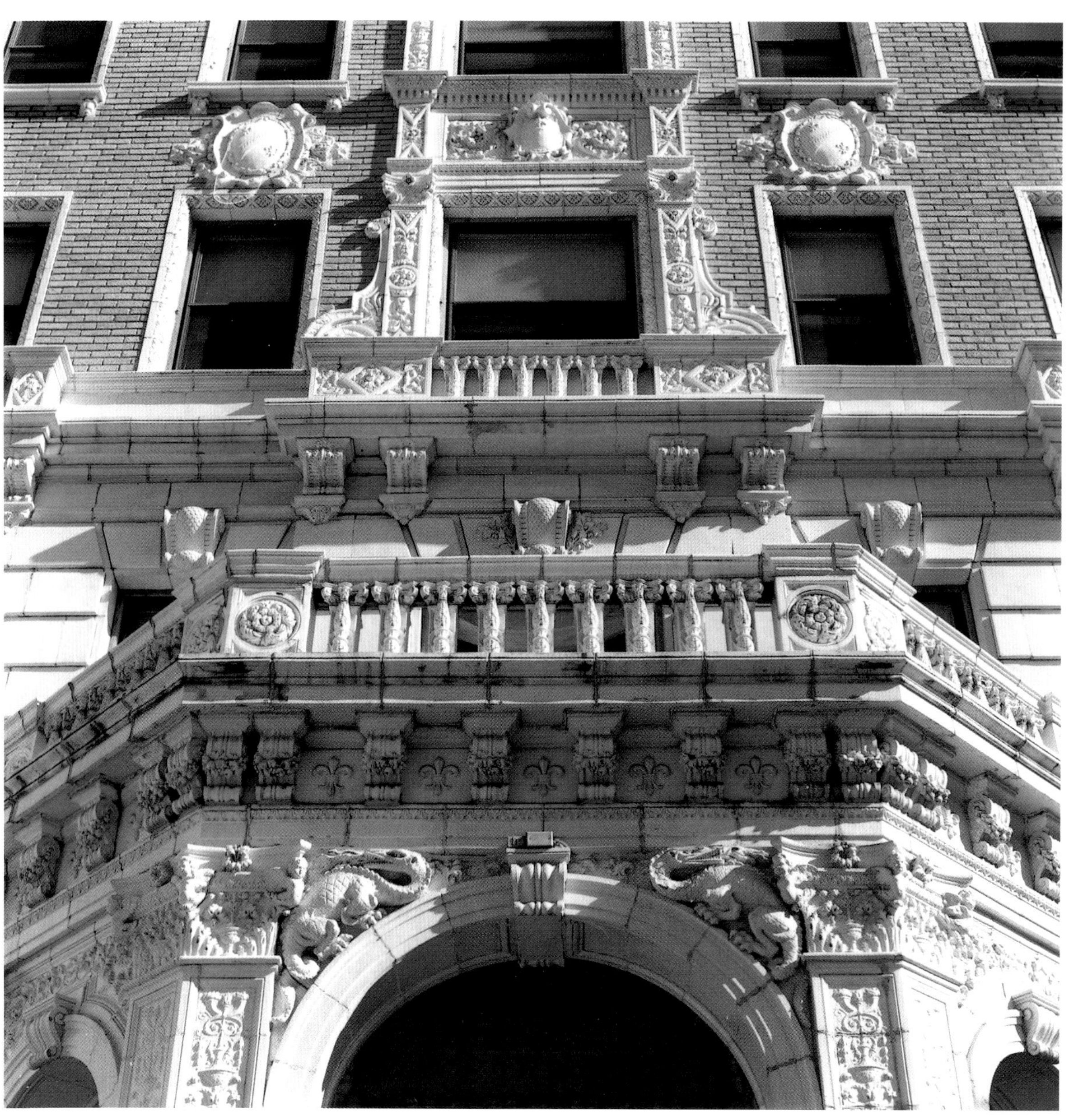

Apartment building, Connecticut Avenue

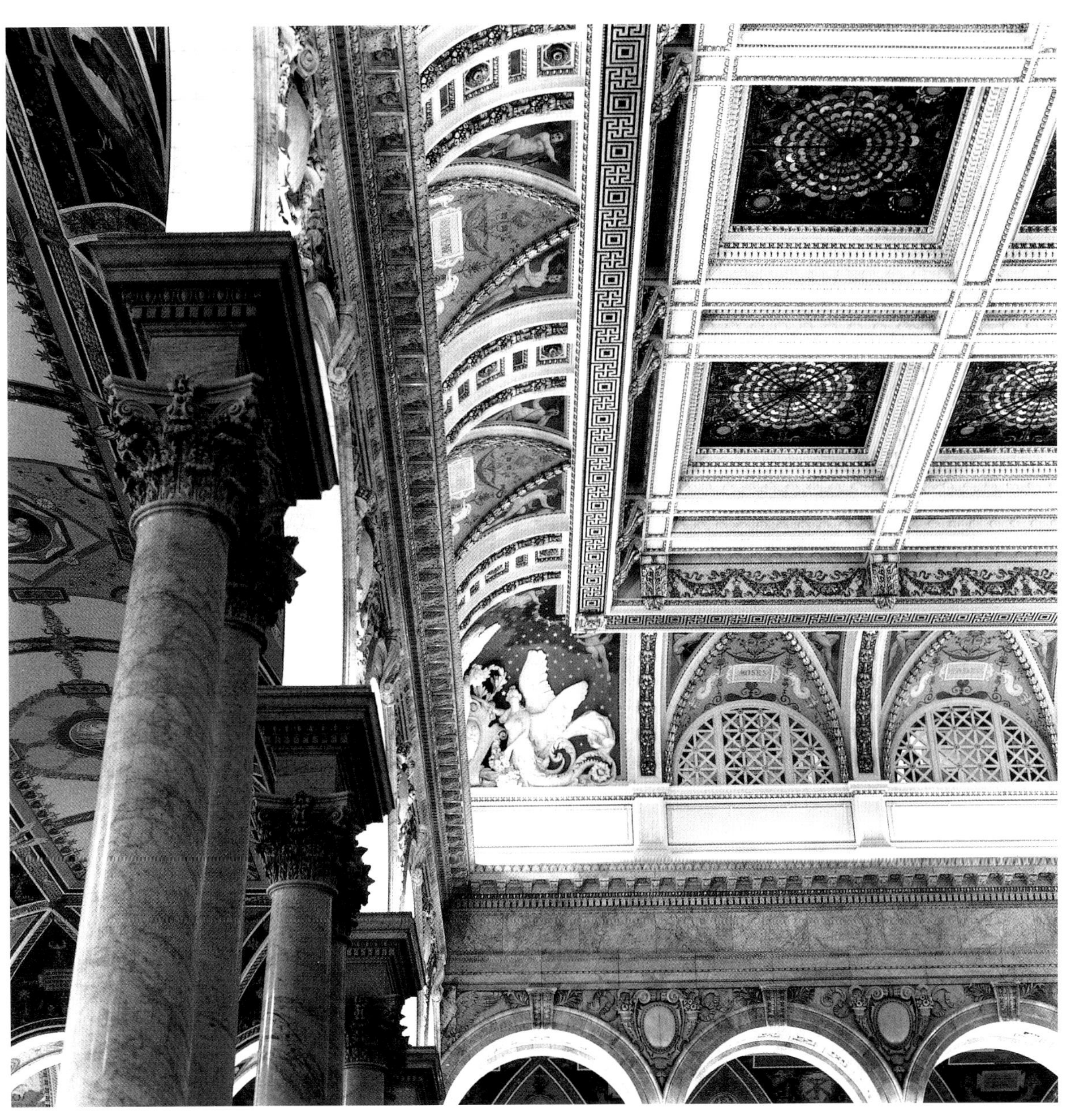

Library of Congress

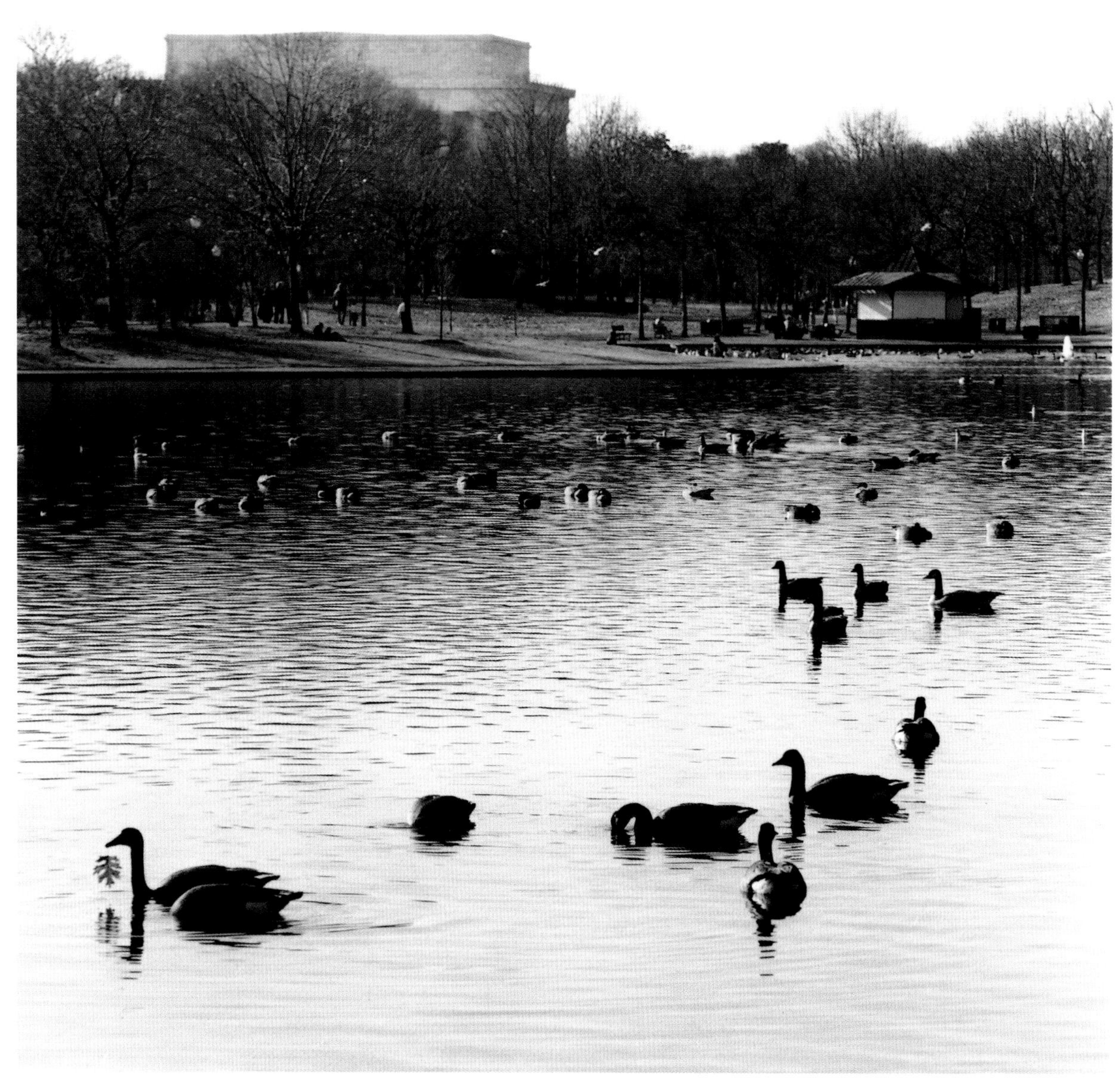

Pond, Constitution Gardens

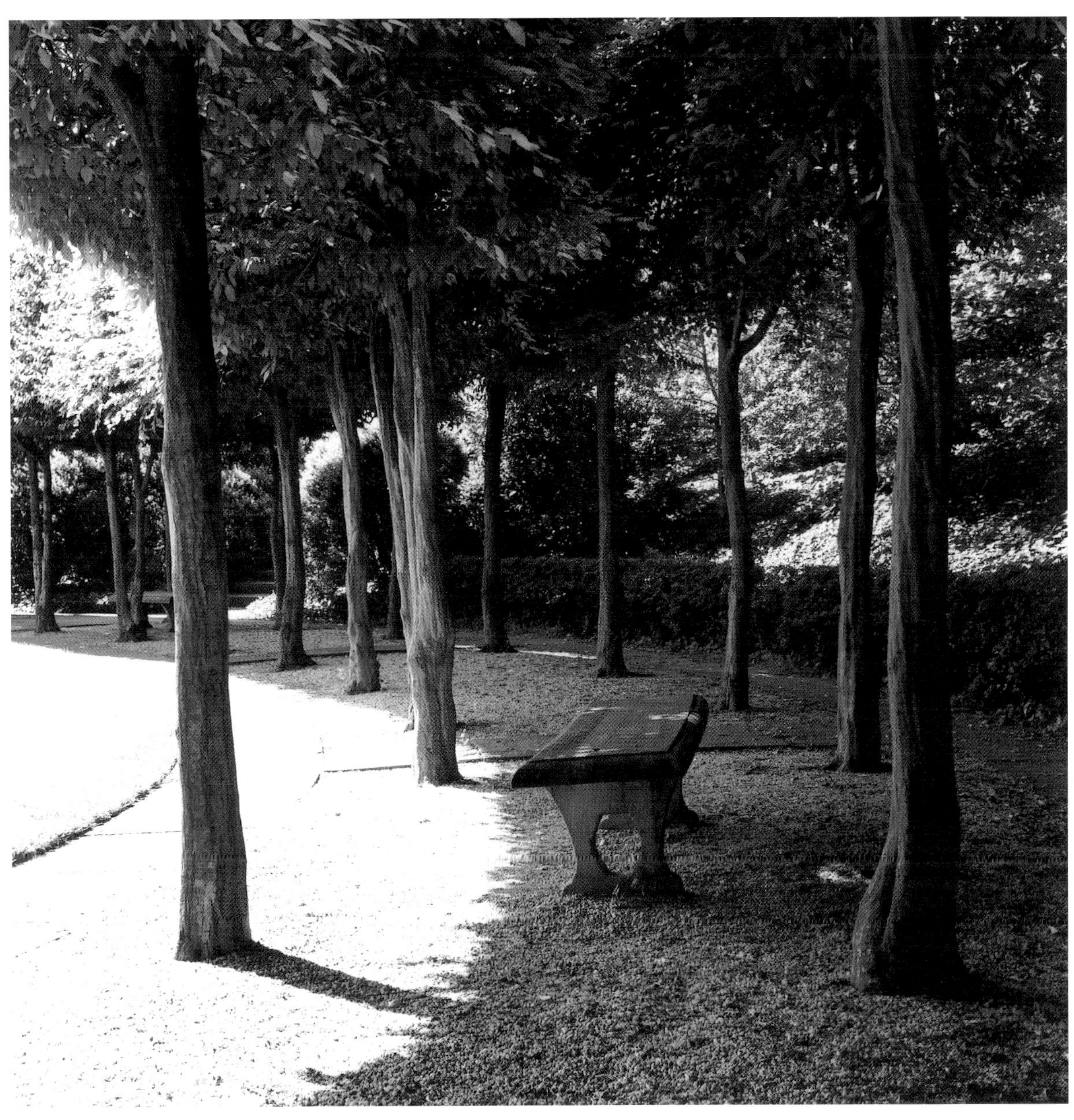

Dumbarton Oaks

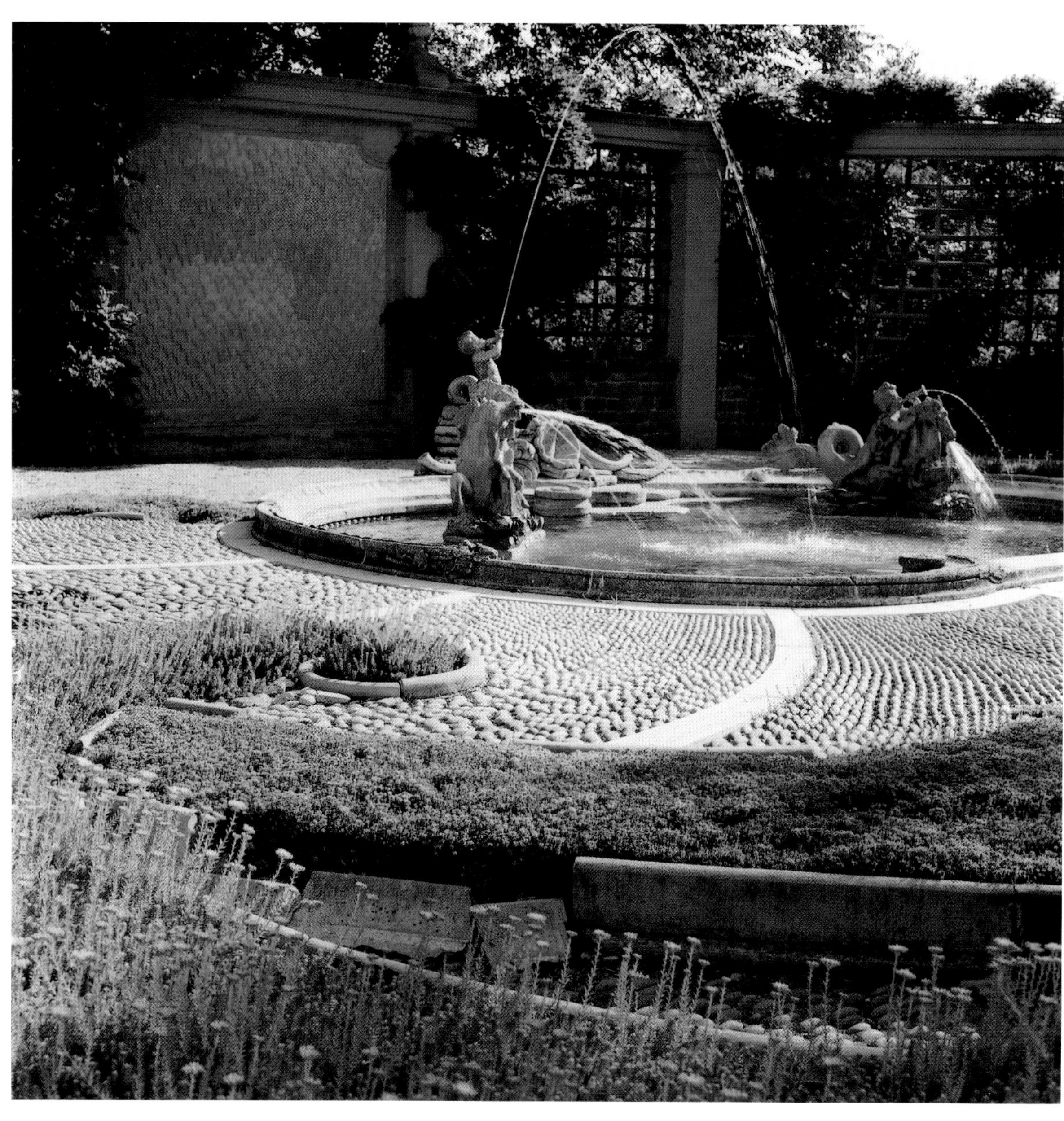

Pebble Garden, Dumbarton Oaks

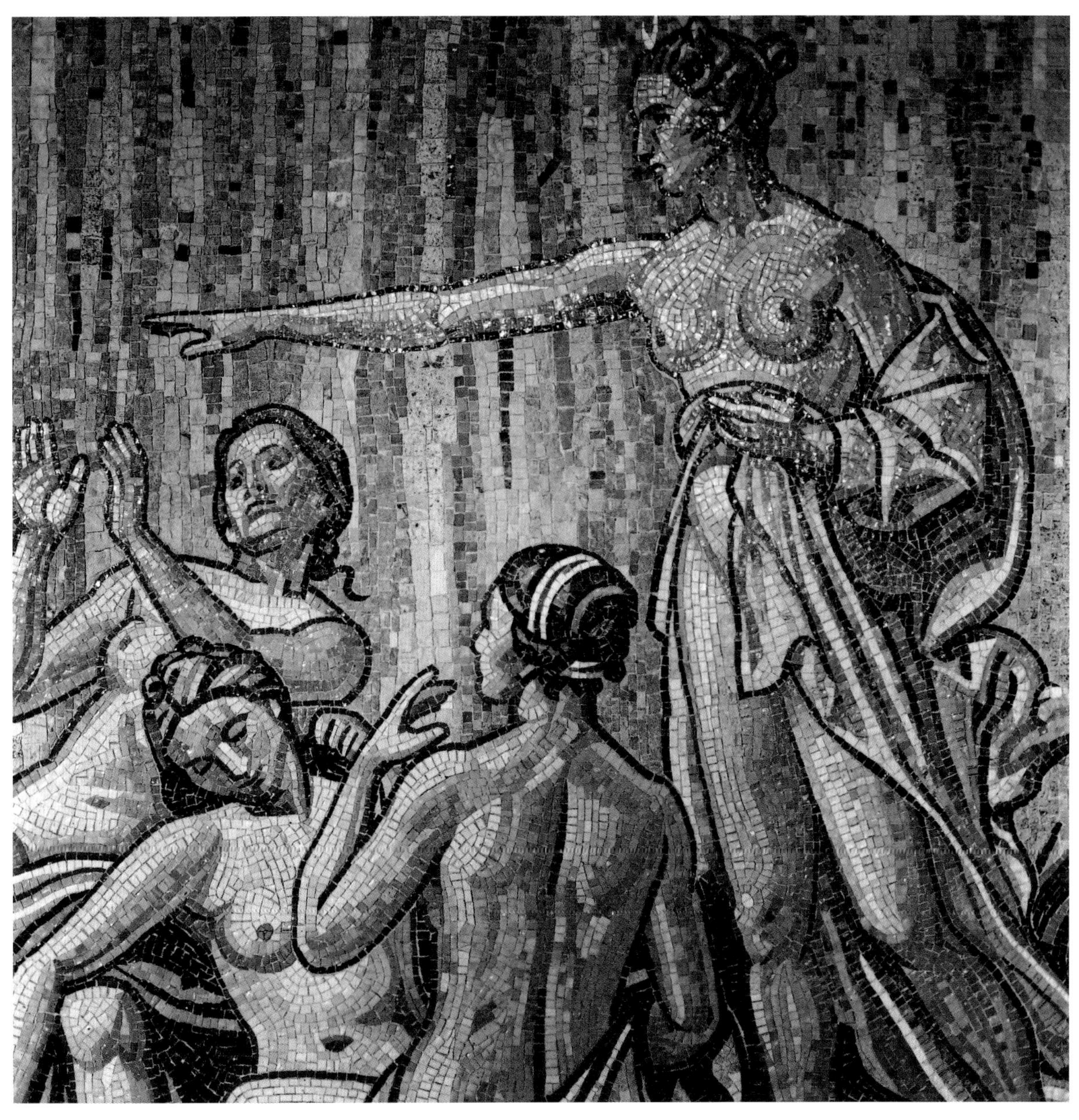

Mosaic, Dumbarton Oaks

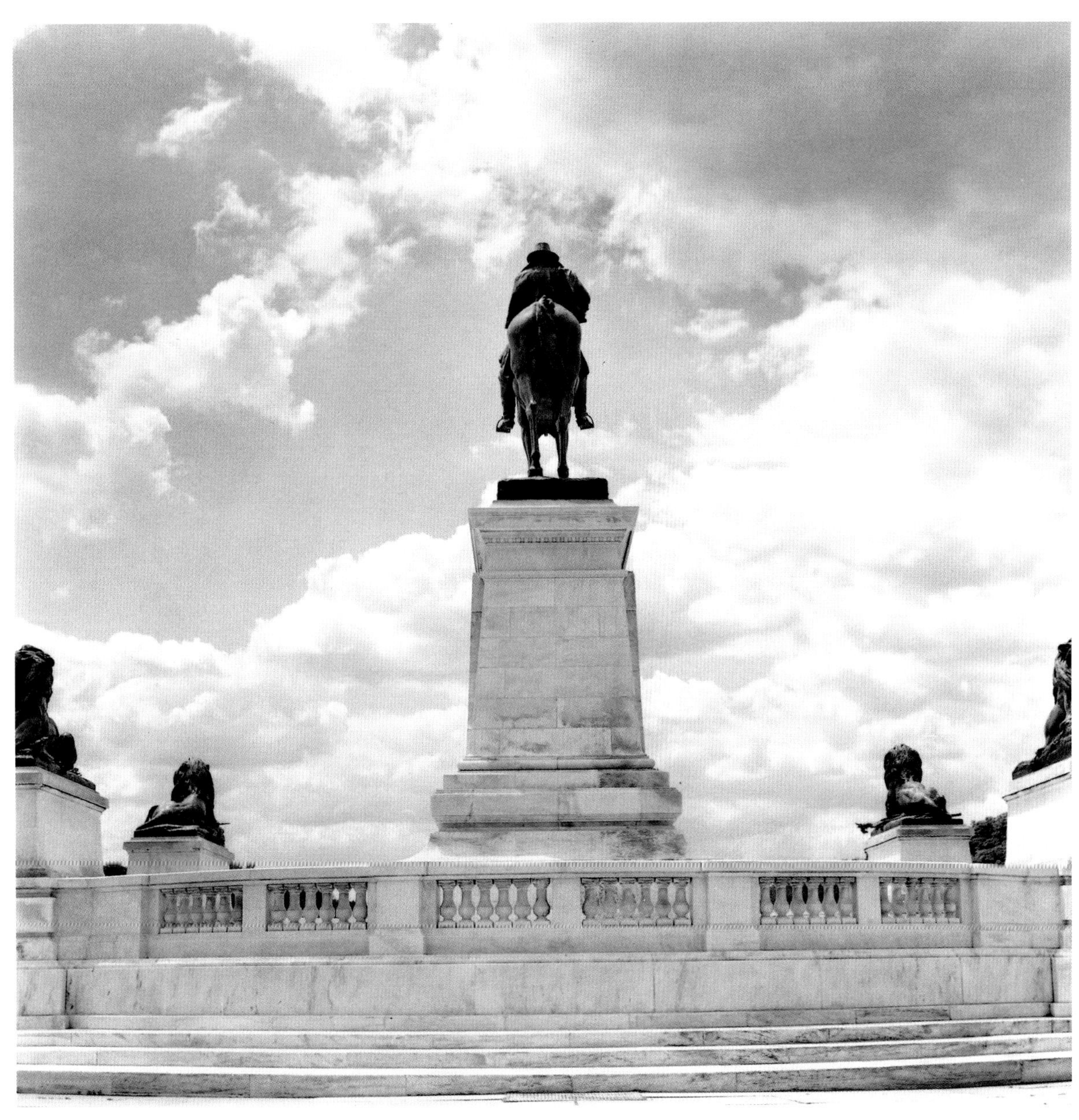

Grant Memorial

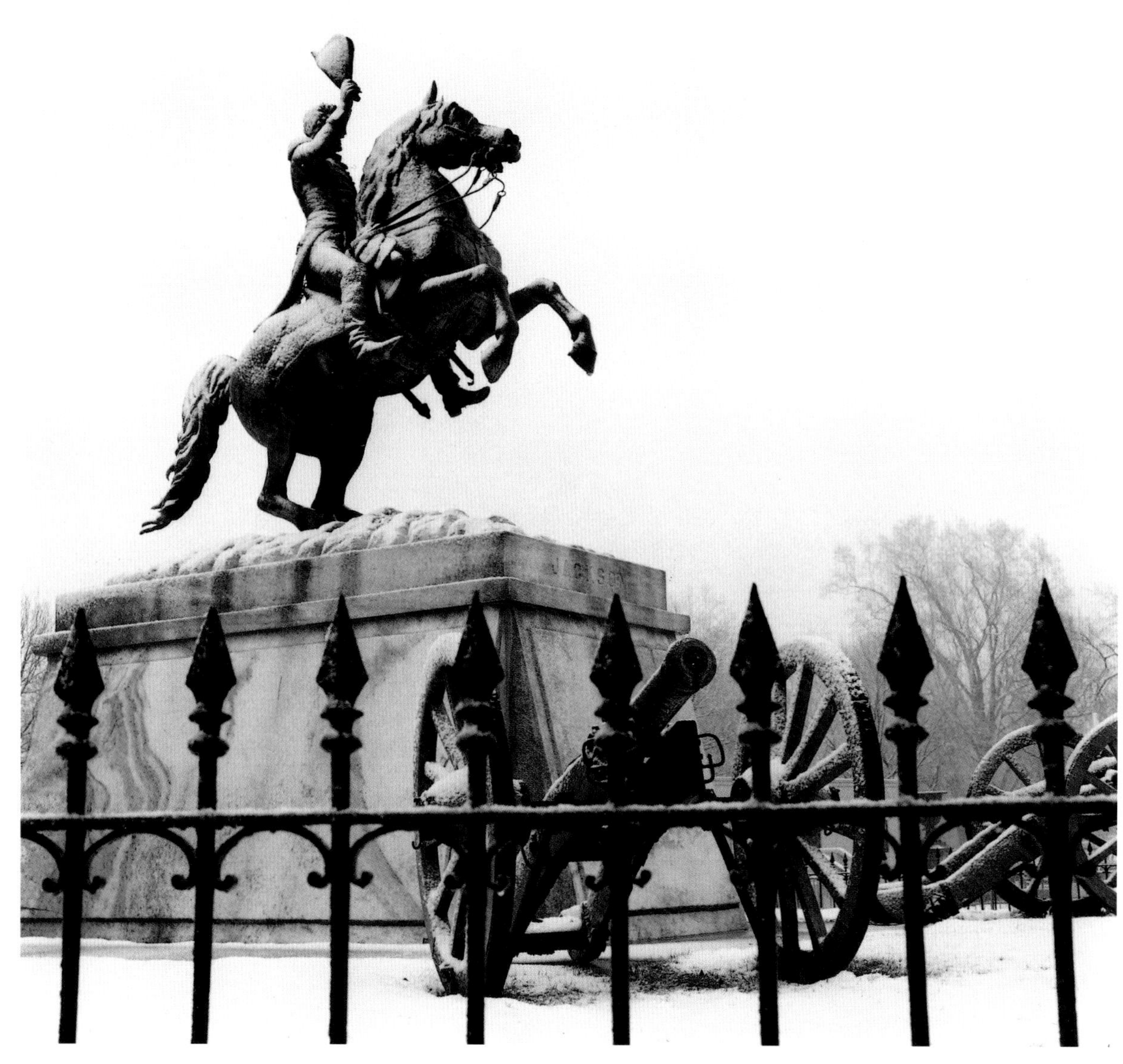

Andrew Jackson Statue

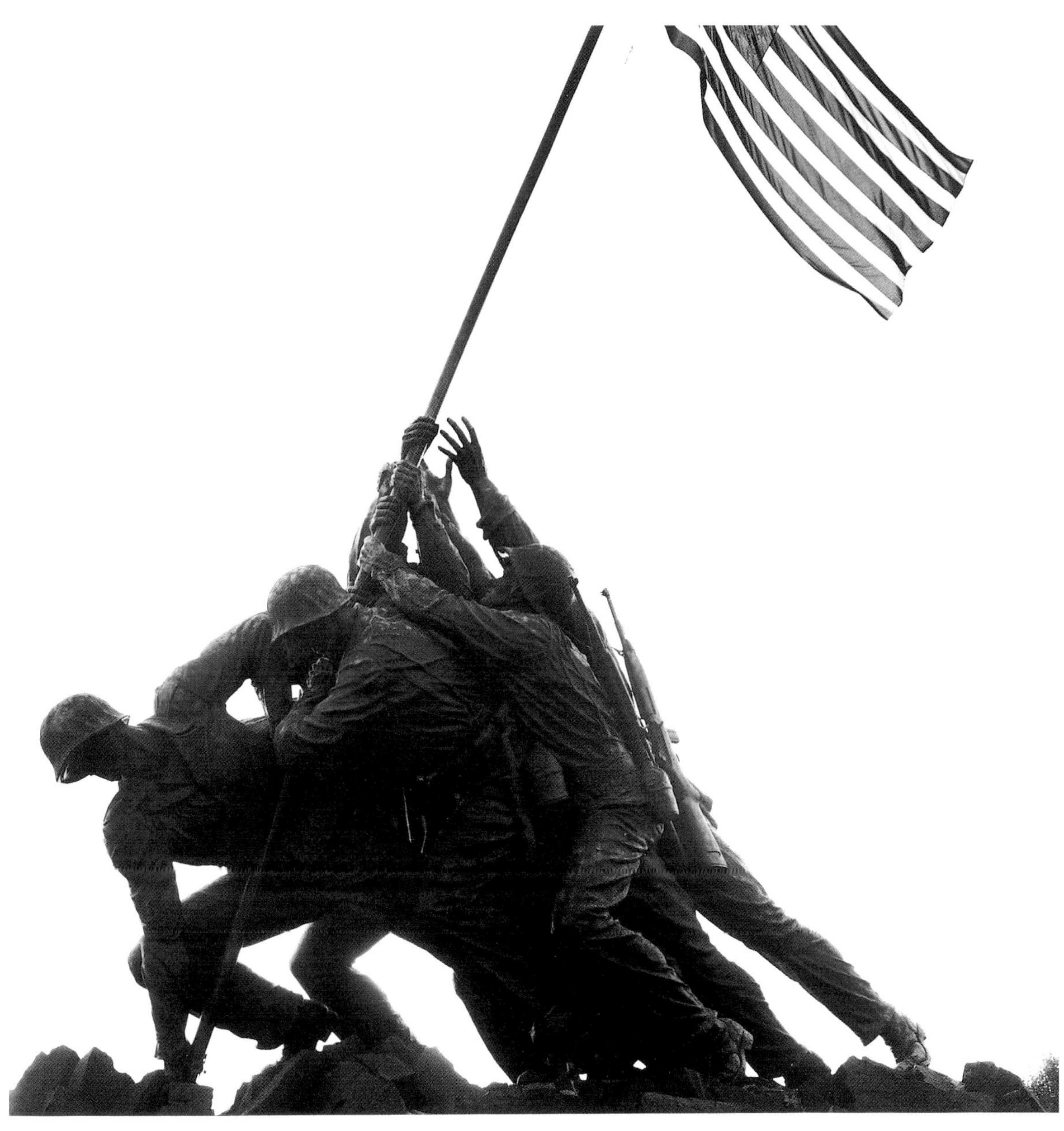

Marine Corps War Memorial

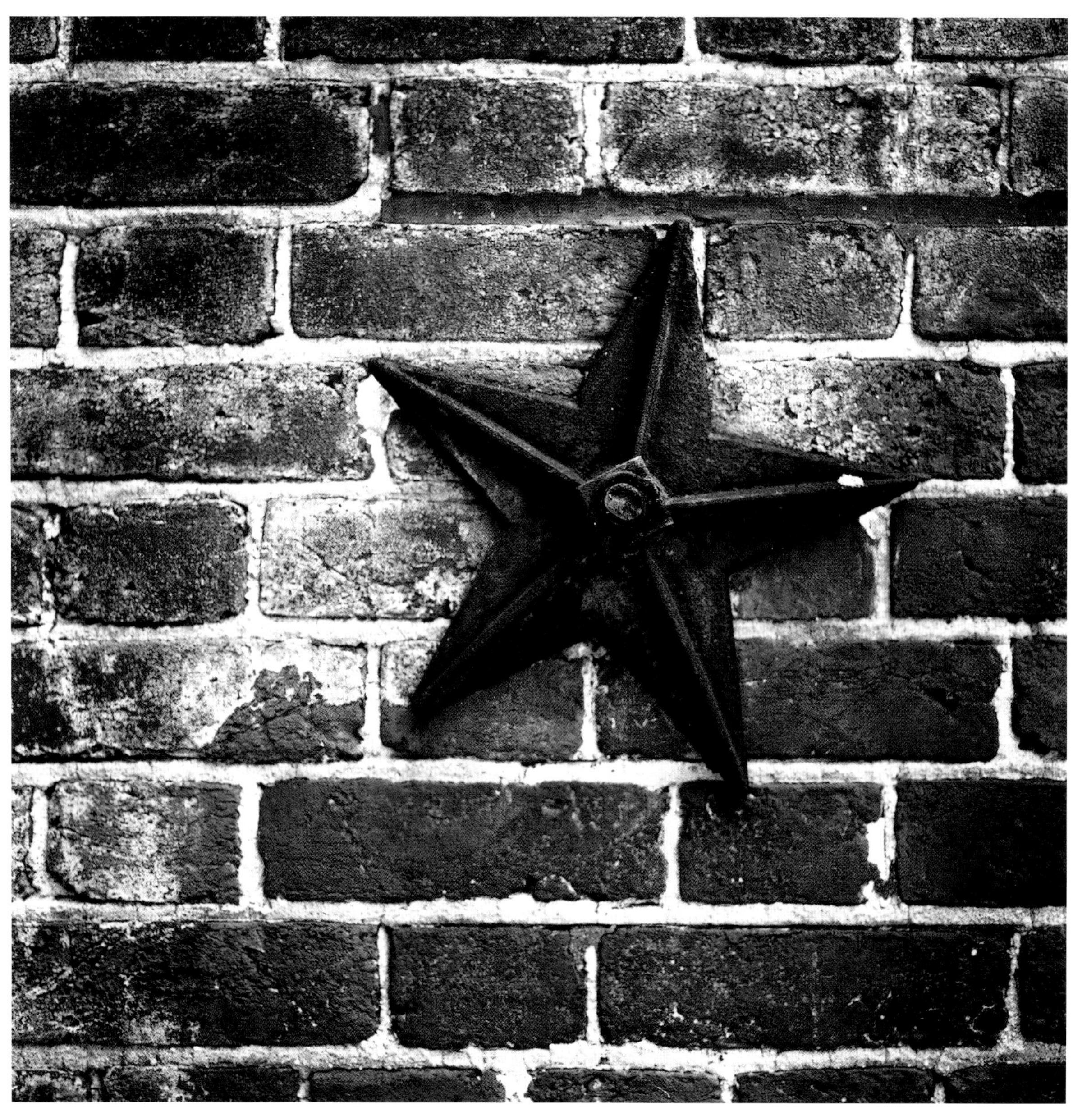

Cast-iron building tie, Georgetown

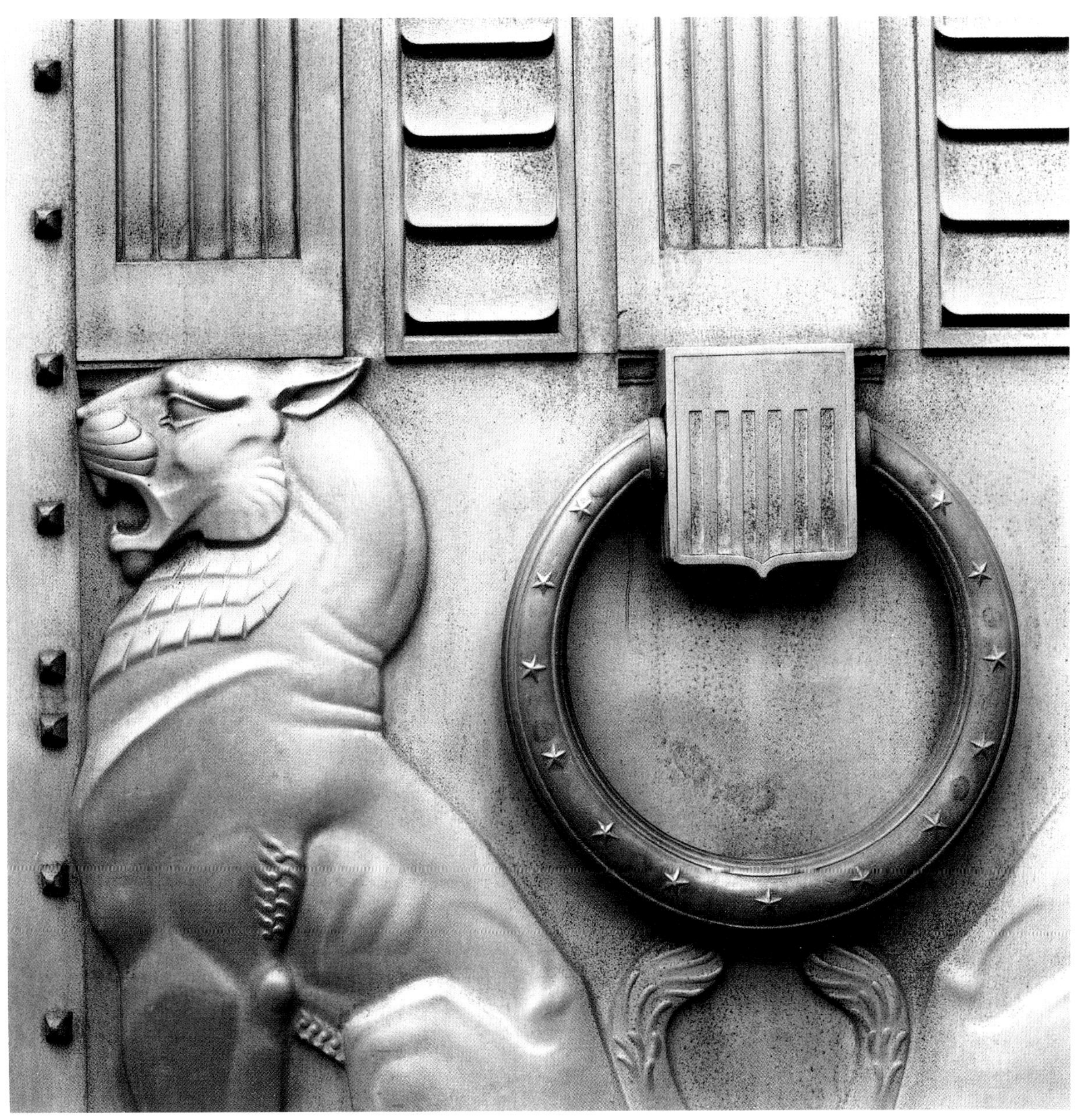

Detail of door, Department of Justice

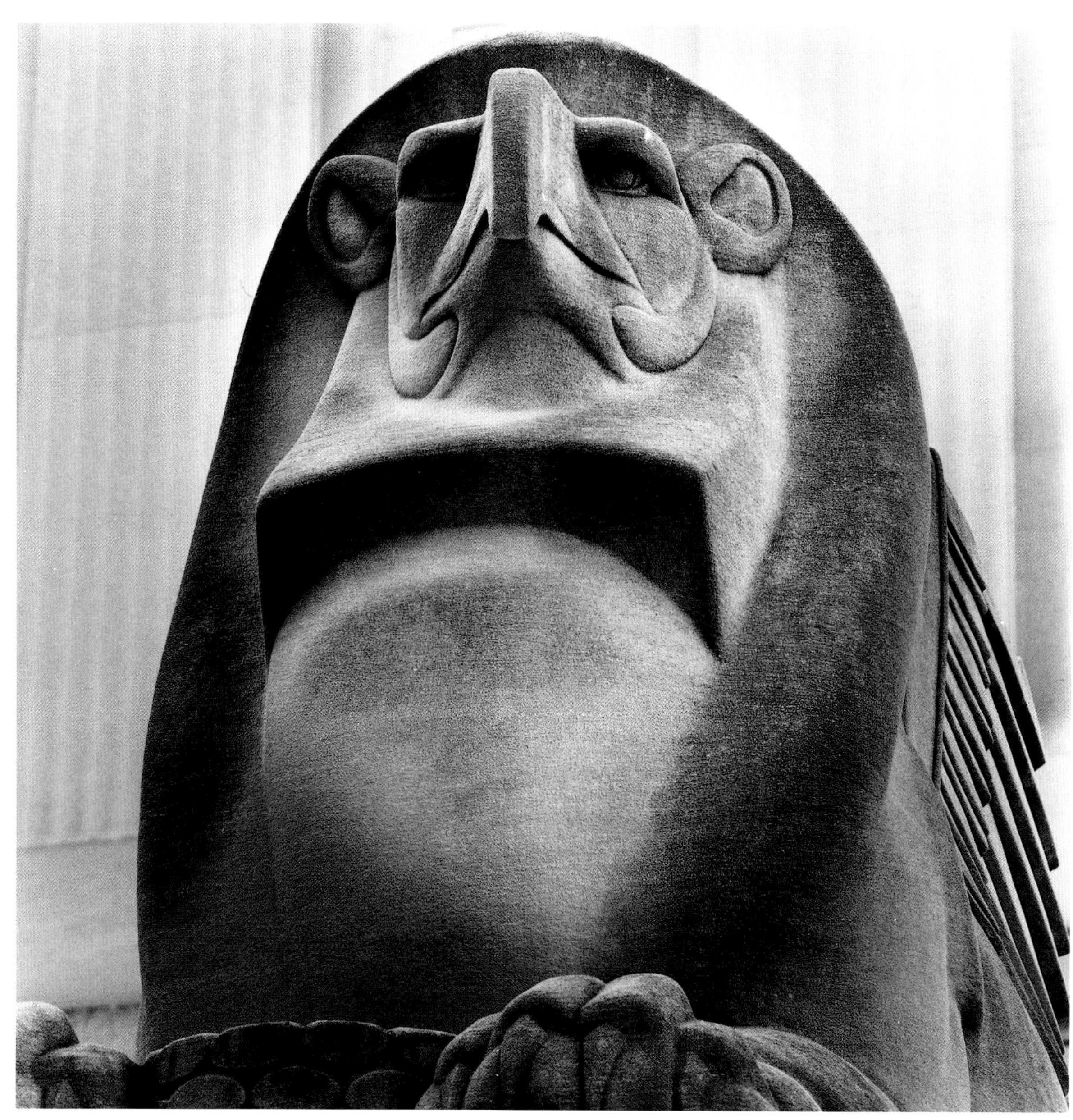

Griffin, Acacia Mutual Life Insurance Building

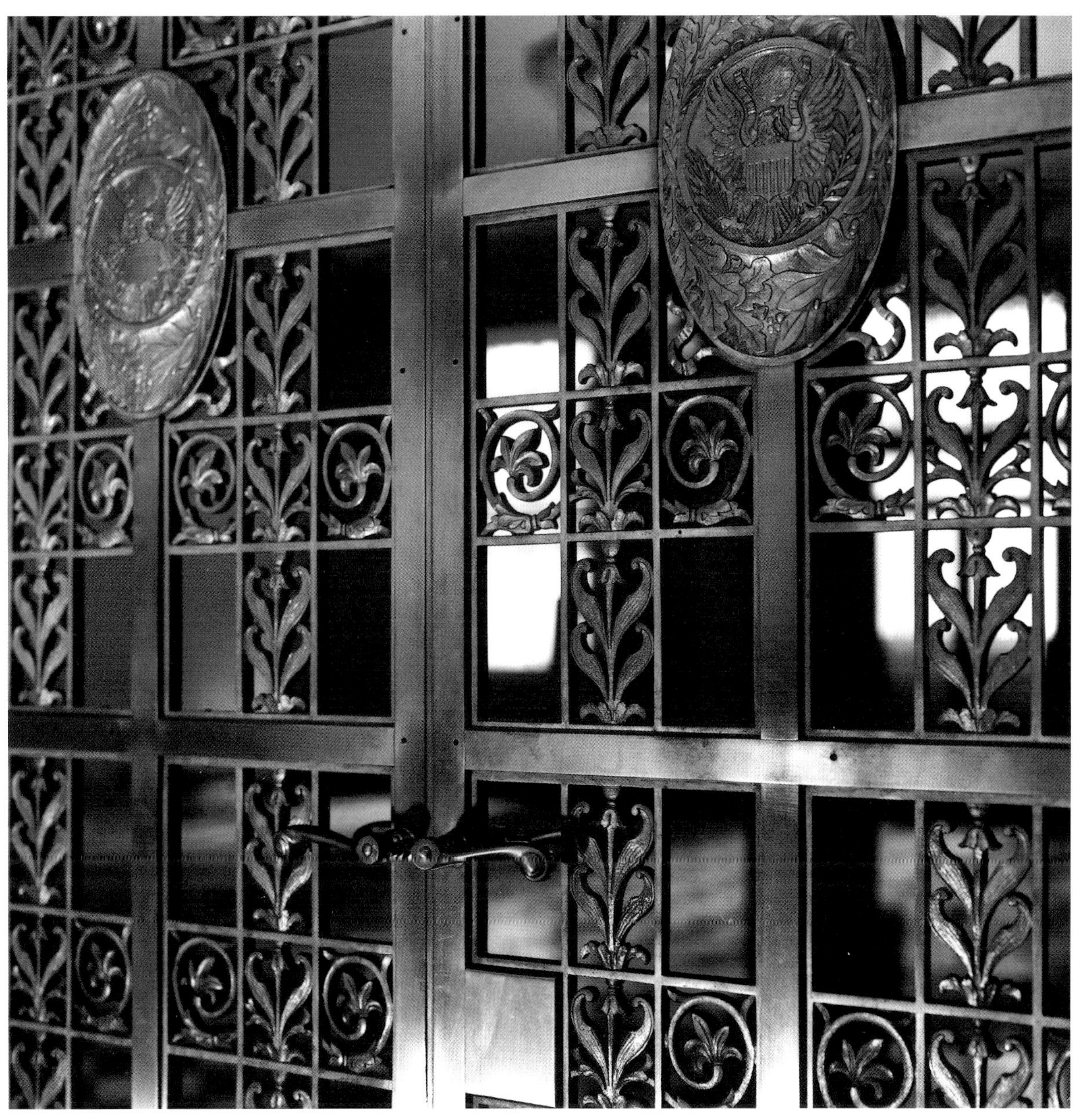

Bronze gate, Treasury Building

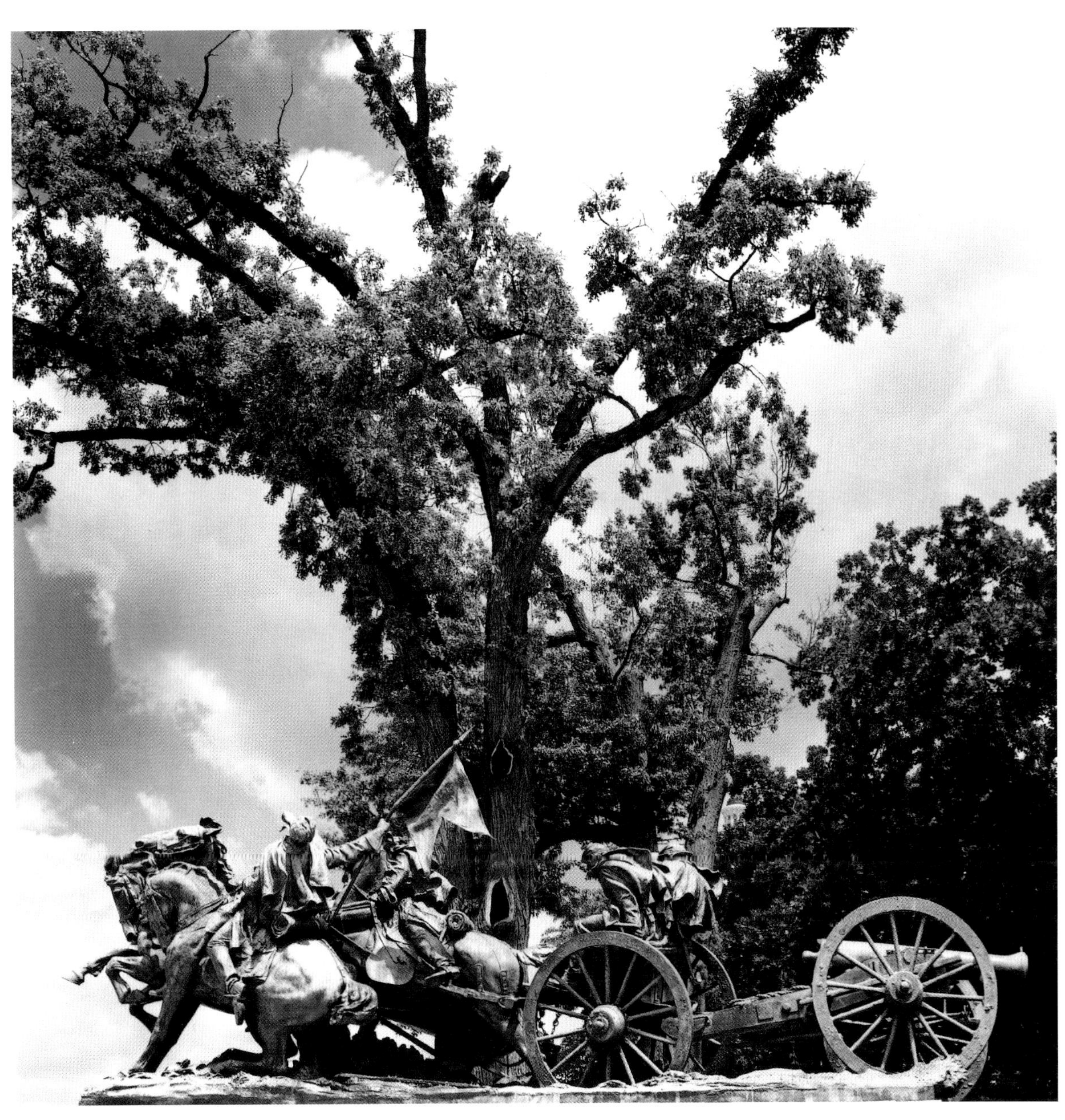

"Artillery Group," Grant Memorial

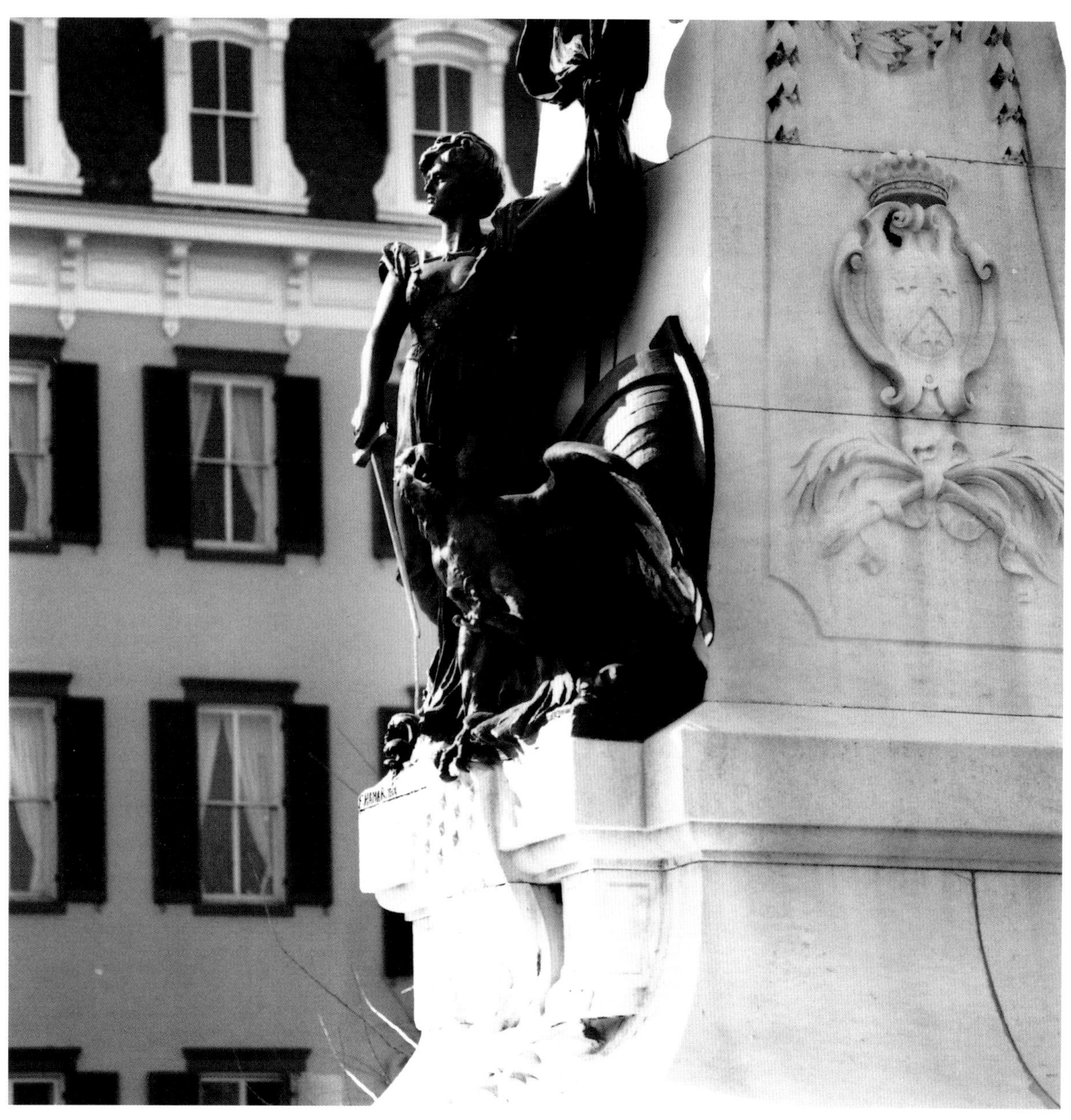

"Liberty," Lafayette Park

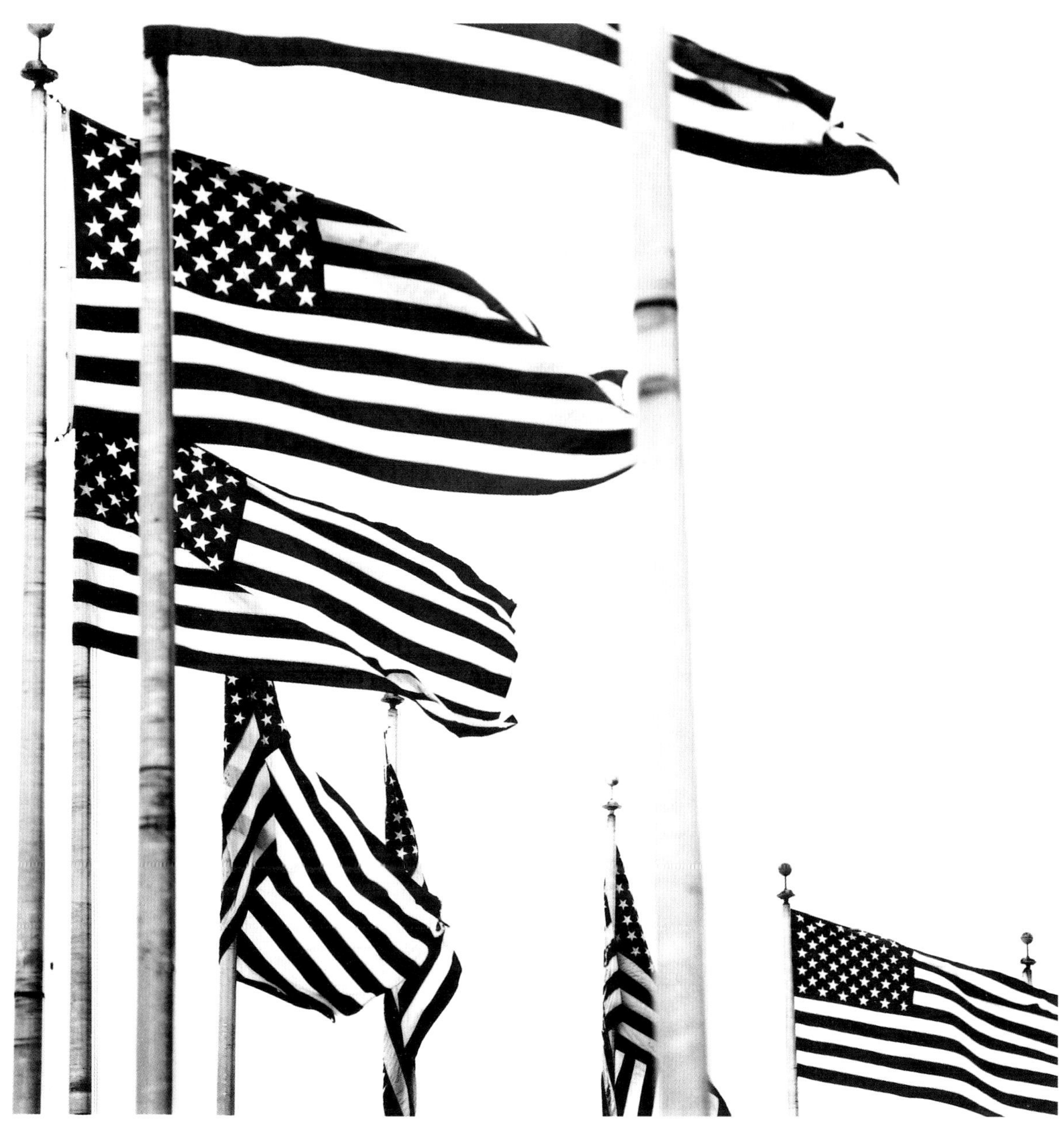

American flags, Washington Monument

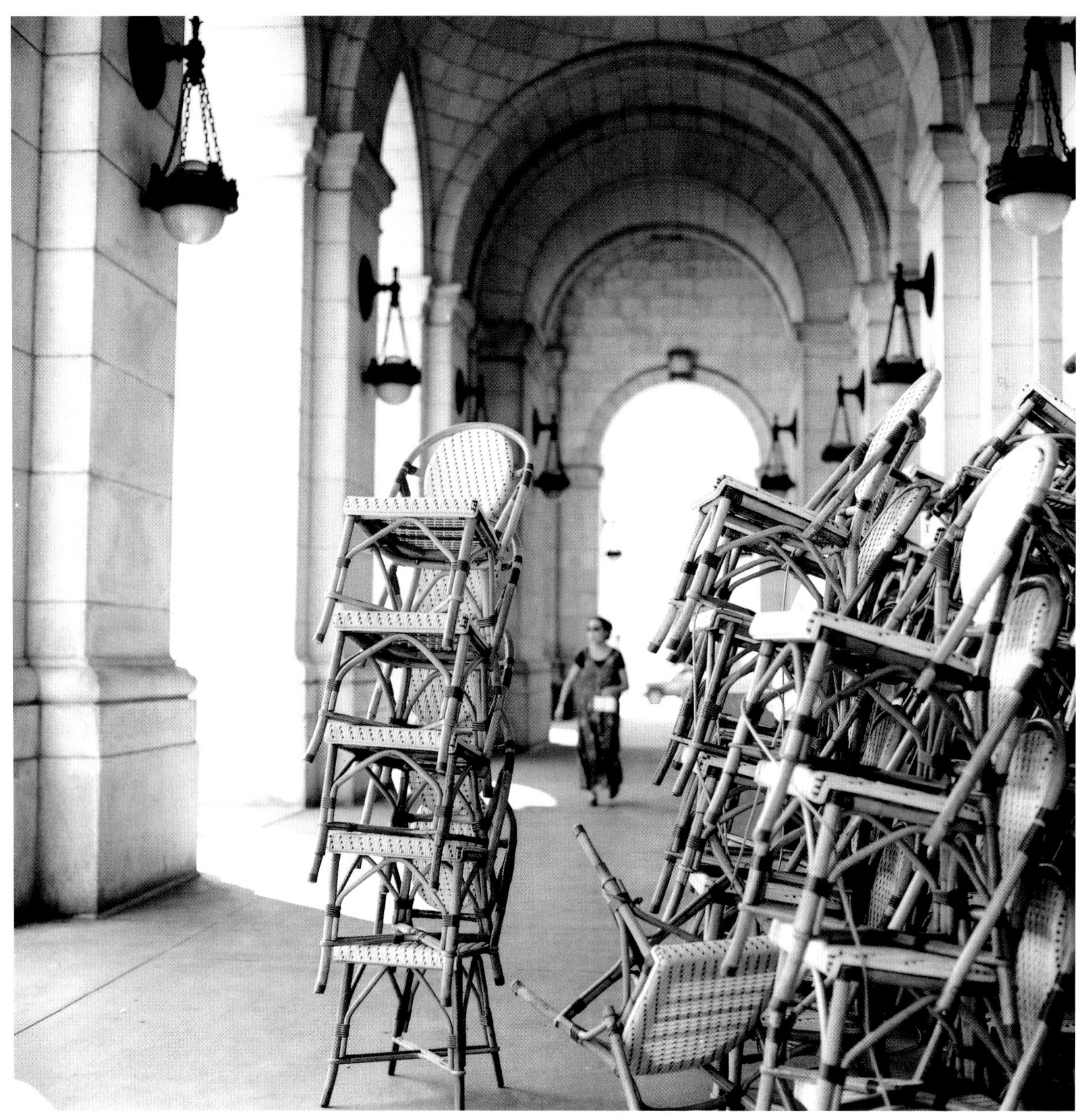

Union Station

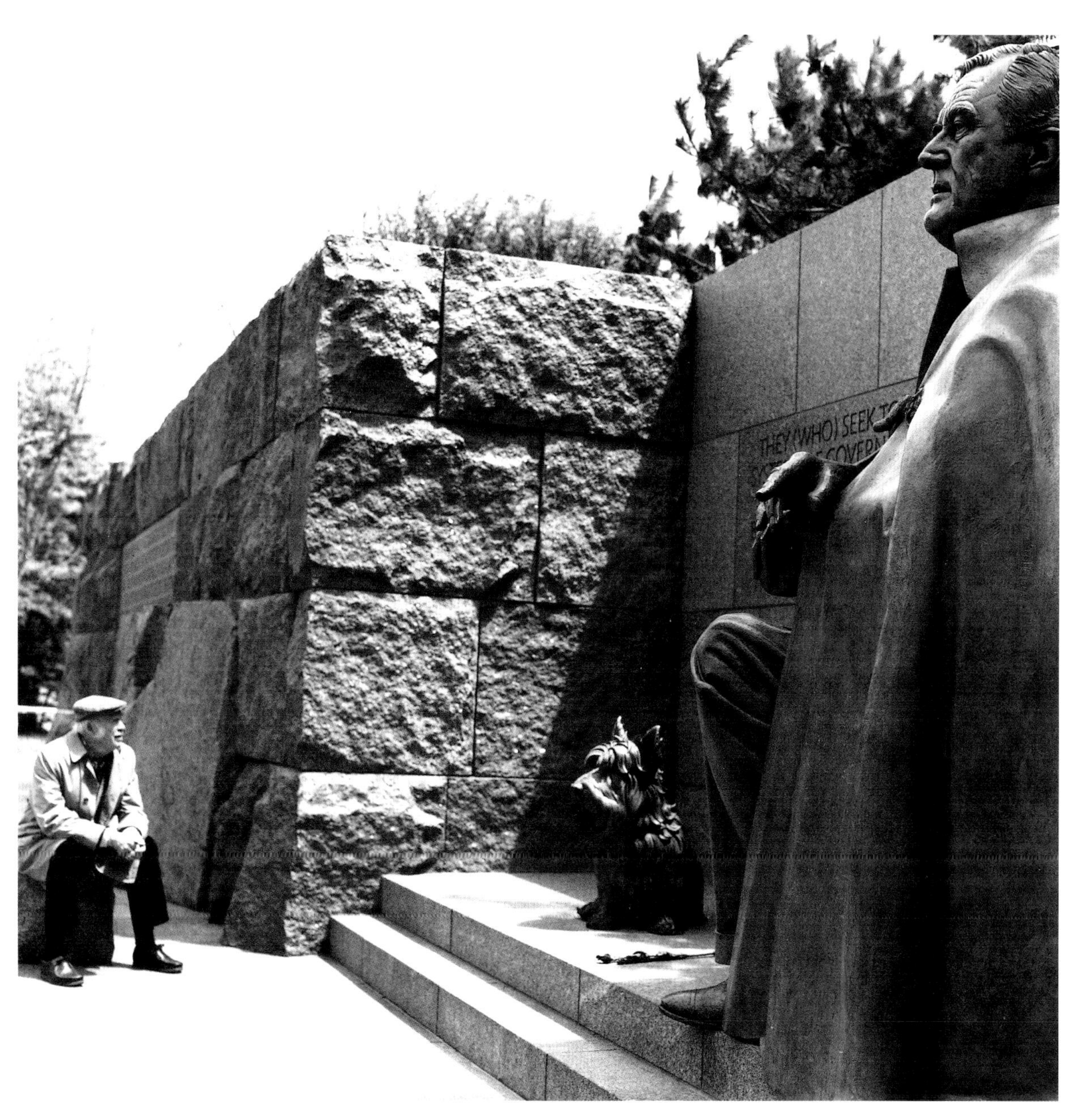

F.D.R. Memorial

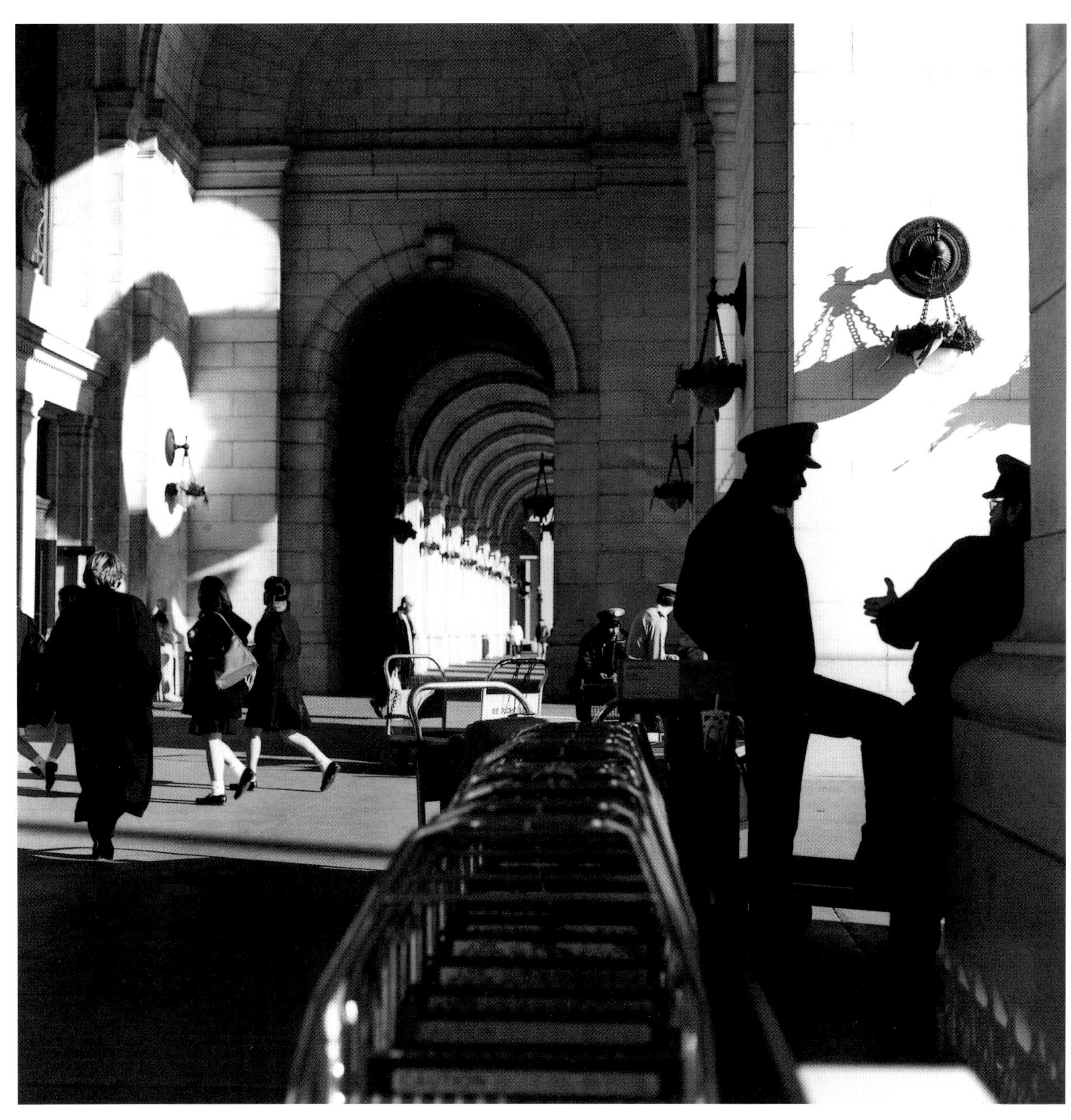

Red Caps, Union Station

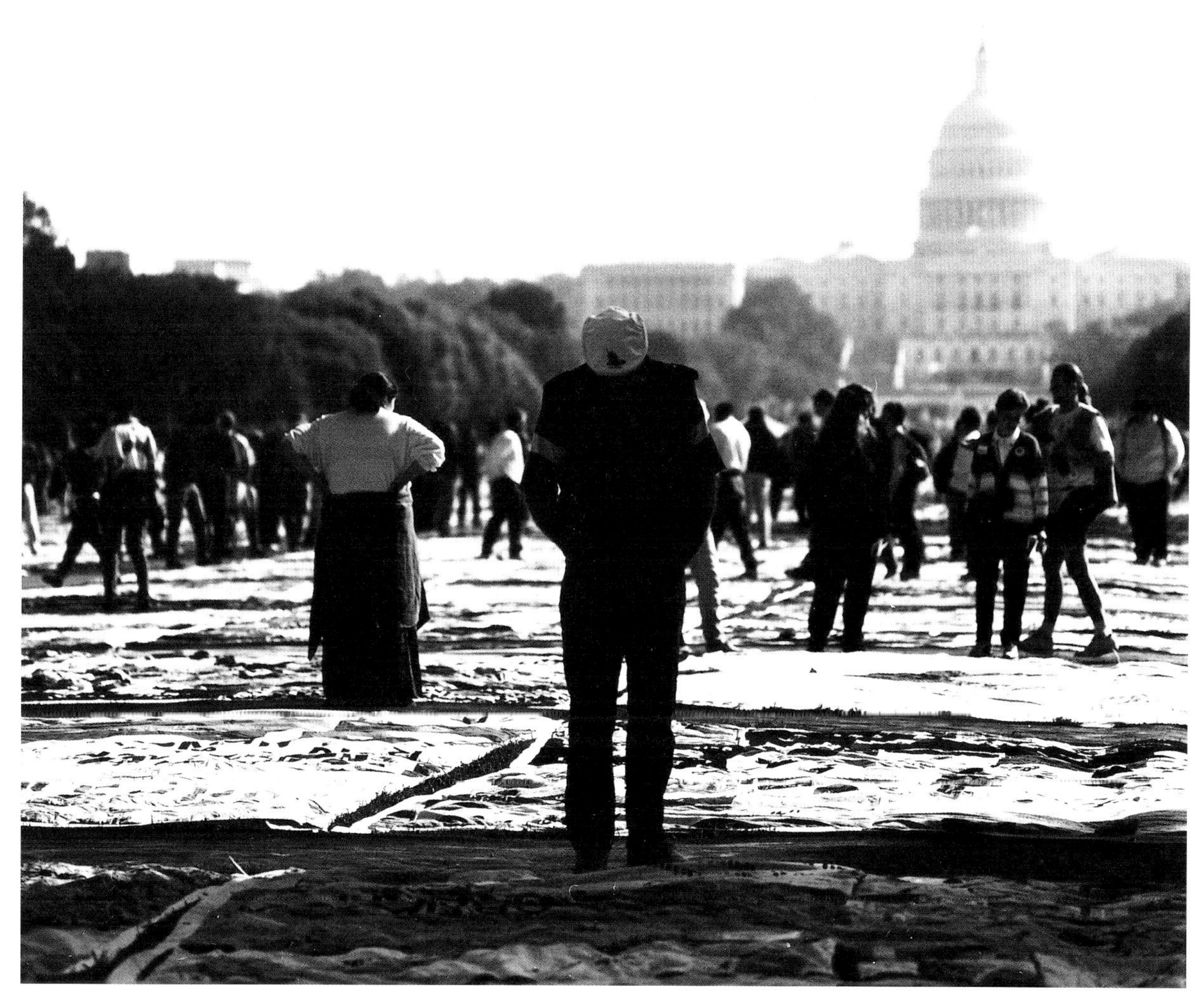

AIDS memorial quilts, the Mall

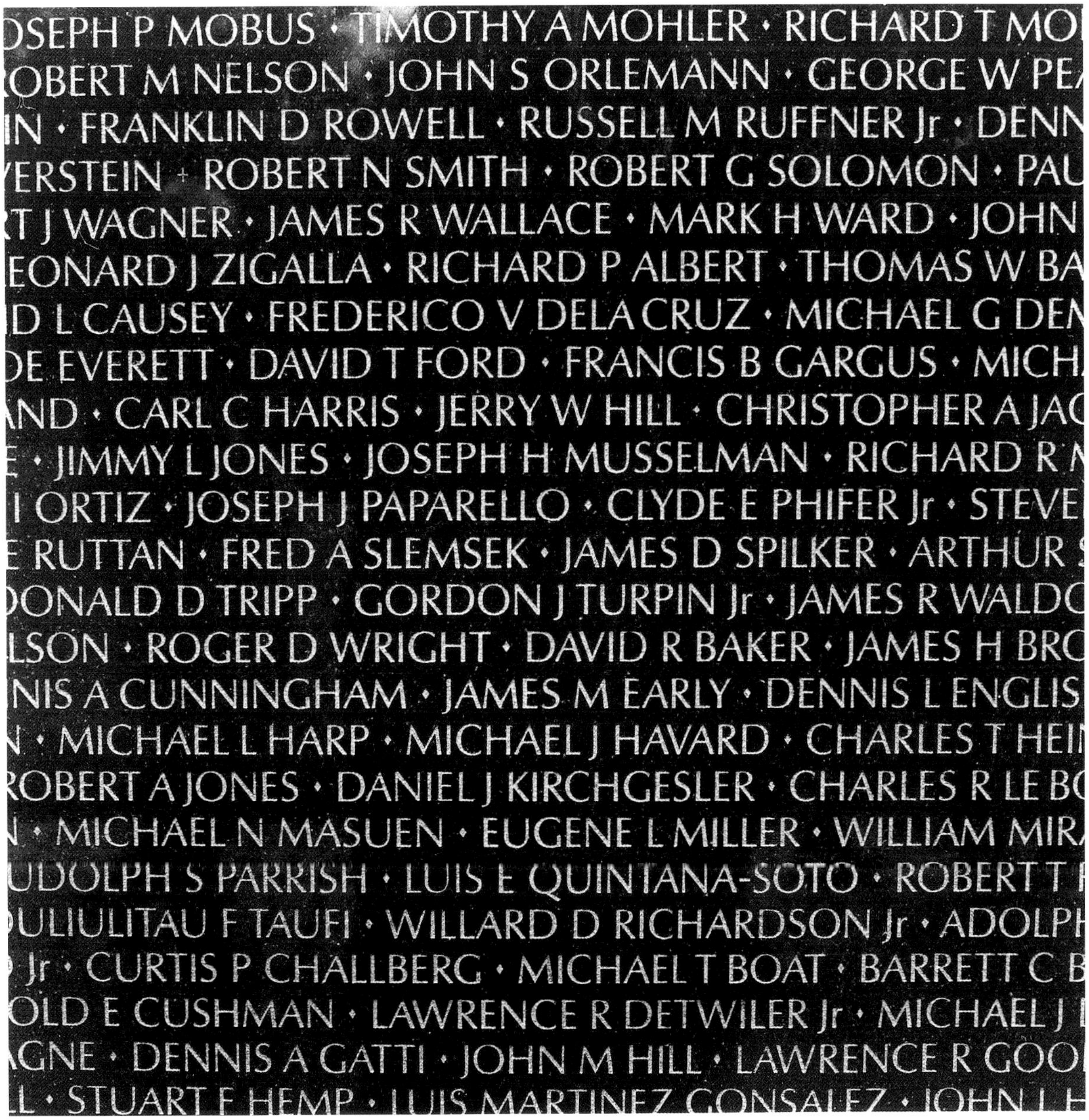

DSEPH P MOBUS • TIMOTHY A MOHLER • RICHARD T MO
OBERT M NELSON • JOHN S ORLEMANN • GEORGE W PE
IN • FRANKLIN D ROWELL • RUSSELL M RUFFNER Jr • DENN
ERSTEIN • ROBERT N SMITH • ROBERT G SOLOMON • PAU
T J WAGNER • JAMES R WALLACE • MARK H WARD • JOHN
EONARD J ZIGALLA • RICHARD P ALBERT • THOMAS W BA
D L CAUSEY • FREDERICO V DELA CRUZ • MICHAEL G DE
DE EVERETT • DAVID T FORD • FRANCIS B GARGUS • MICH
ND • CARL C HARRIS • JERRY W HILL • CHRISTOPHER A JA
E • JIMMY L JONES • JOSEPH H MUSSELMAN • RICHARD R
I ORTIZ • JOSEPH J PAPARELLO • CLYDE E PHIFER Jr • STEVE
E RUTTAN • FRED A SLEMSEK • JAMES D SPILKER • ARTHUR
DONALD D TRIPP • GORDON J TURPIN Jr • JAMES R WALDO
LSON • ROGER D WRIGHT • DAVID R BAKER • JAMES H BRO
NIS A CUNNINGHAM • JAMES M EARLY • DENNIS L ENGLIS
N • MICHAEL L HARP • MICHAEL J HAVARD • CHARLES T HEI
ROBERT A JONES • DANIEL J KIRCHGESLER • CHARLES R LE B
N • MICHAEL N MASUEN • EUGENE L MILLER • WILLIAM MIR
UDOLPH S PARRISH • LUIS E QUINTANA-SOTO • ROBERT T
ULIULITAU F TAUFI • WILLARD D RICHARDSON Jr • ADOLPH
Jr • CURTIS P CHALLBERG • MICHAEL T BOAT • BARRETT C B
OLD E CUSHMAN • LAWRENCE R DETWILER Jr • MICHAEL J
GNE • DENNIS A GATTI • JOHN M HILL • LAWRENCE R GOO
L • STUART F HEMP • LUIS MARTINEZ GONSALEZ • JOHN L H

Vietnam Veterans Memorial

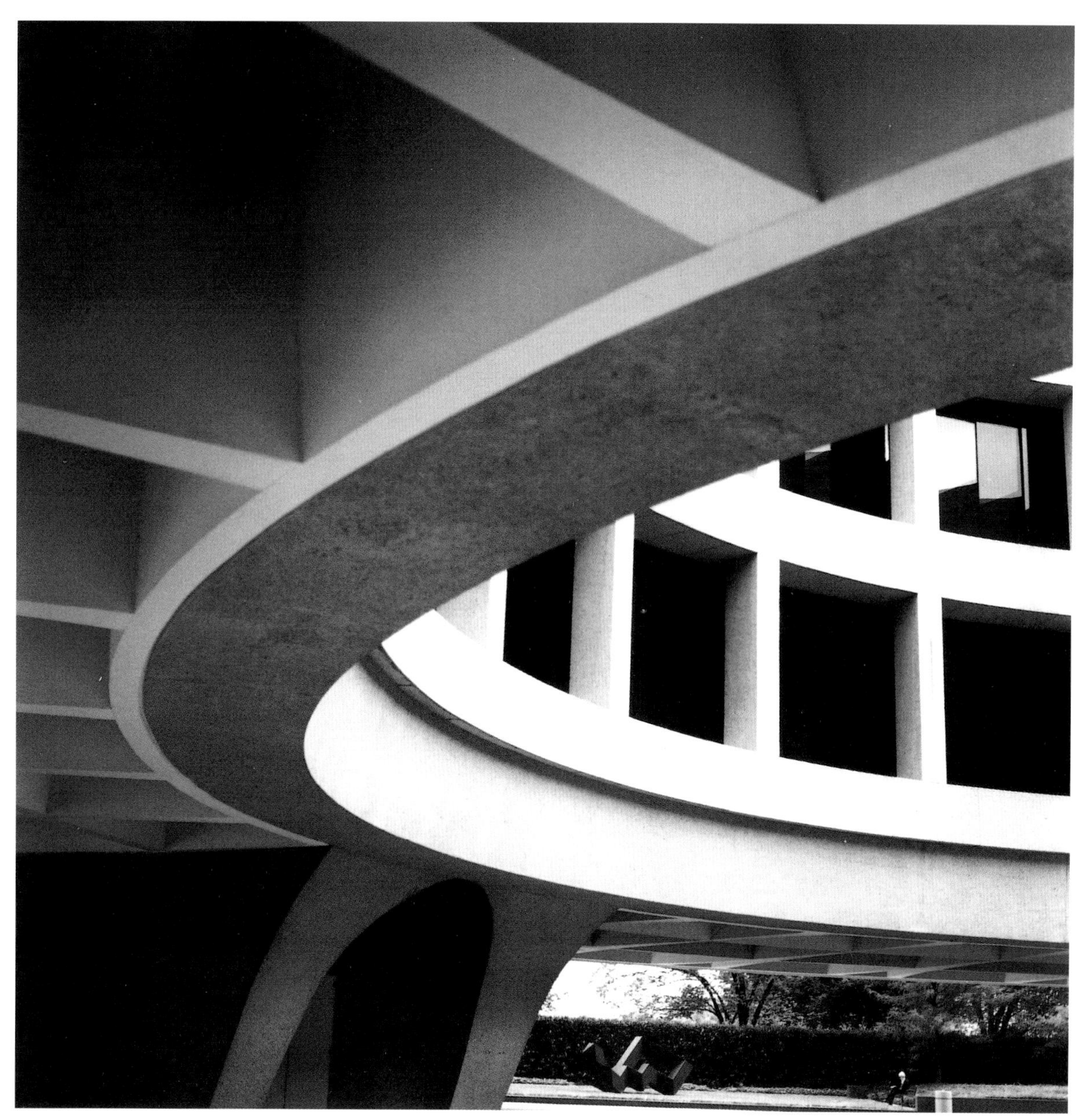

Hirchhorn Museum

Lincoln Memorial

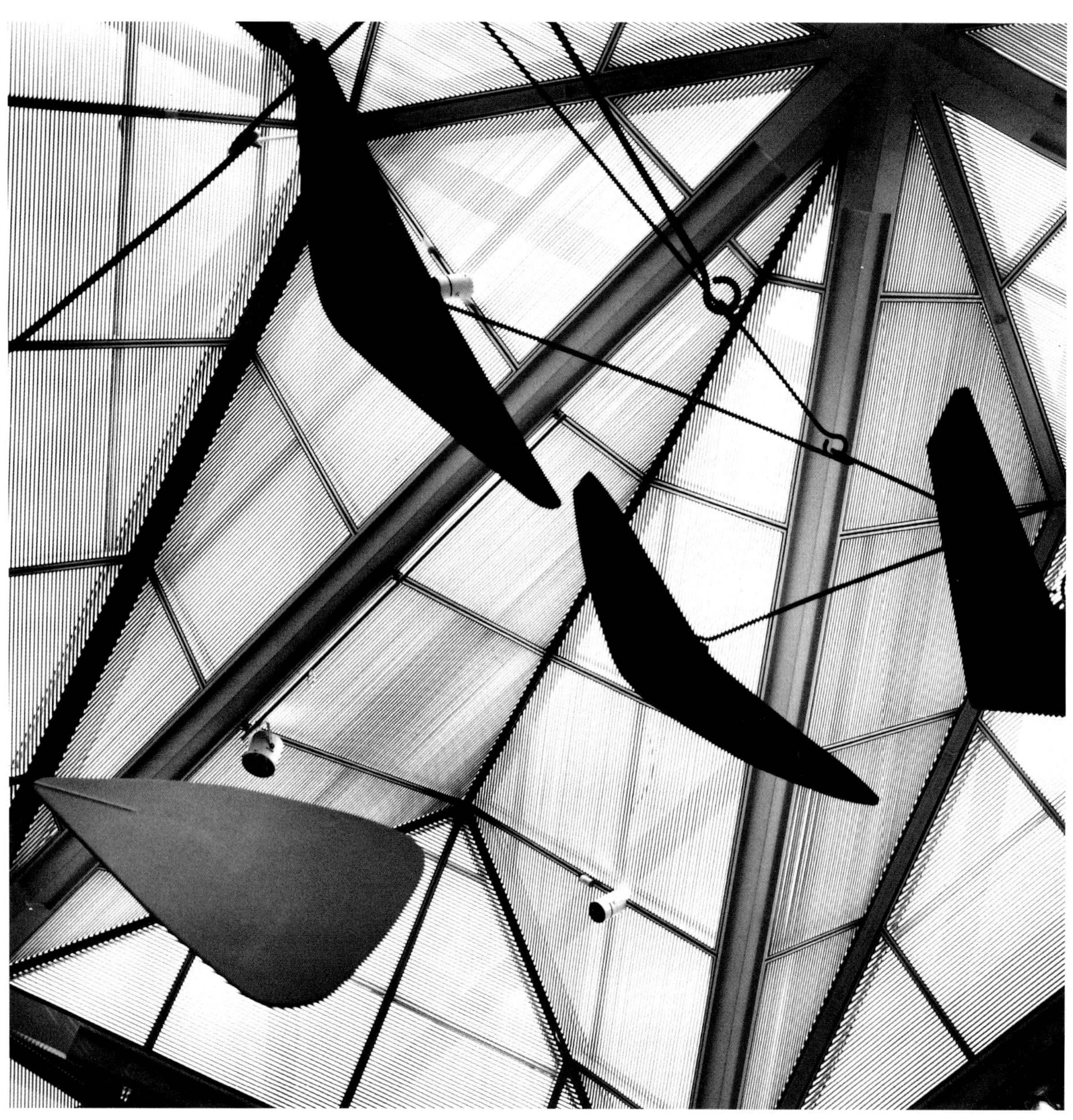

East Building, National Gallery of Art

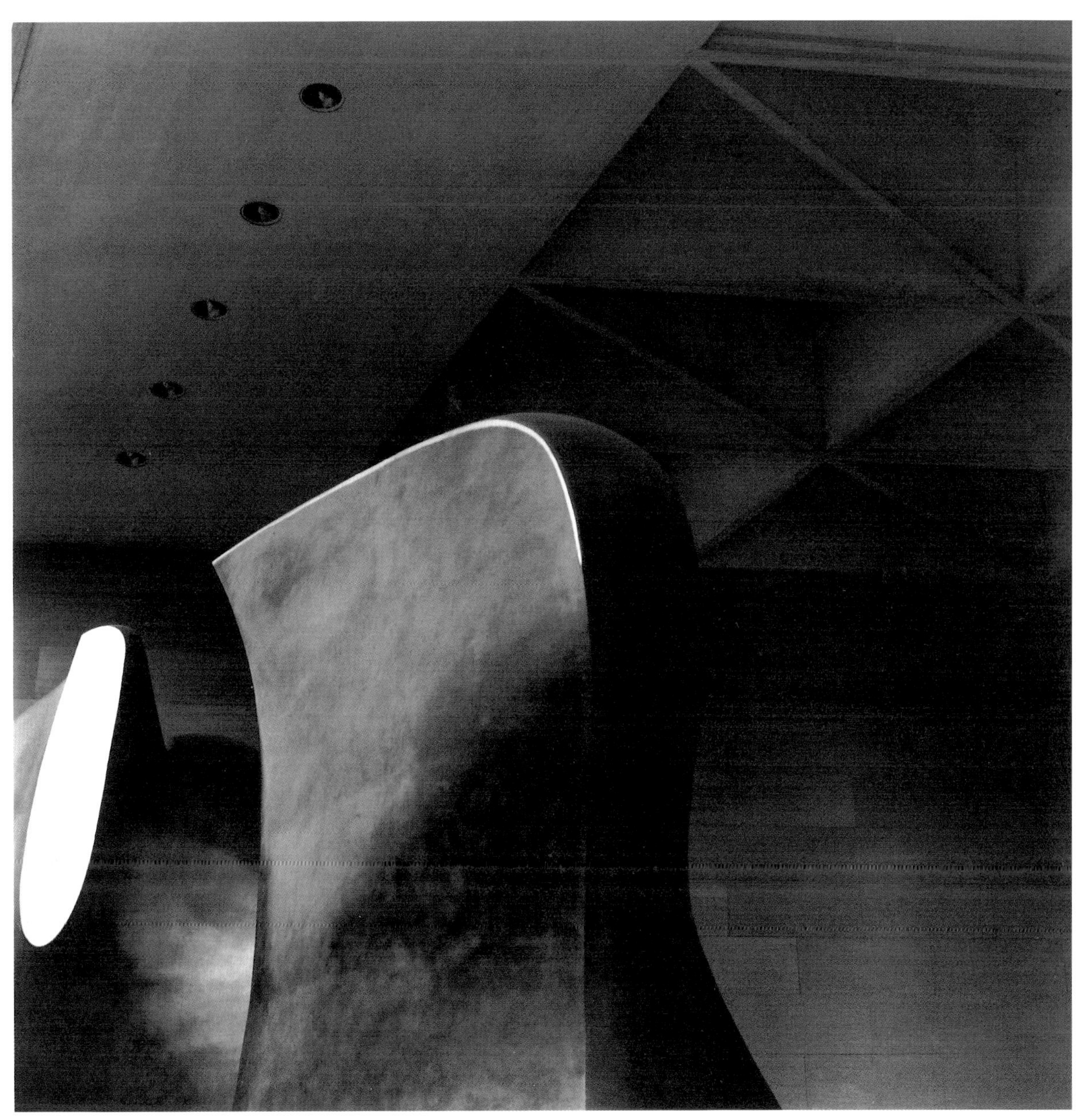

East Building, National Gallery of Art

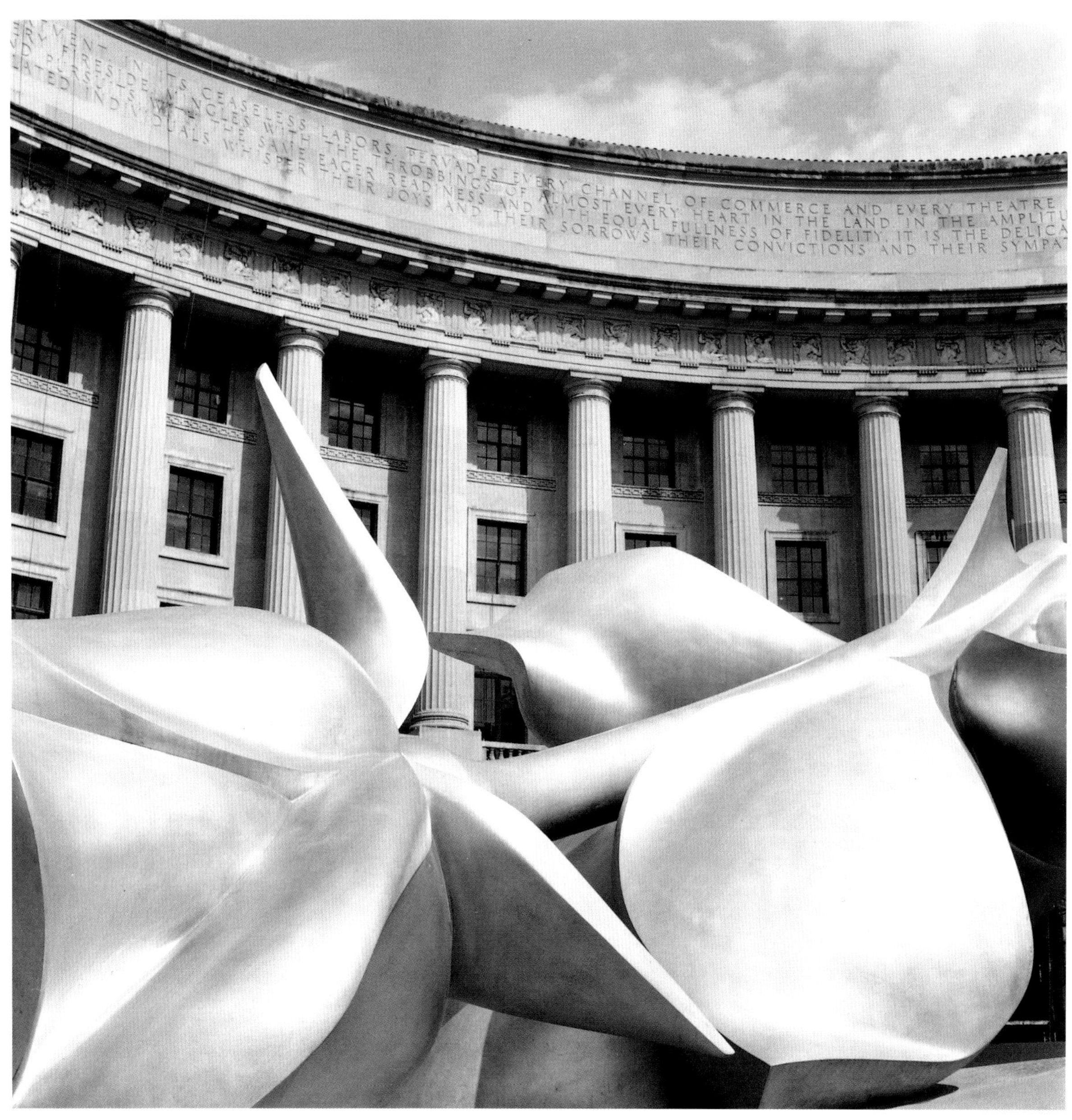

Ariel Rios Building

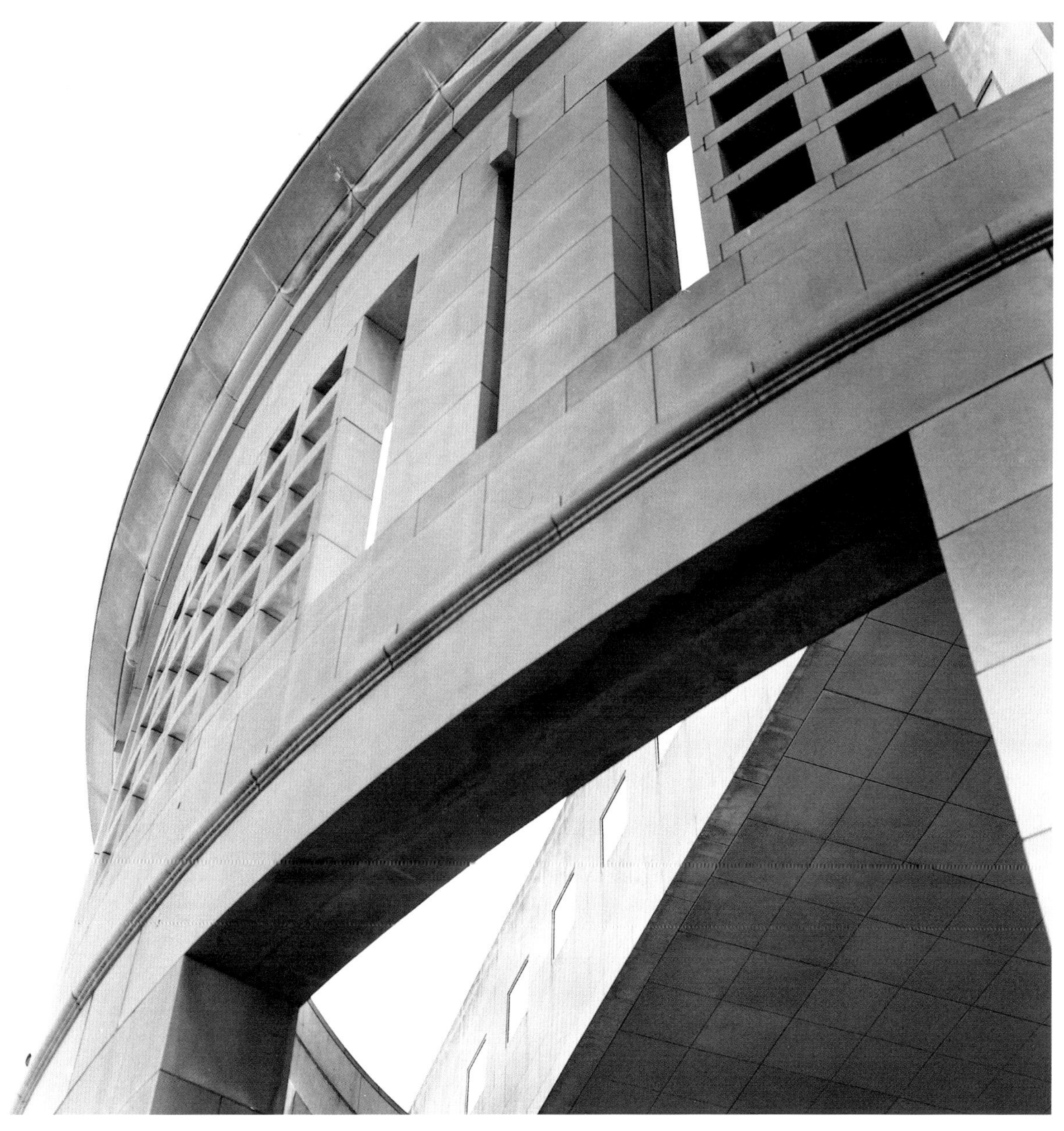

U.S. Holocaust Memorial Museum

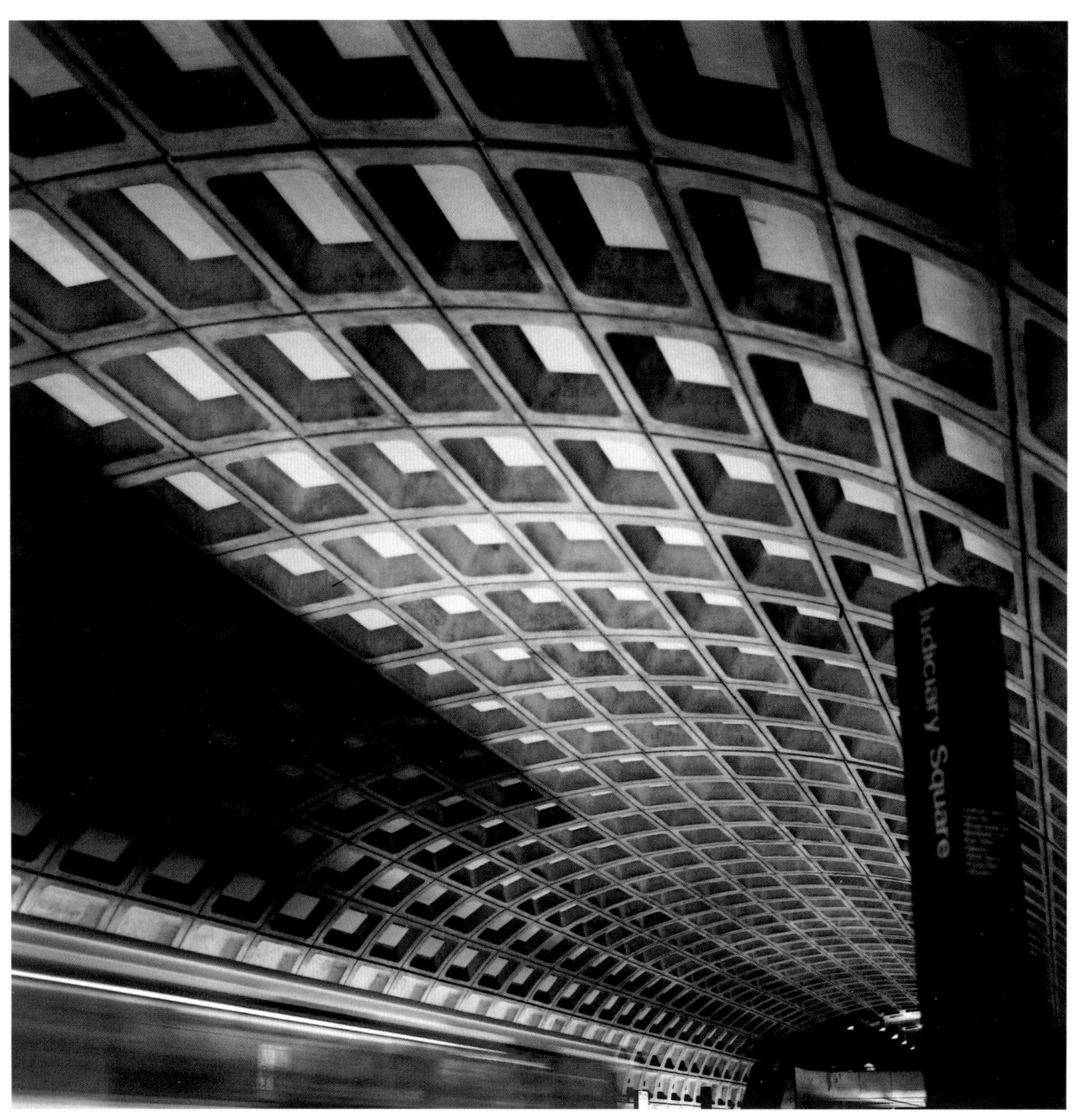

Judiciary Square Station, the Metro

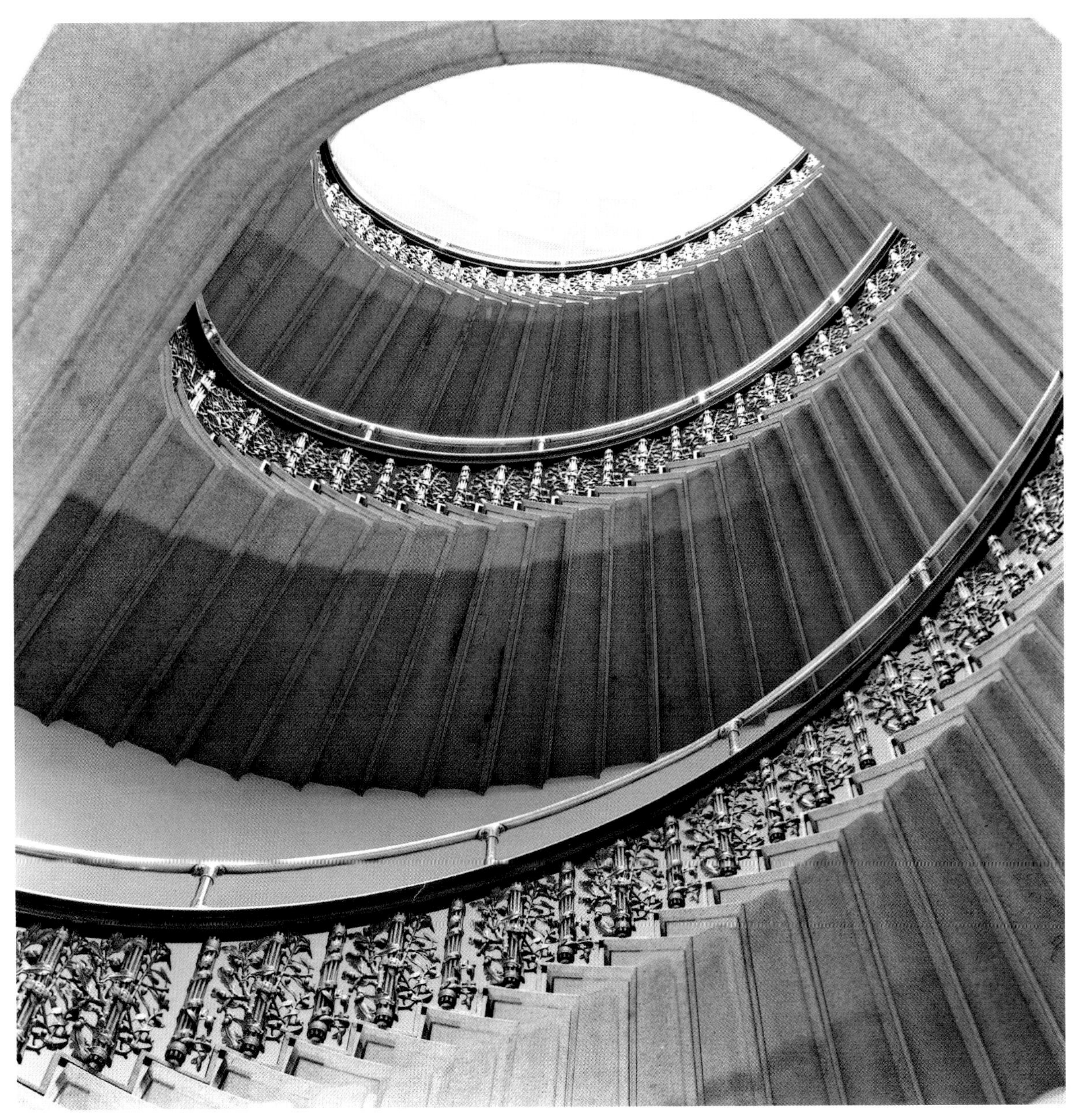

Treasury Building

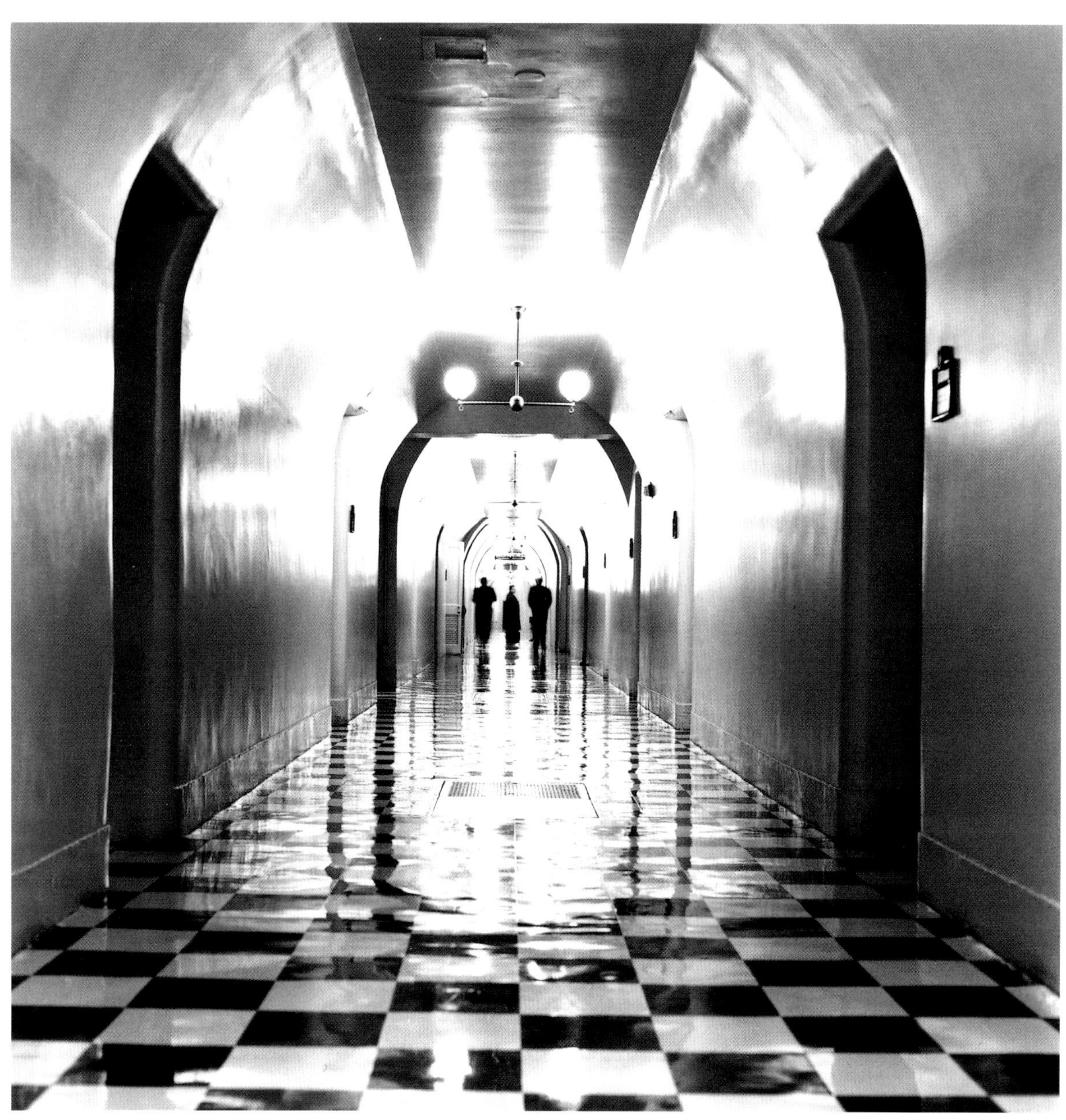

Basement, Treasury Building

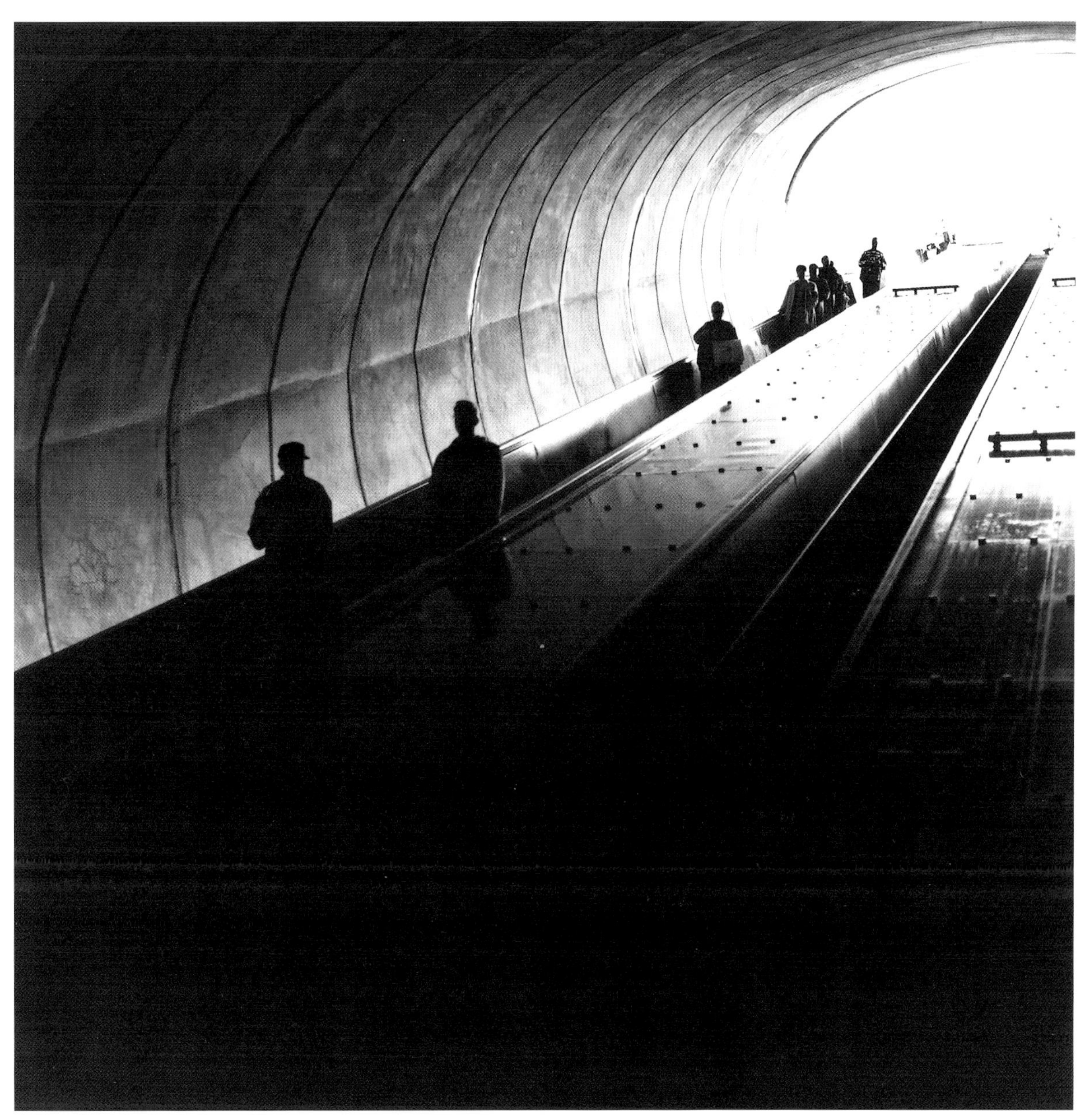

Dupont Circle, the Metro

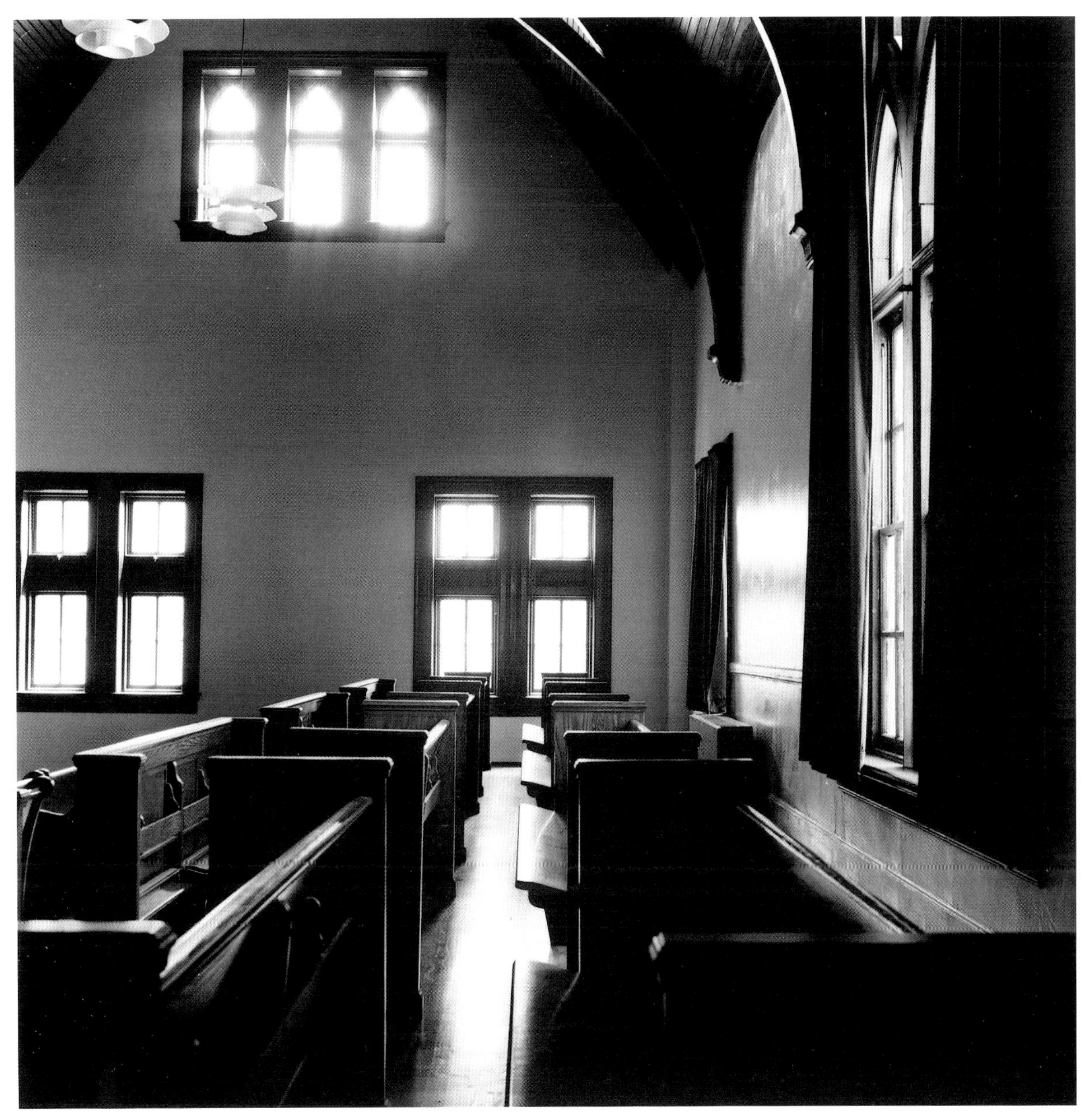

Chapel, U.S. Soldiers' and Airmen's Home

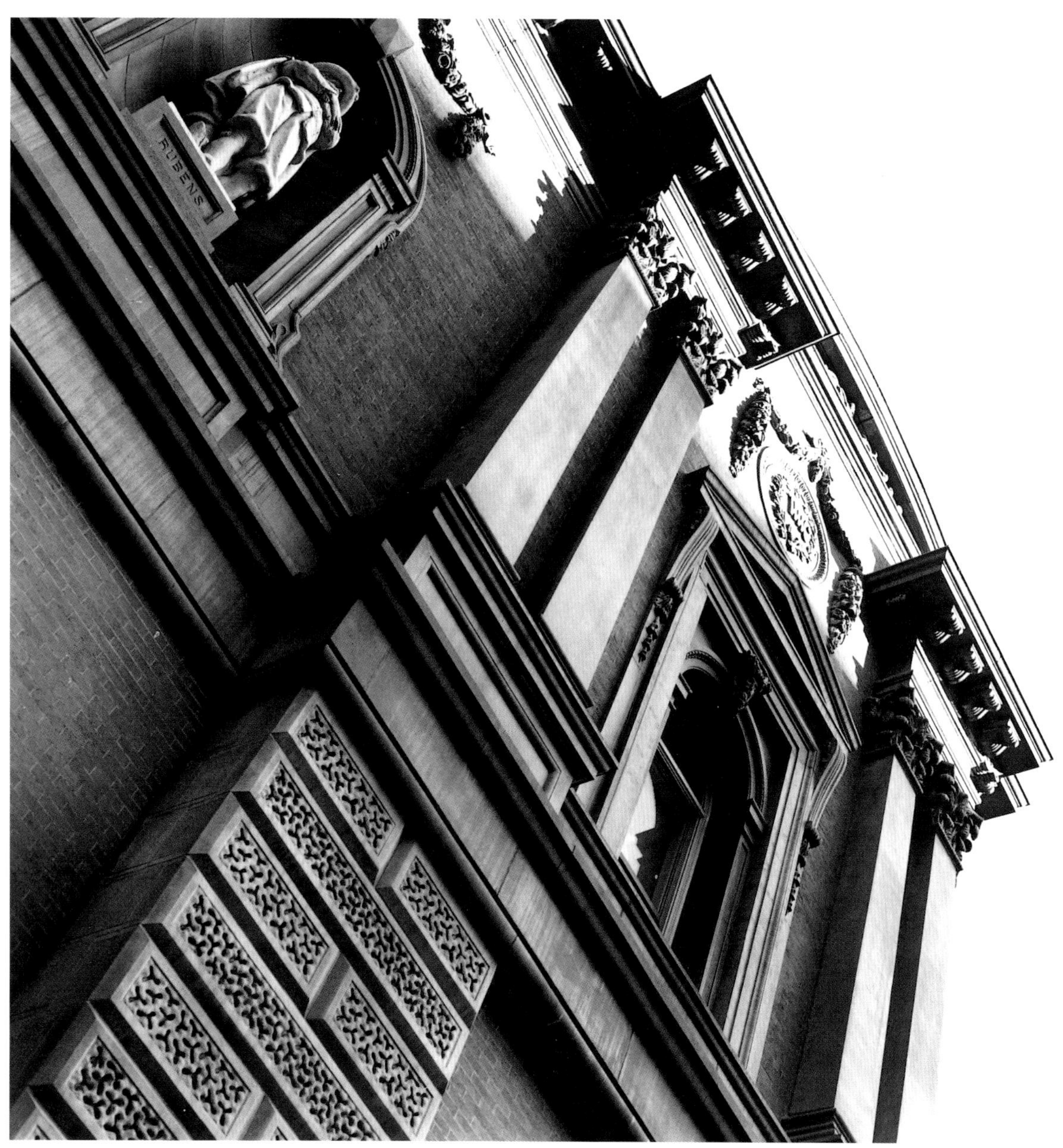

Renwick Gallery

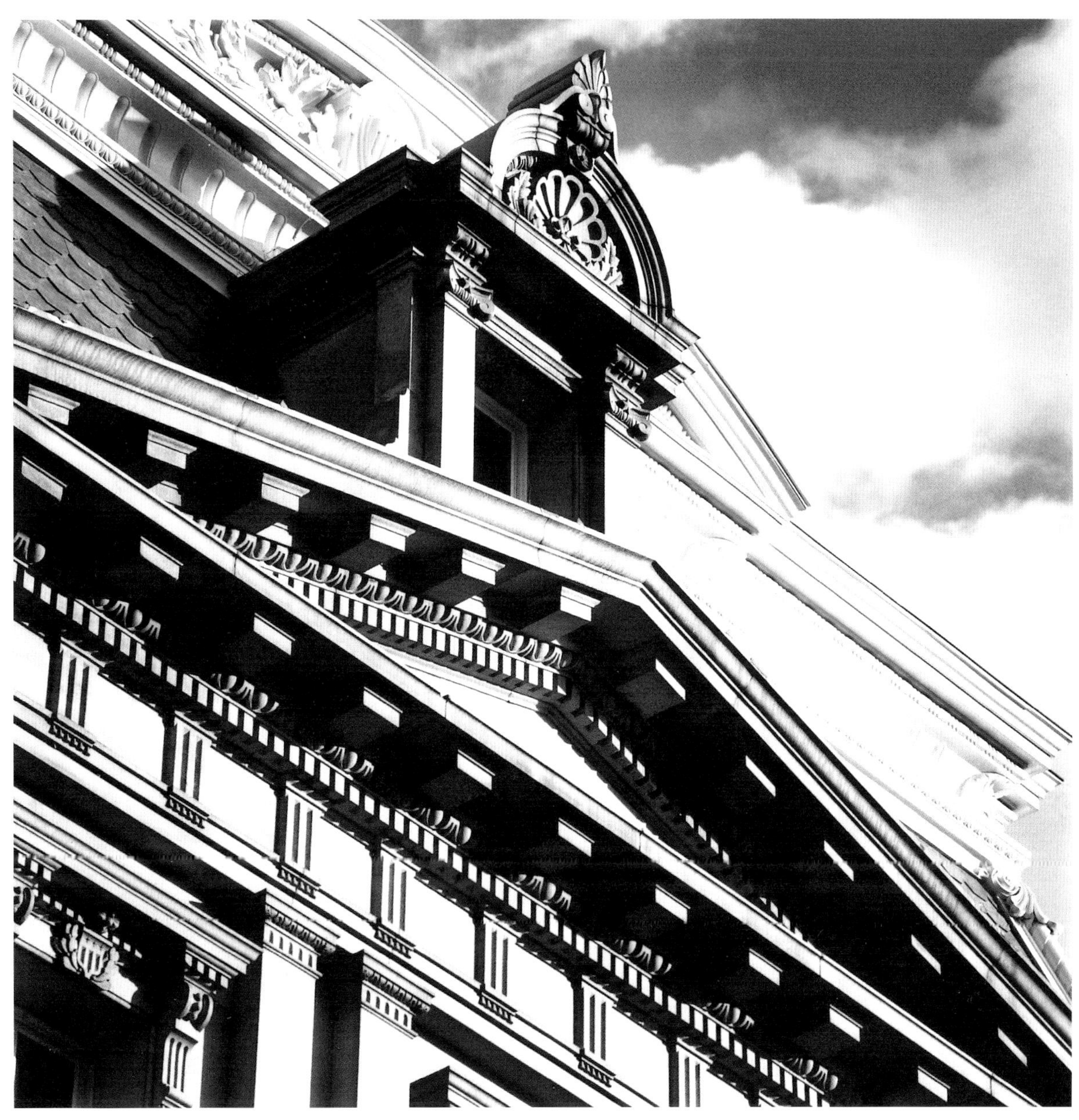

Old Executive Office Building

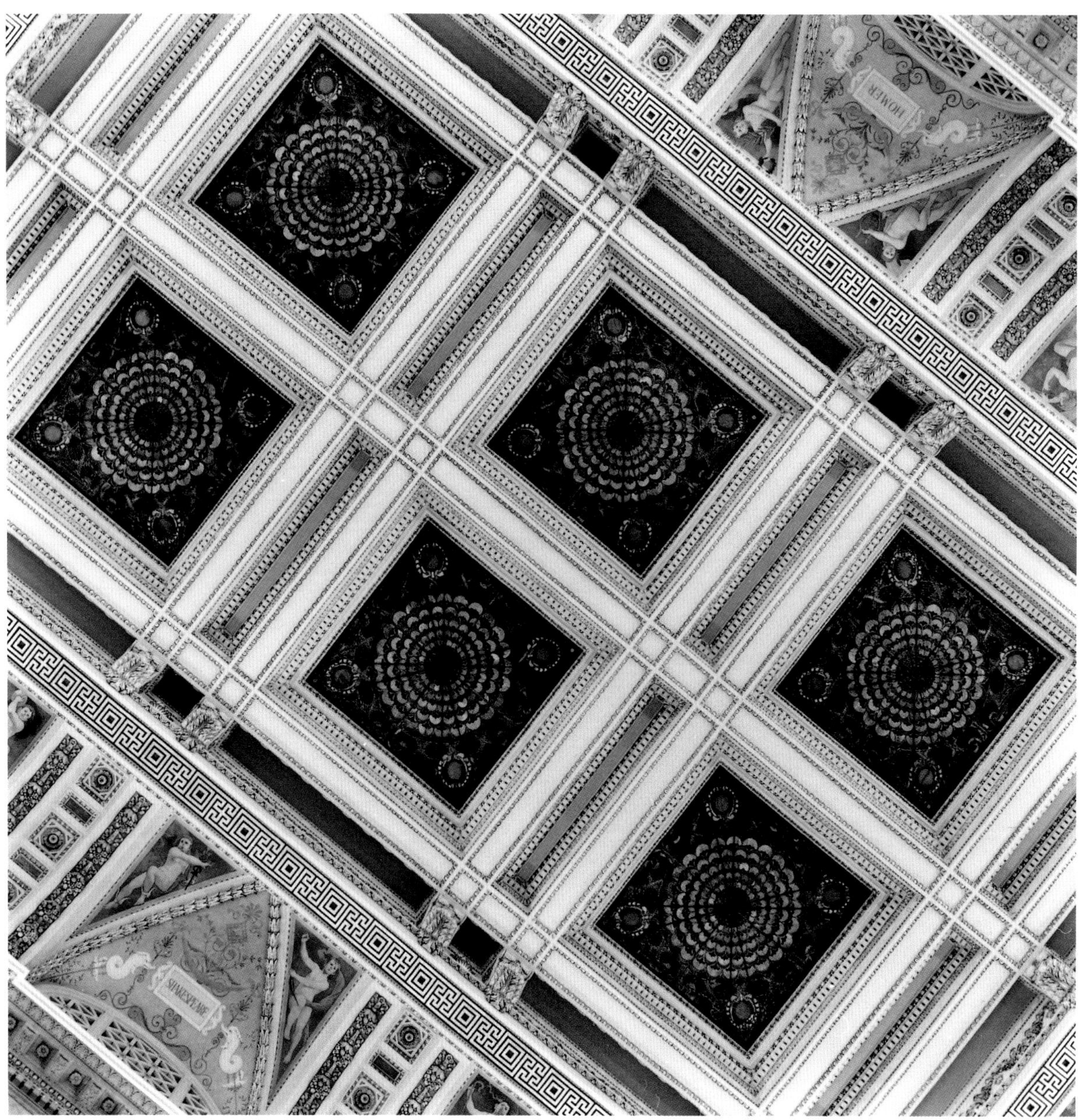

Ceiling, Library of Congress

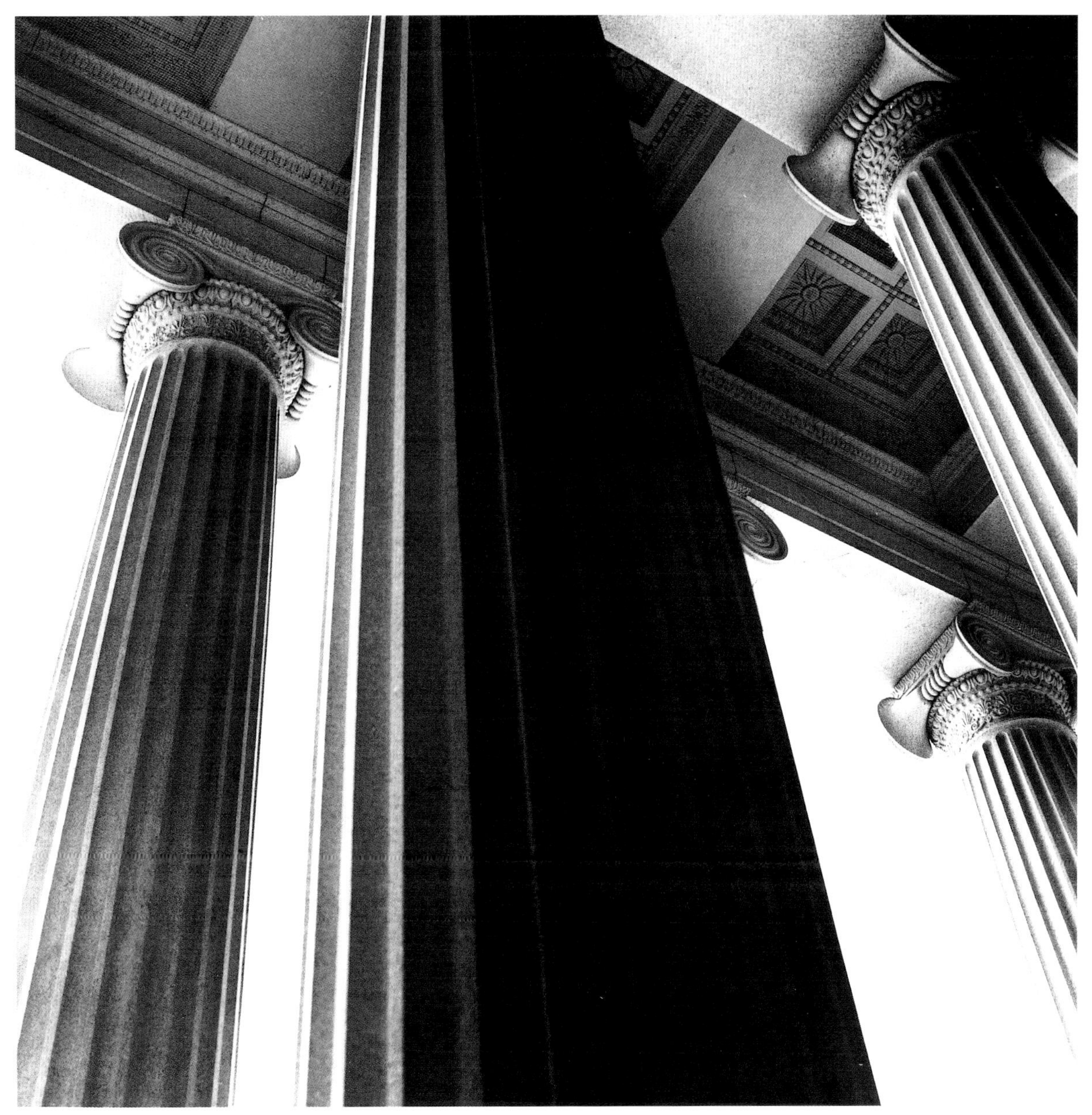

Treasury Building

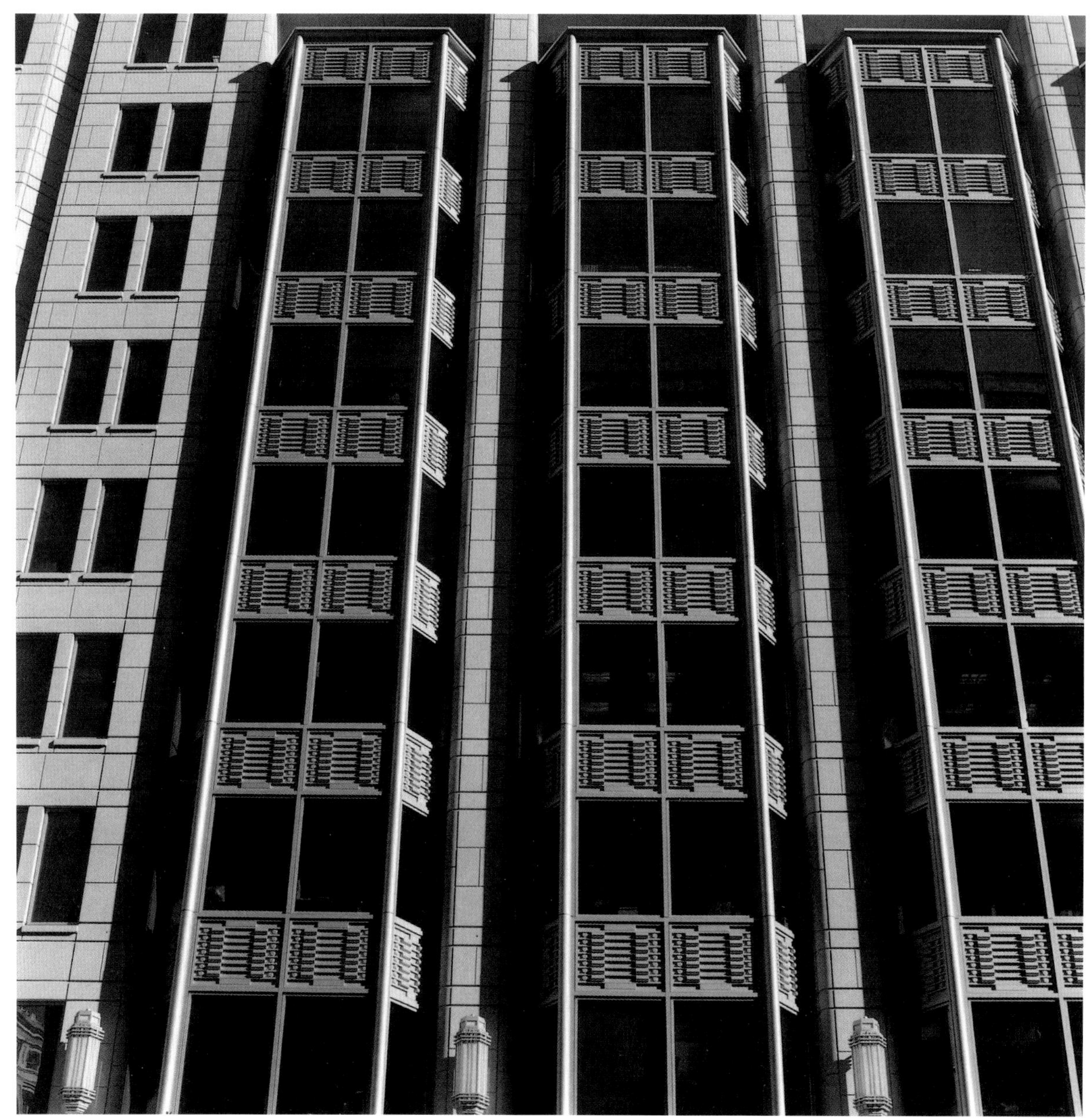

555 Twelfth Street

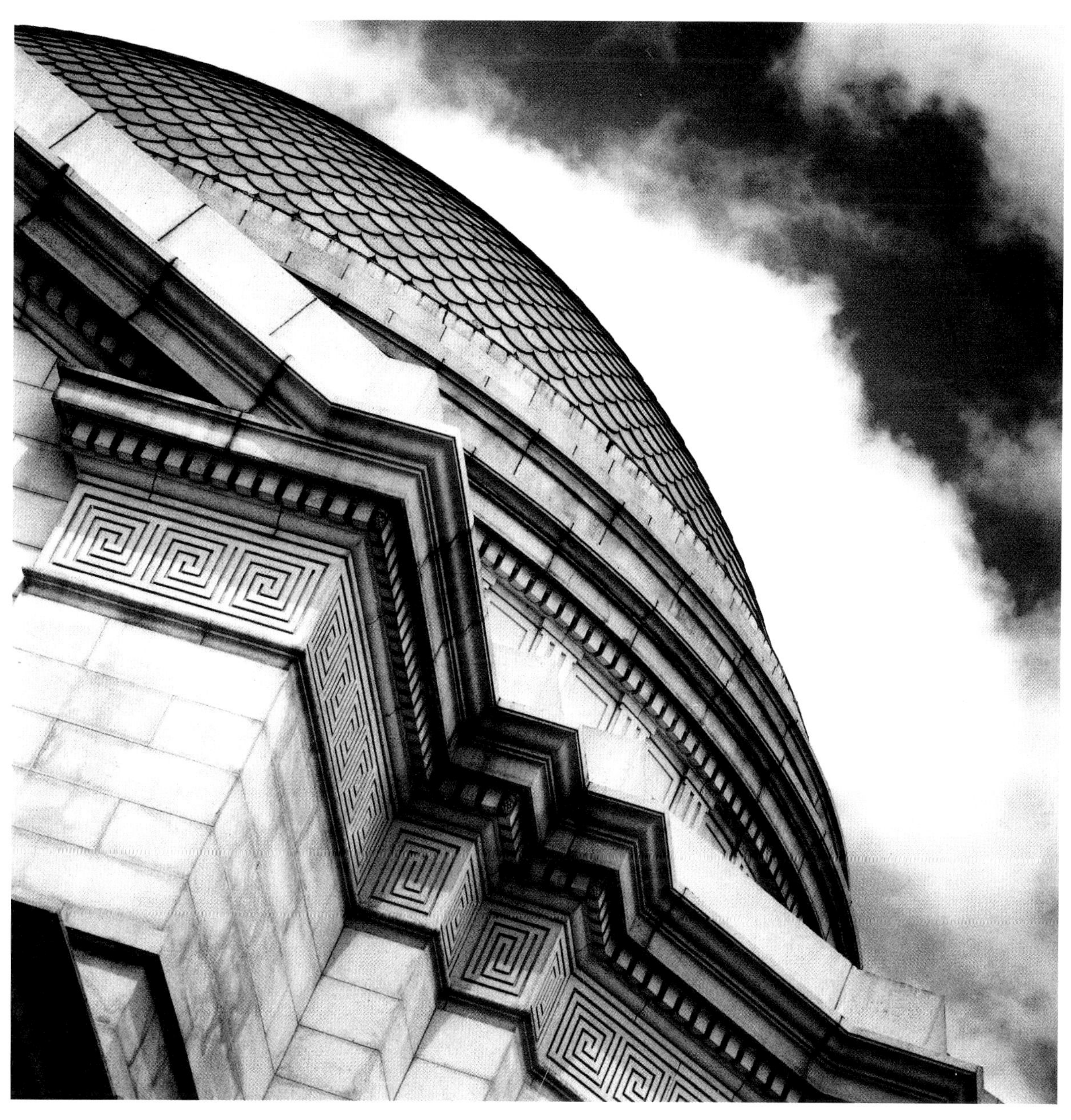

Museum of Natural History

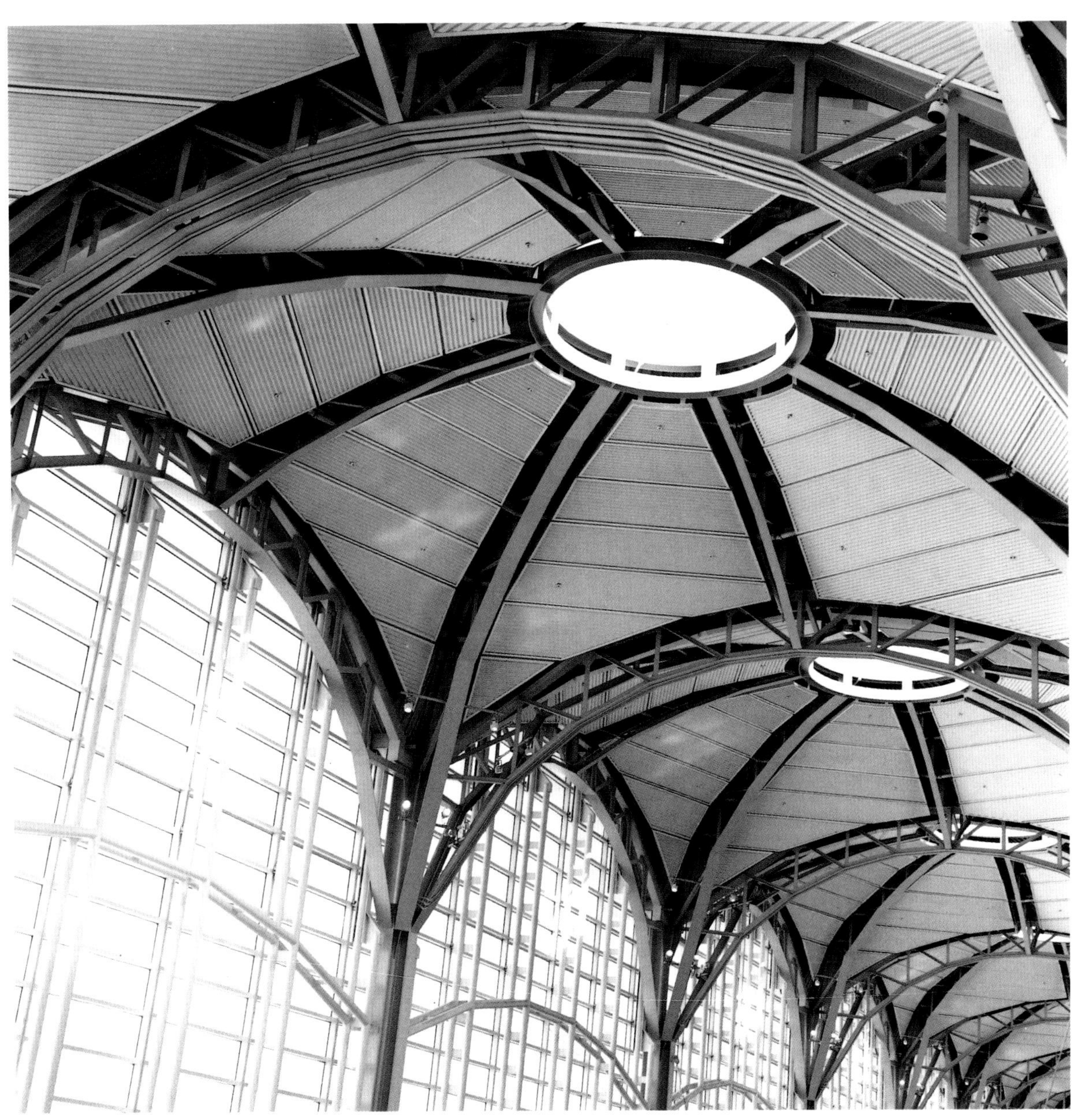

Reagan National Airport

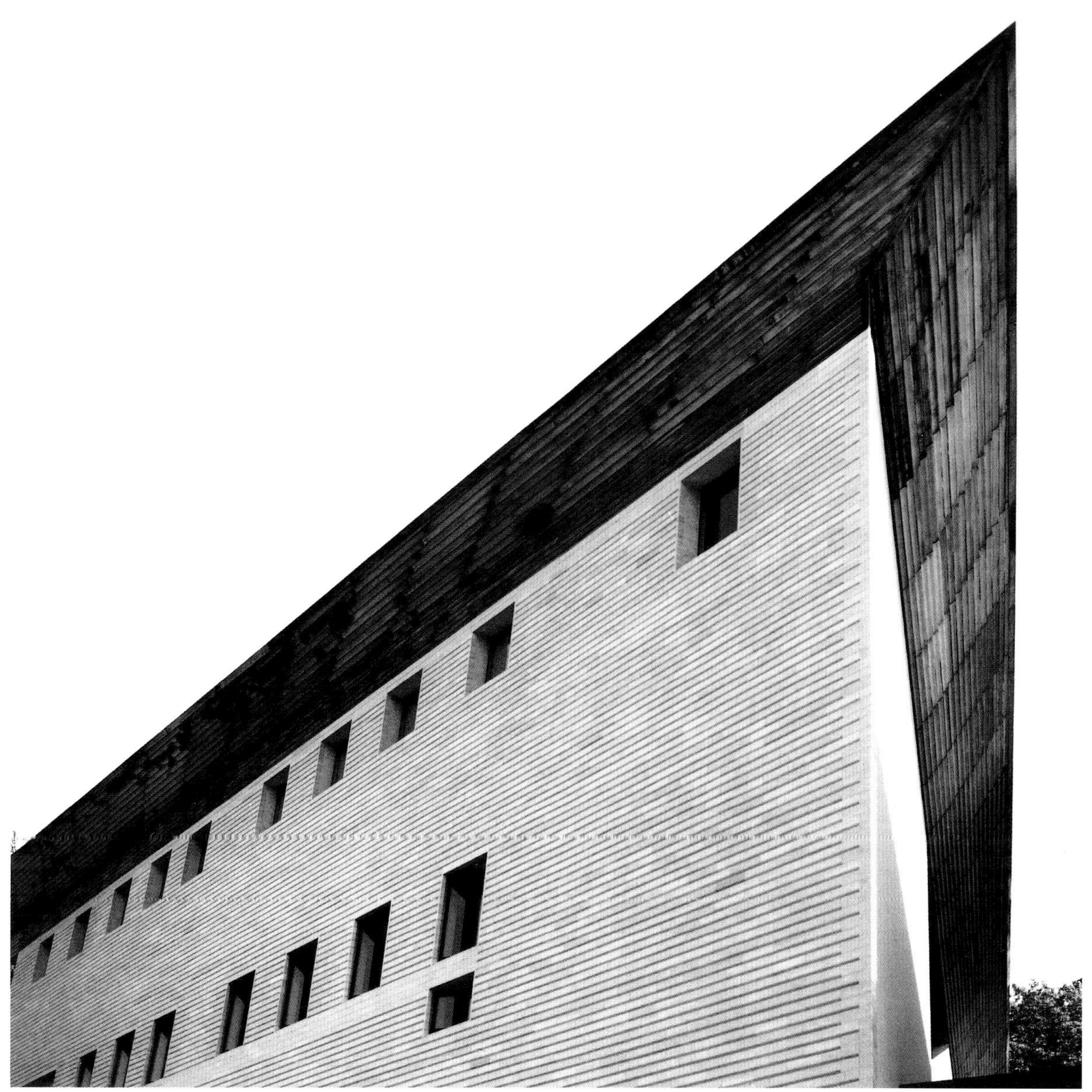

Italian Embassy

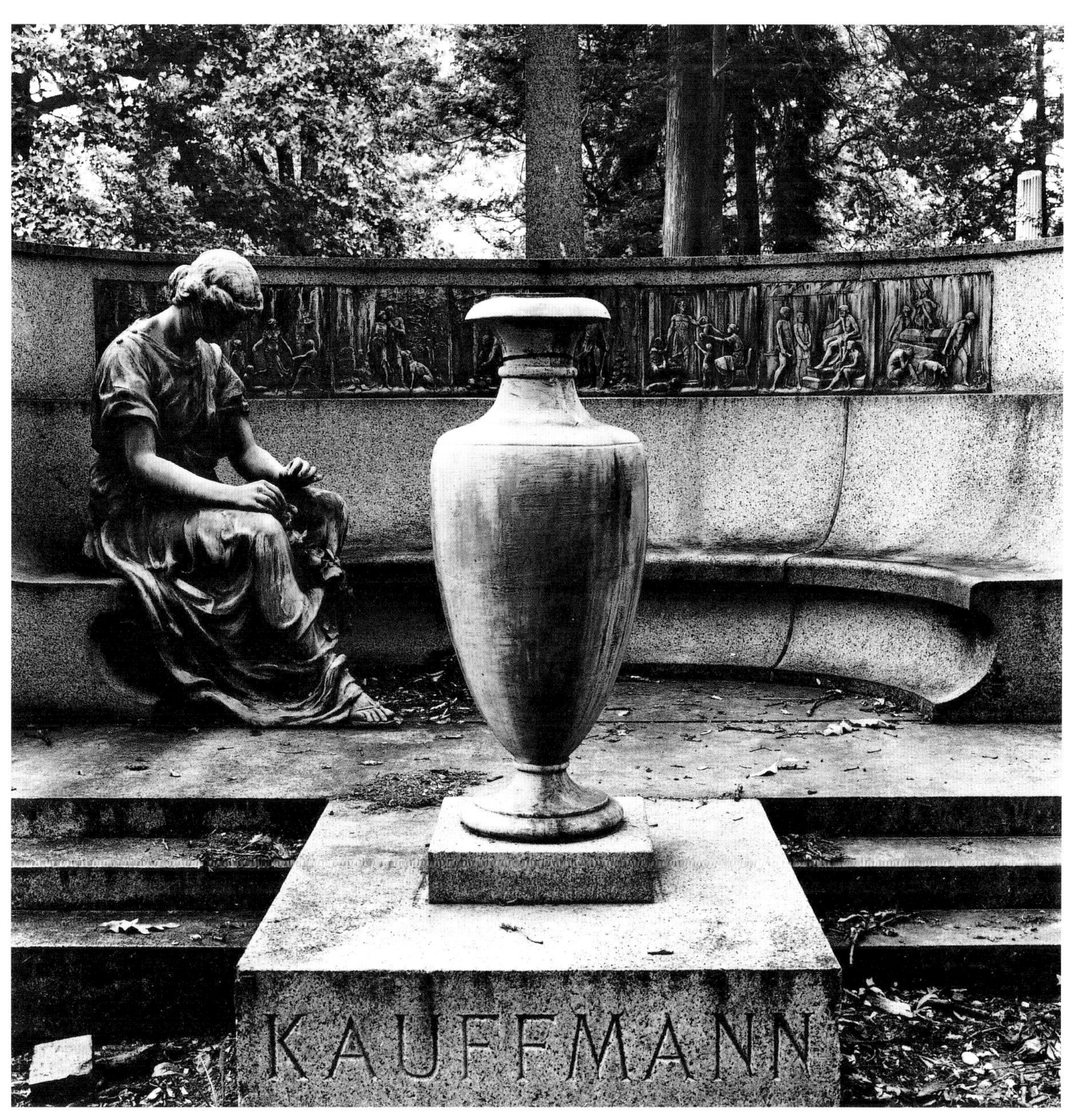

Rock Creek Cemetery

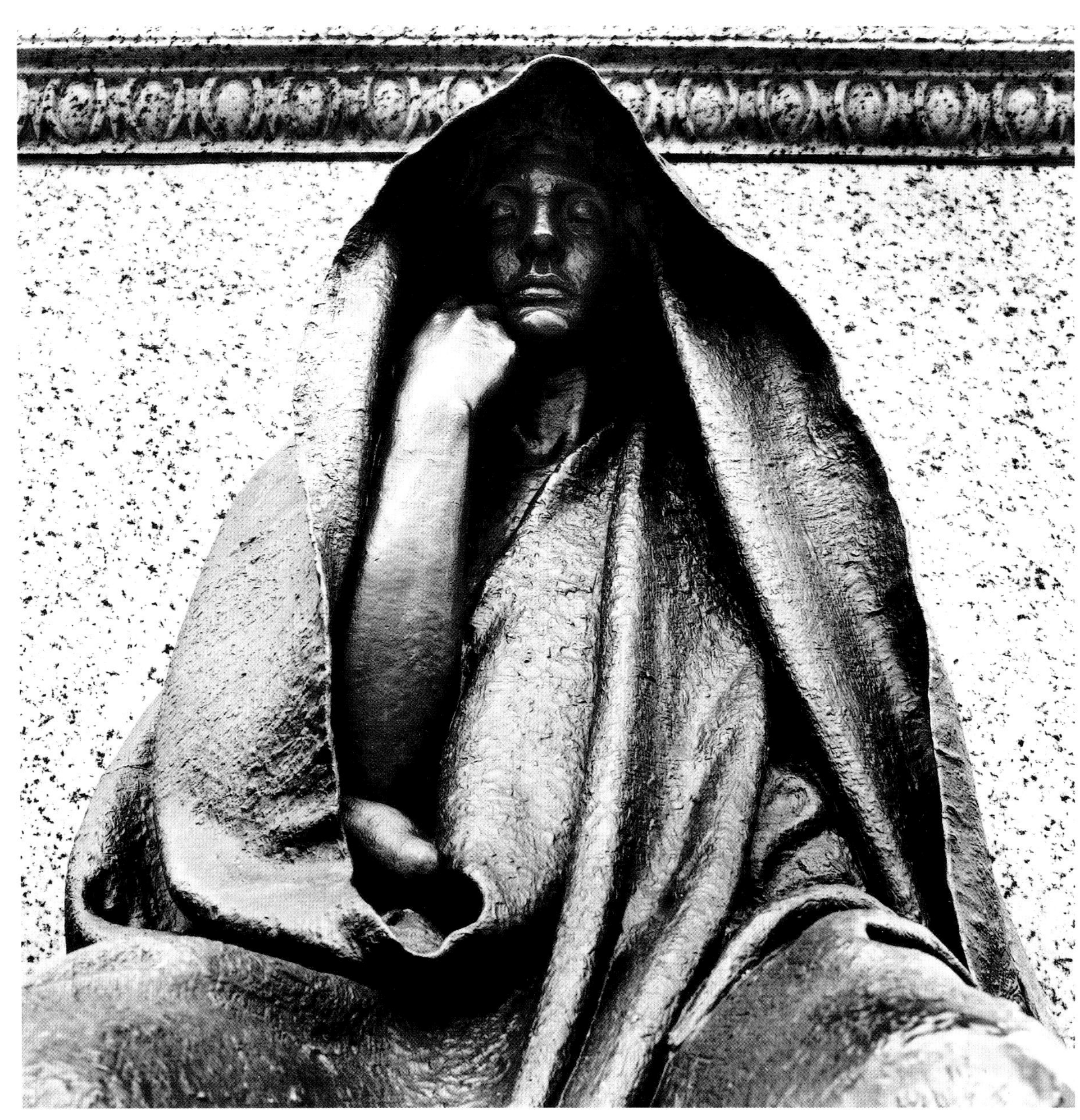

Adams Monument, Rock Creek Cemetery

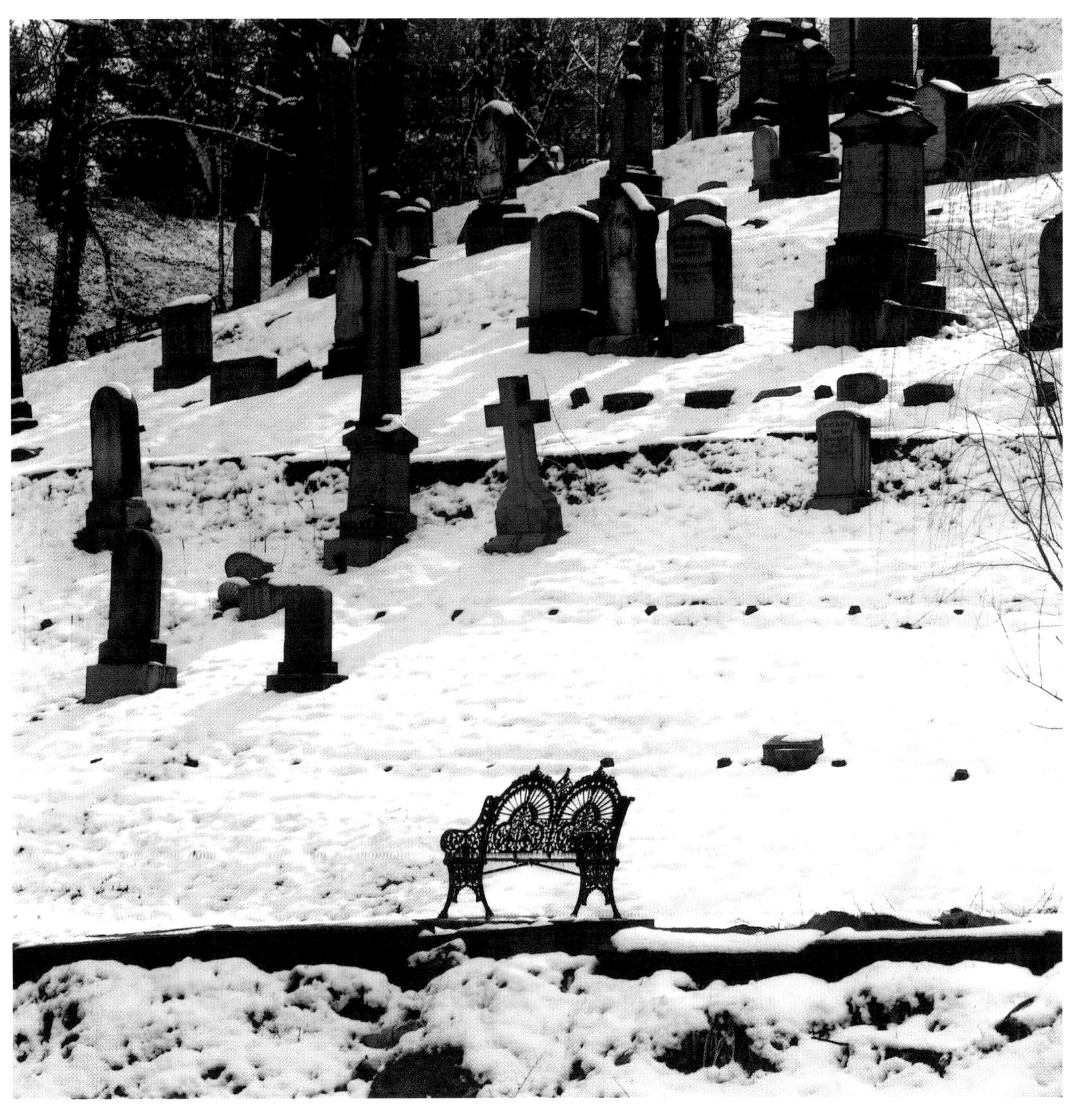

Mount Zion Cemetery

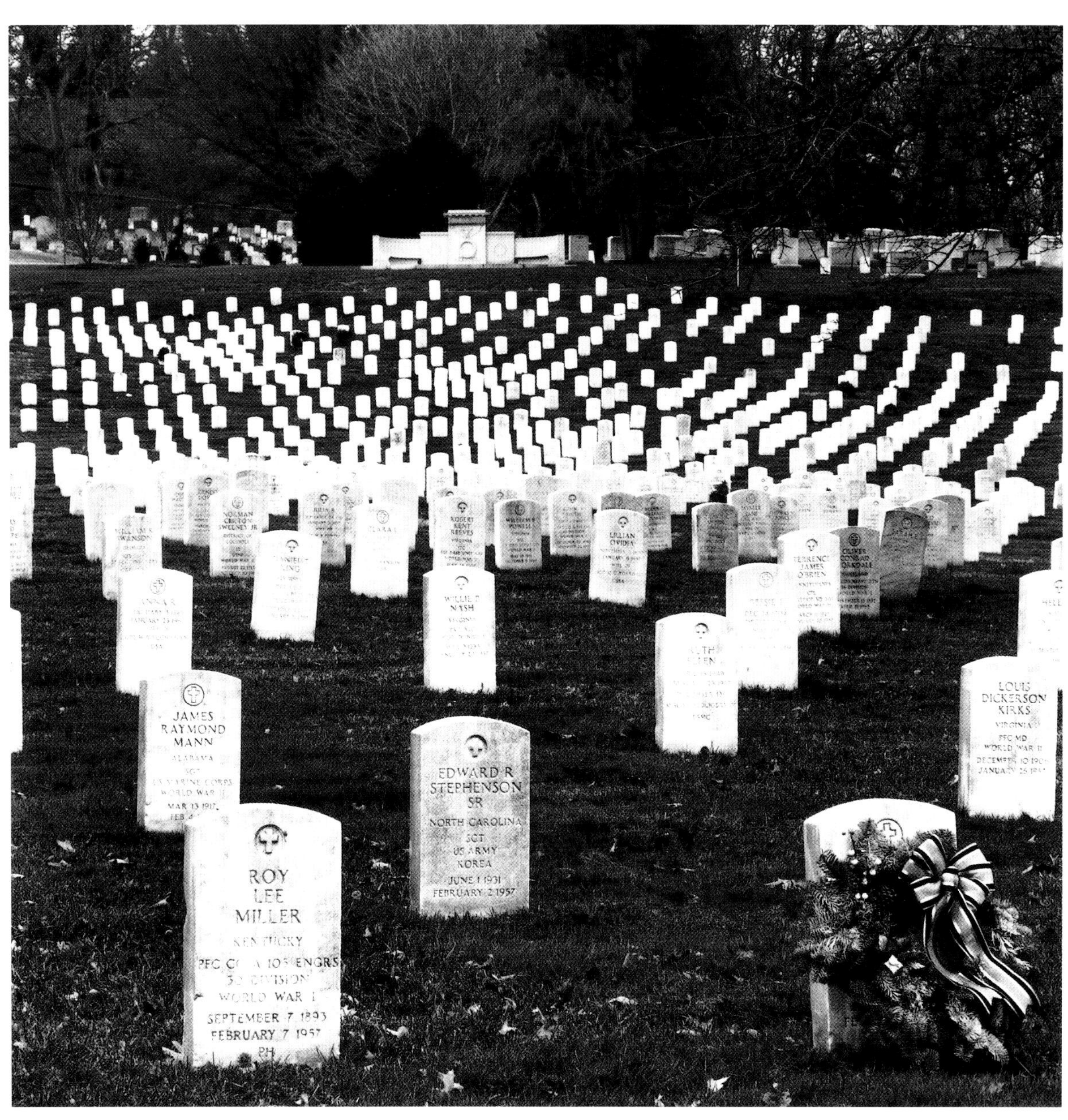

Arlington National Cemetery

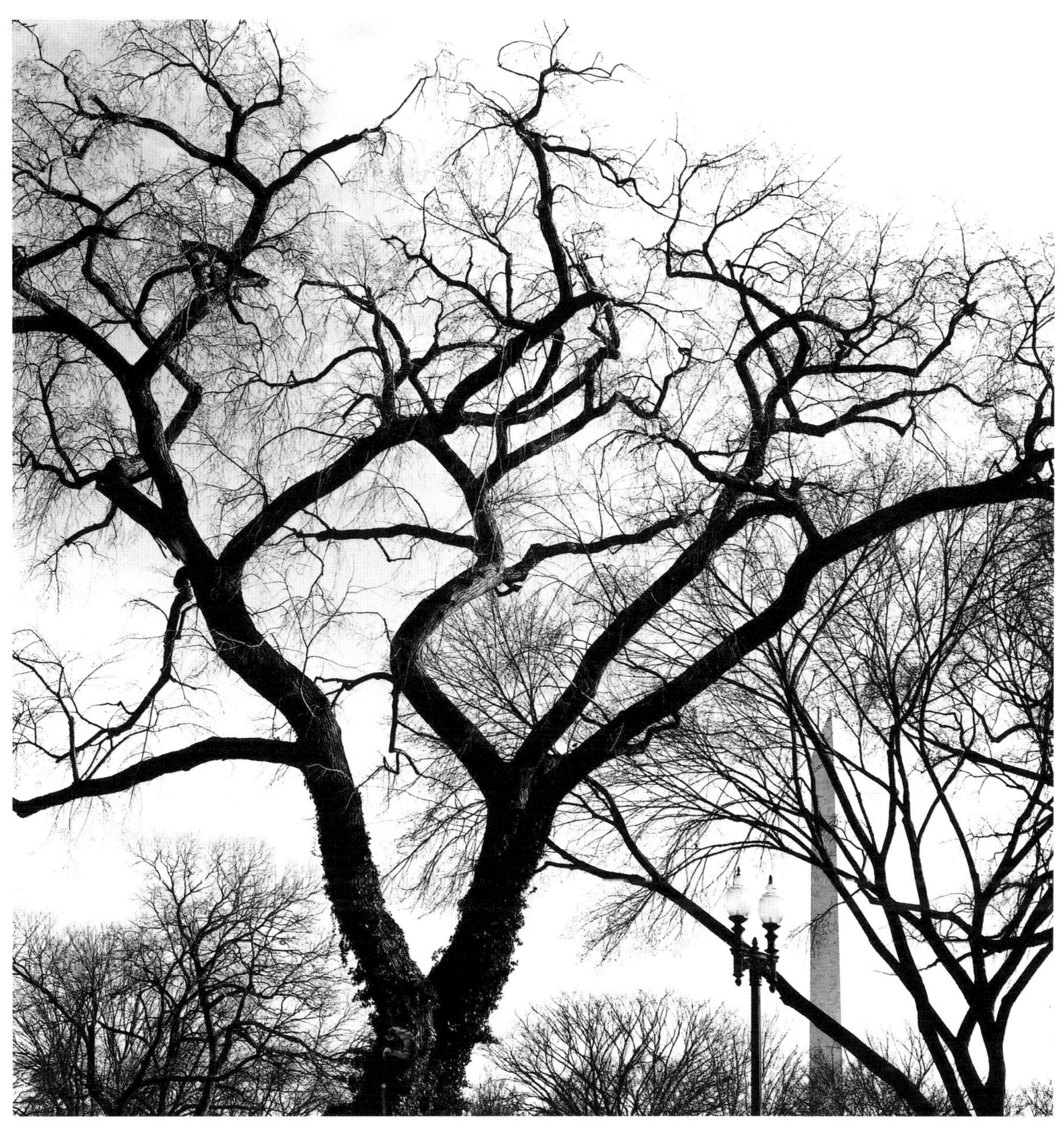

Washington Monument

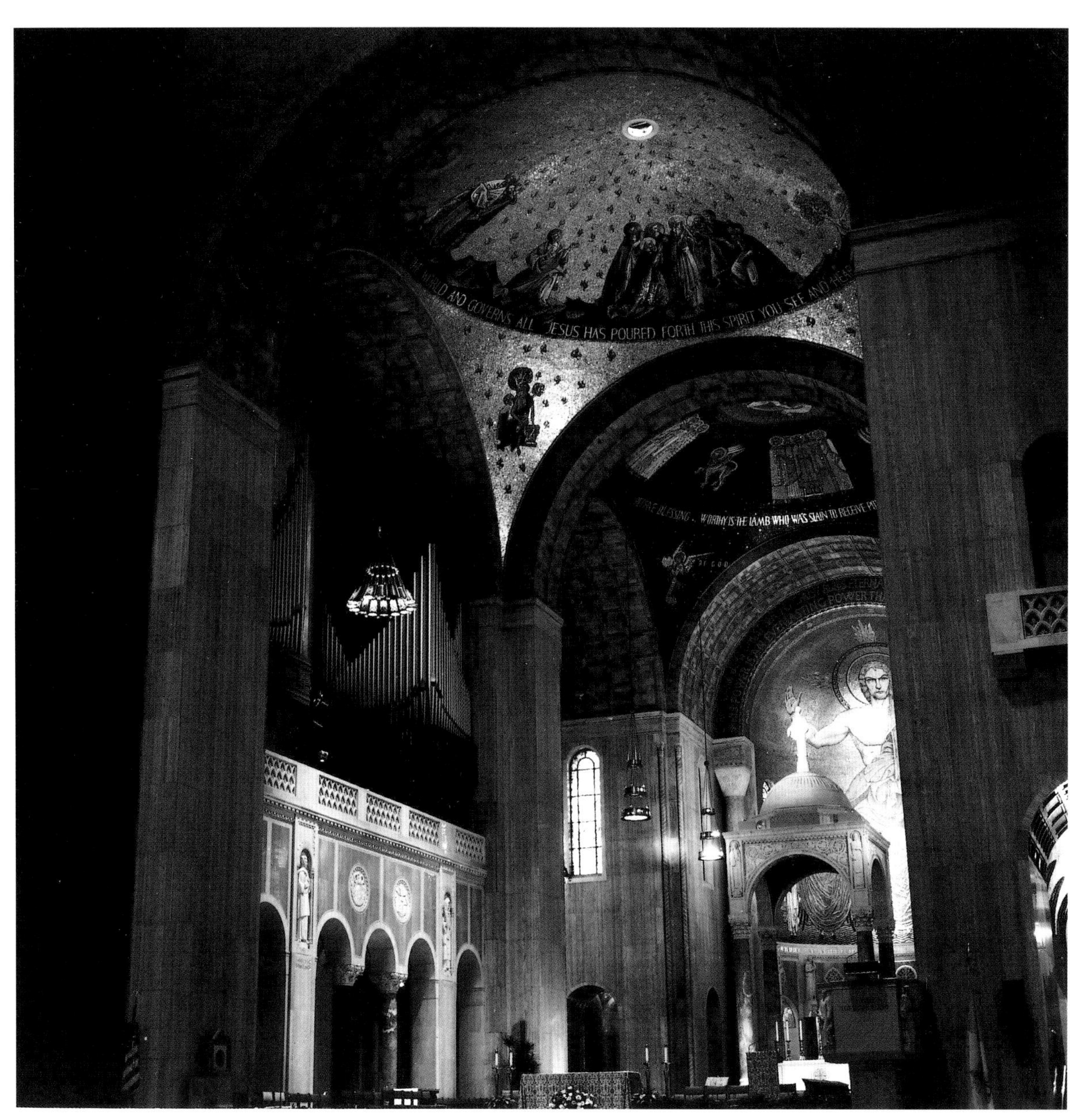

National Shrine of the Immaculate Conception

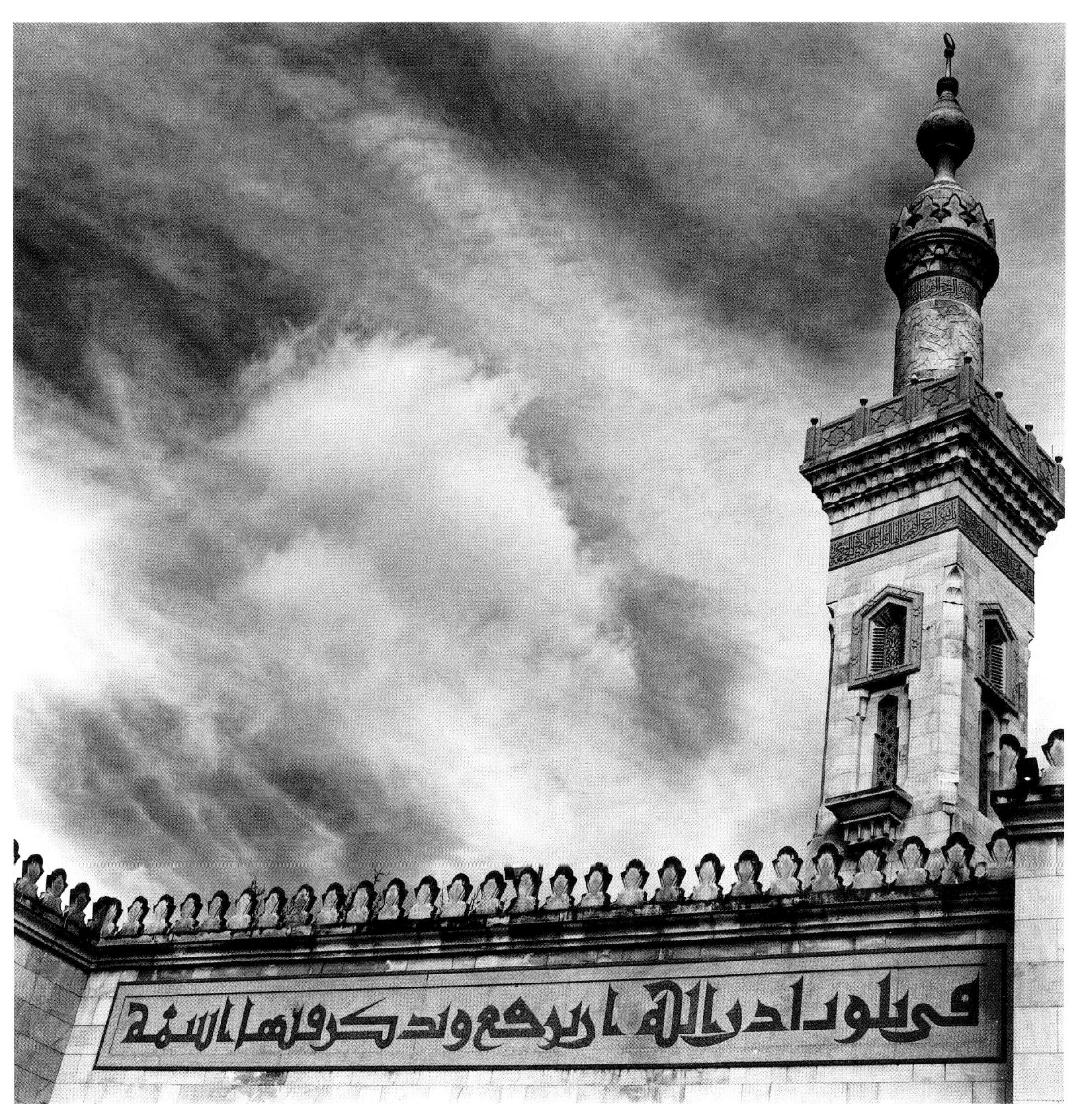

Islamic Center

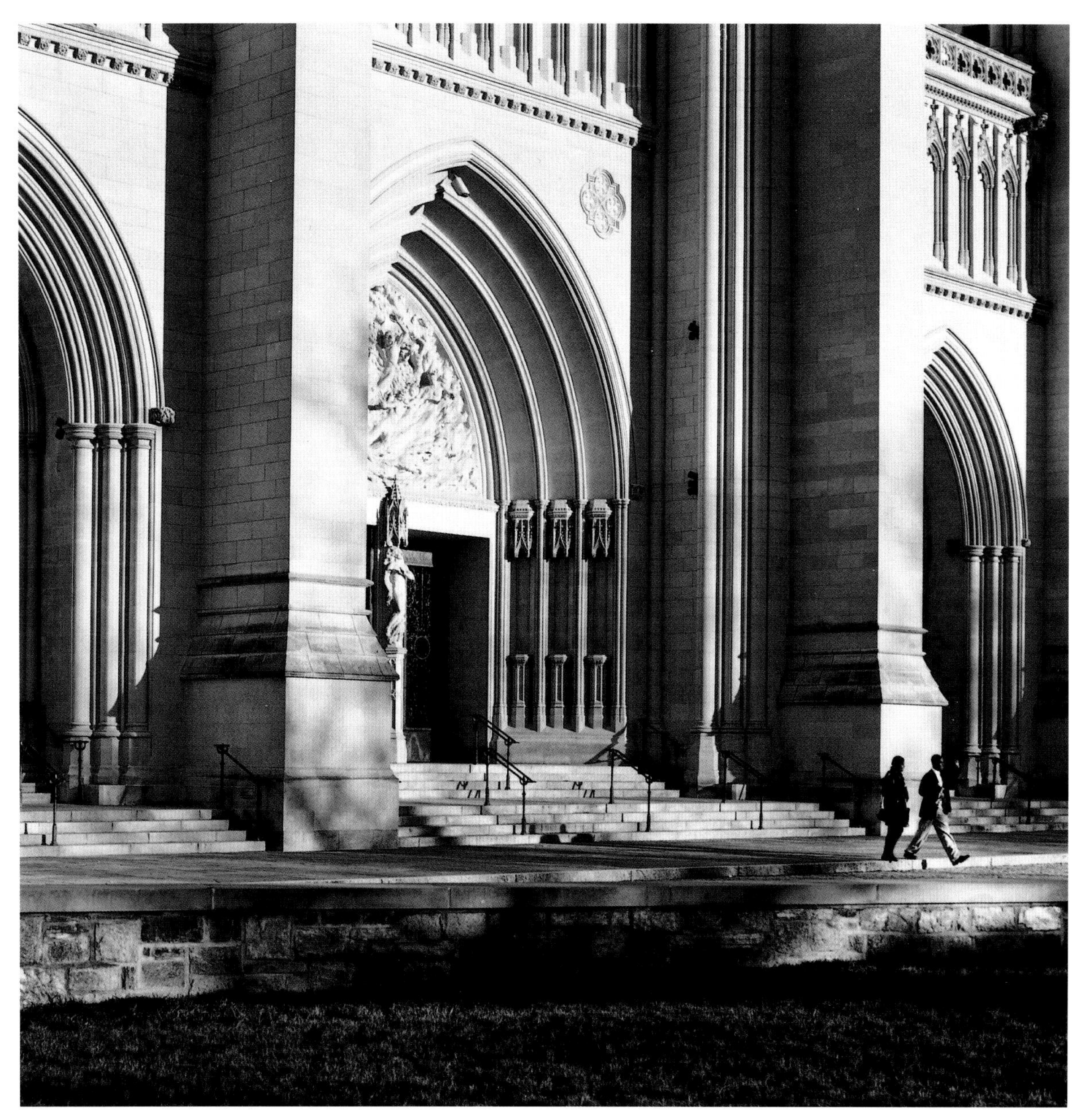

Washington National Cathedral

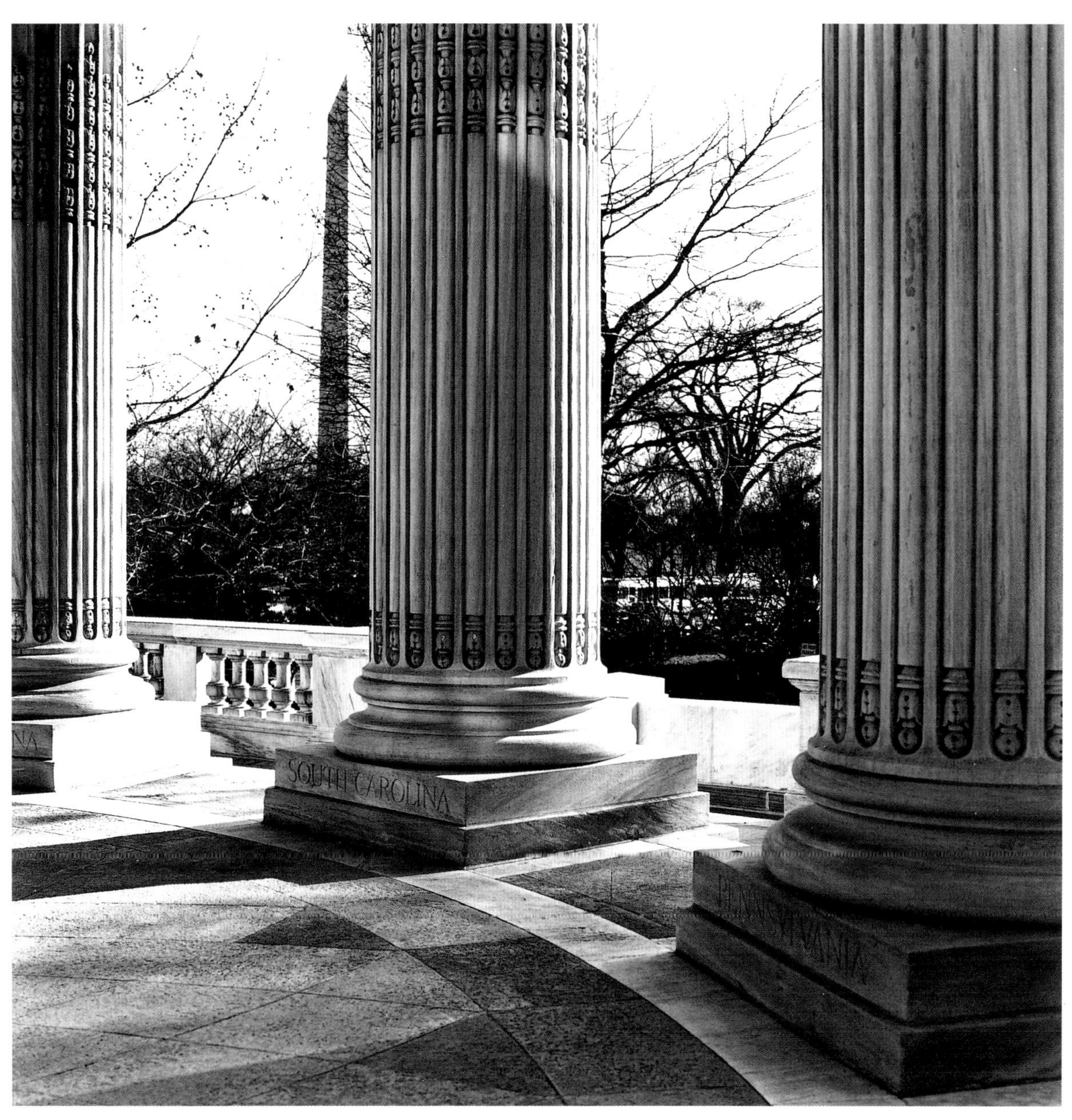

South portico, Continental Hall

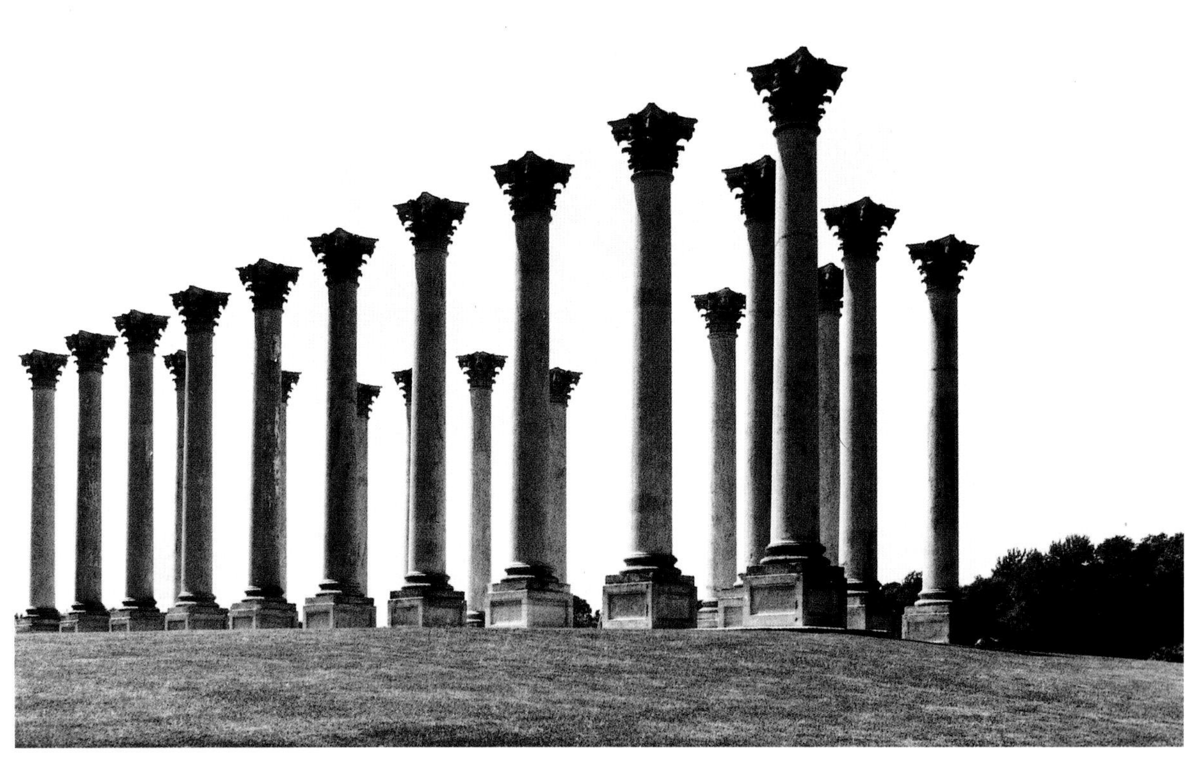

Columns, National Arboretum

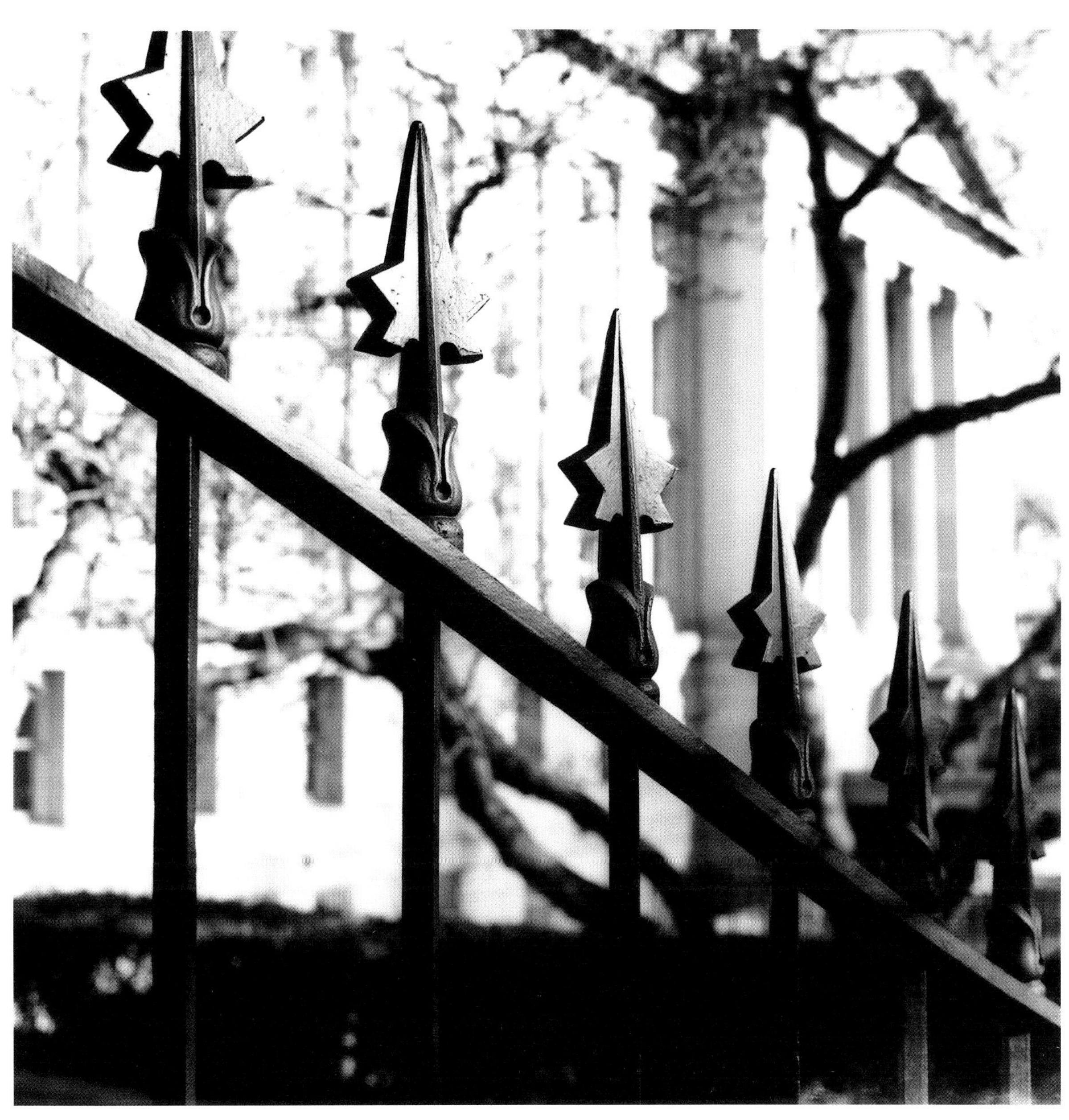

Iron fence, Treasury Building

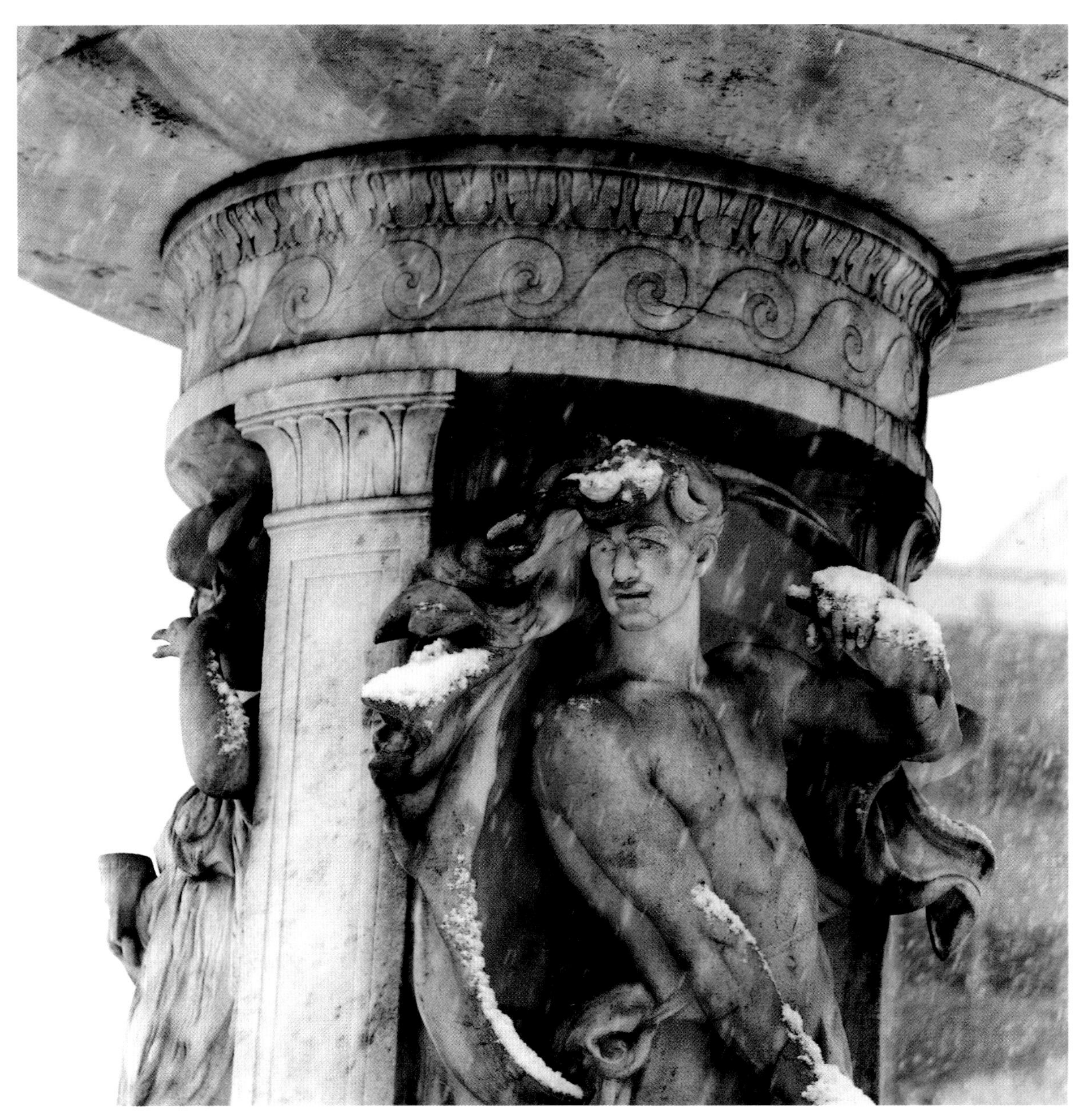

Fountain, Dupont Circle

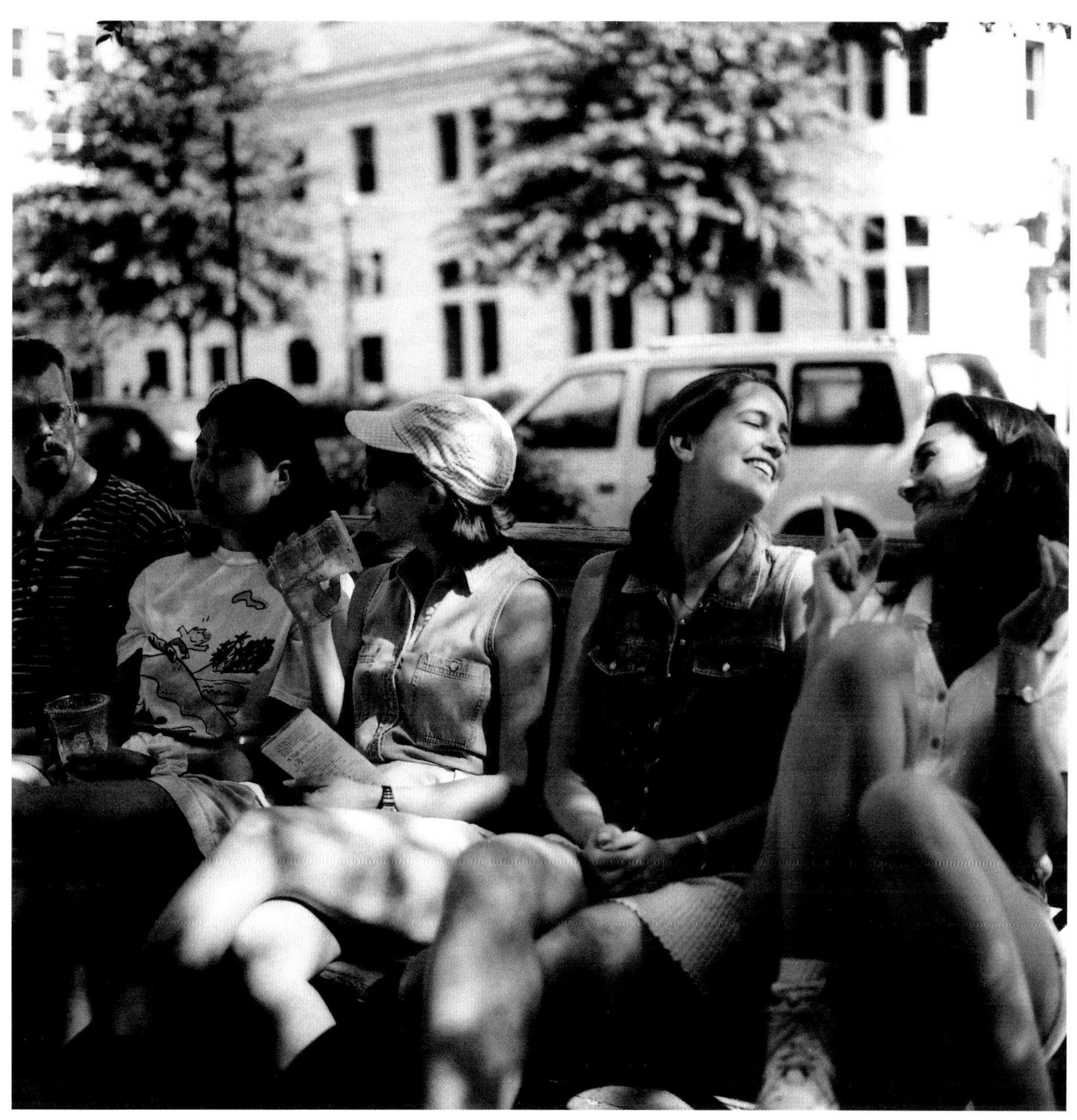

Indiana Avenue

WASHINGTON REFERENCE

(Page numbers are in bold)

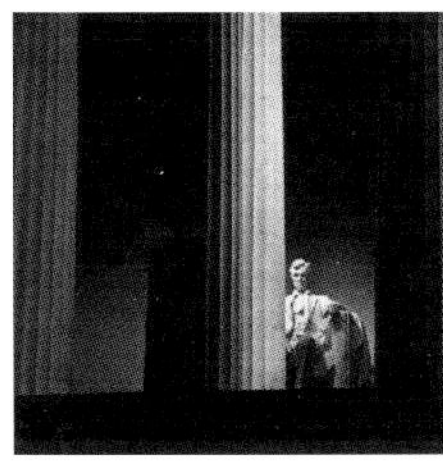

2 Lincoln Memorial, 1911-1922, West Potomac Park at west end of the Mall. Designed by Henry Bacon (with sculpture by Daniel Chester French and murals by Jules Guerin), this heroic, monumental, and moving creation ranks among the most famous works of art in America. French himself said it best: "The memorial tells you just what manner of man you are coming to pay homage to—his simplicity, his grandeur, and his power." See **99**

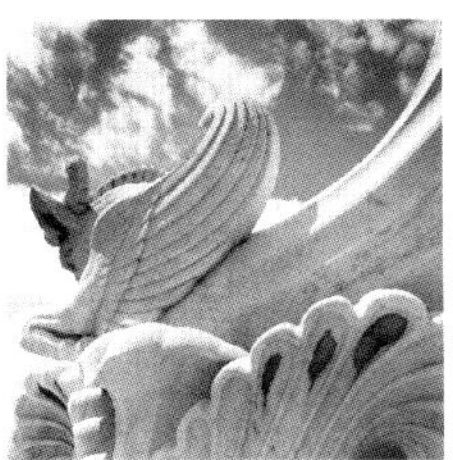

6 One of four enormous marble vases that flank the east and west façades of the Rayburn House Office Building, First Street and Independence Avenue. The vases, modeled on ancient Hellenic drinking horns, were sculpted in 1964 by W. H. Livingston, Sr.

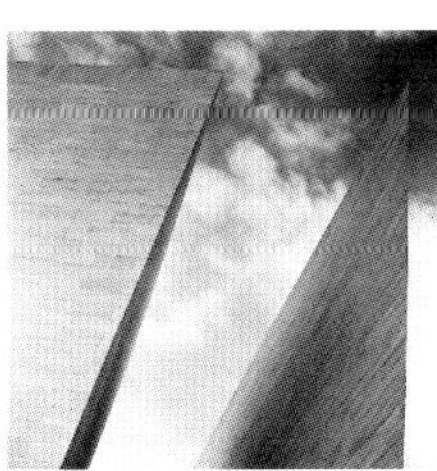

8 National Gallery of Art (East Building), Constitution Avenue and Fourth Street, 1978. A masterpiece from the pen of architect I. M. Pei, this abstract, sculptural work is a lesson in geometry and site planning. Pei took an awkward trapezoidal piece of ground and designed a building of two overlapping pieces: an isosceles triangle to house the lobby and gallery spaces and a right triangle for offices. It makes a wonderful contrast to the gallery's staid and serious West Building. See **100**, **101**

9 Canadian Embassy, 501 Pennsylvania Avenue, 1989. Architect Arthur Erickson, winner of many medals for design, created this semi-neoclassical, semi-modernist masterpiece to blend in with its neighbors. He cleverly gave the building's rotunda twelve columns, one for each of Canada's provinces and territories.

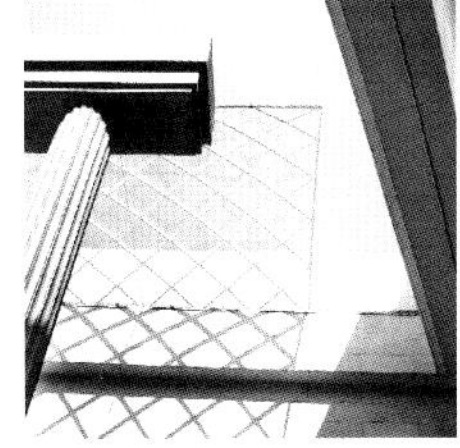

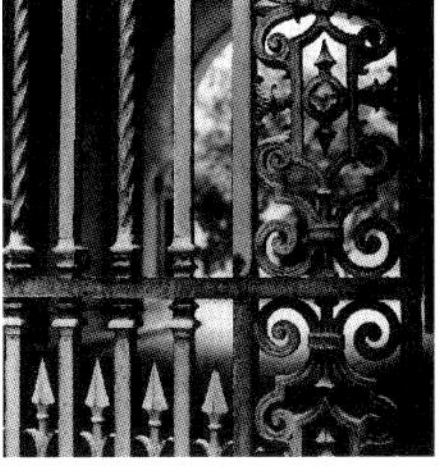

10 Detail of gate, Ariel Rios Building, Pennsylvania Avenue and Twelfth Streets, 1934. Delano & Aldrich, architects. A concave façade and thoughtful detail make this structure the most genteel of those that comprise the otherwise rather stolid Federal Triangle. Interior has superb WPA murals. See **102**

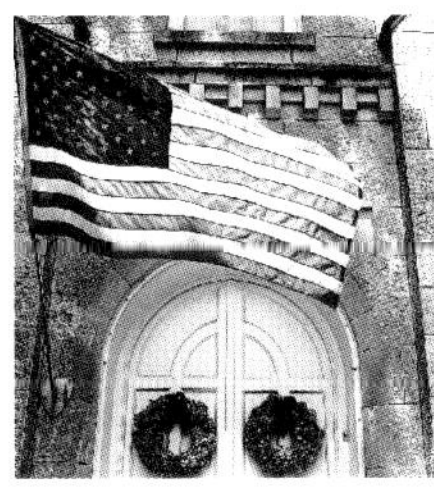

11 Entrance to the Commandant's Home, U. S. Soldiers' and Airmen's Home, circa 1890, architect unknown. See **109**, **26**, **148**

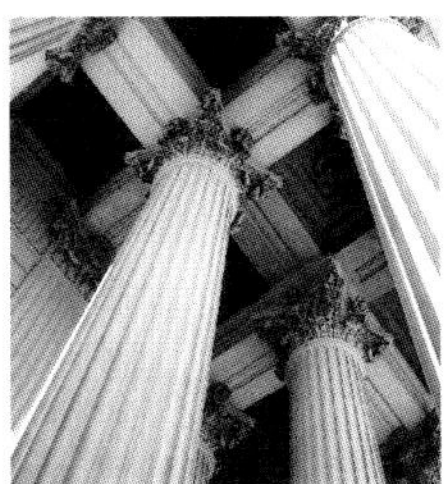

12 Detail of columns, National Archives. See **35**

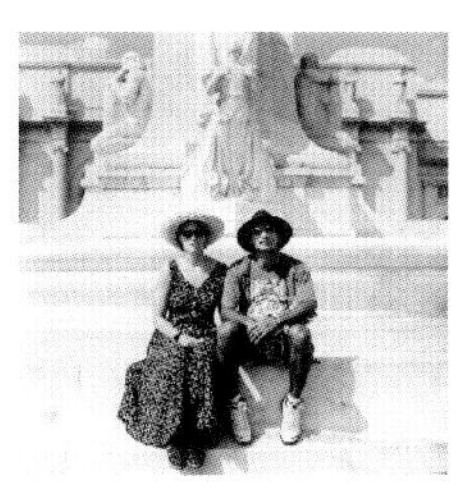

14 Columbus Fountain in front of Union Station. Lorado Taft (sculptor) and Daniel Burnham (architect) created this popular landmark in 1912.

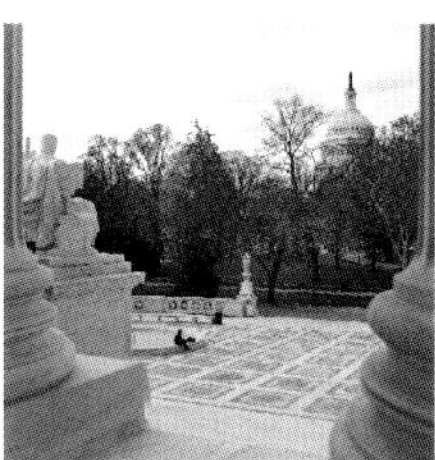

17 View towards the Capitol from the steps of the Supreme Court. See **41**

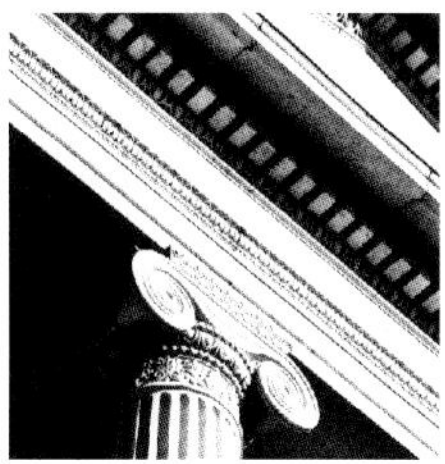

18 Detail of the Treasury Building, 1500 Pennsylvania Avenue. L'Enfant laid out Pennsylvania Avenue so the White House and Capitol would enjoy a "reciprocity of views." That lasted until the 1830s when President Andrew Jackson, searching for a spot for a new Treasury headquarters, saw this site and cried, "Build it here!" The building's original architect was Robert Mills, who gave Jackson a masterpiece. The building, now sprawling across five acres, stands as the largest Greek-revival structure in the world. See **87**, **105**, **106**, **113**, **129**

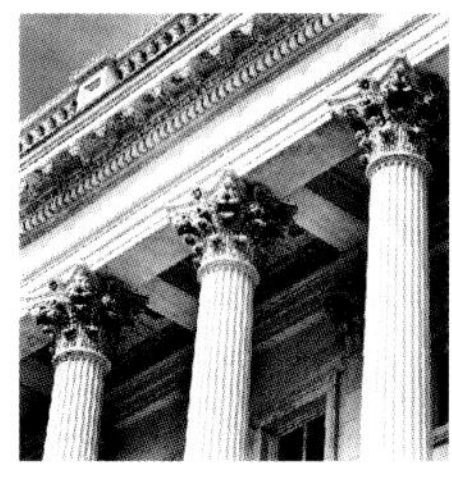

19 Senate Wing, the Capitol. See **33**, **20**, **21**

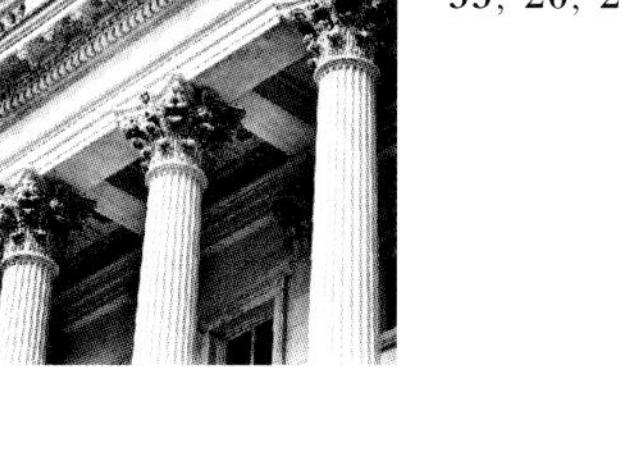

20 The majestic central dome of the Capitol, 1859, Thomas U. Walter, architect. See **33**, **21**

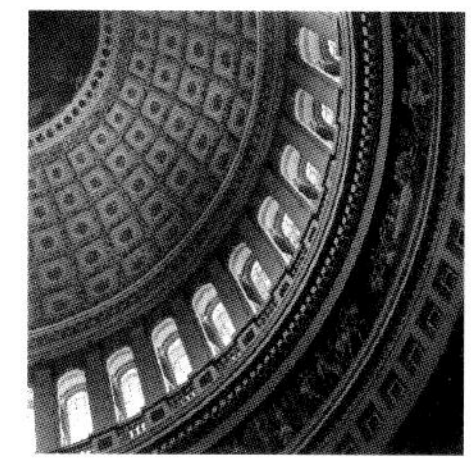

21 The soaring interior of the central dome of the Capitol with Constantin Brumidi's allegorical frieze. See **33**, **20**

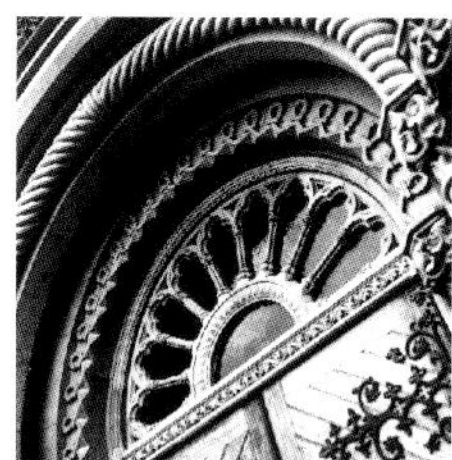

22 Detail of a door and lunette window and its fine Gothic tracery, Smithsonian Building, 1855. See **71**

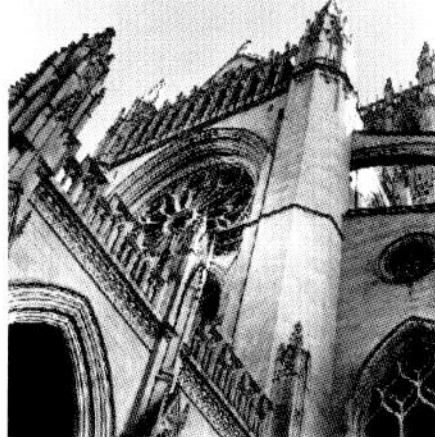

23 Washington National Cathedral, Massachusetts and Wisconsin Avenues. If the Capitol was—and to a degree still is—a work in progress for more than two centuries, its ecclesiastic counterpart, the nation's cathedral, managed to wrap things up in 83 busy years. Initially, there was much jockeying over which architectural style such an emblematic structure should take, but by the time construction began in 1906, the neo-Gothicists had won by a nose over the neoclassicists. Officially the cathedral for the Episcopal Diocese of Washington, it truly serves all and has been the setting for every kind of religious service, Christian and non-Christian alike. See **126**

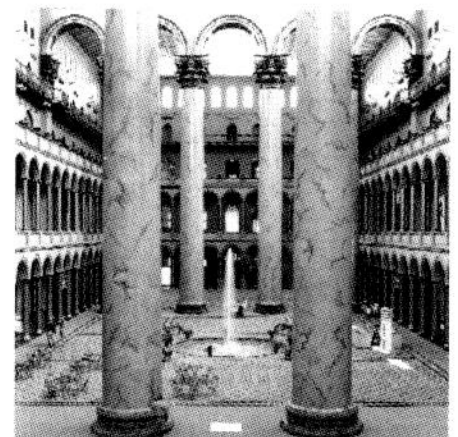

25 National Building Museum interior (also known as the Pension Building), Fourth and F Streets. A quirky masterpiece designed by amateur architect General Montgomery Meigs. His interior plan features one immense room (measuring 316 feet by 116 feet and 159 feet high) with offices around the perimeter. He also incorporated innovative fireproofing. Now a valued part of the cityscape, when "Meigs's old red barn" opened in 1887 it brought universal derision, including a comment from the general's former comrade-in-arms, William Tecumsah Sherman, who took one look and sighed, "the worst of it is, it is fireproof."

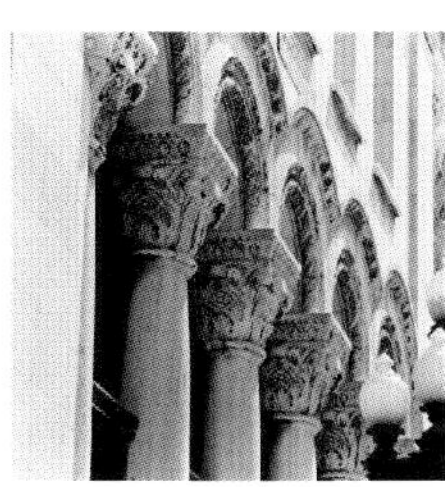

26 The Romanesque Sheridan Building, circa 1890, is part of the picturesque campus at the U.S. Soldiers' and Airmen's Home. See **109**, **11**, **148**

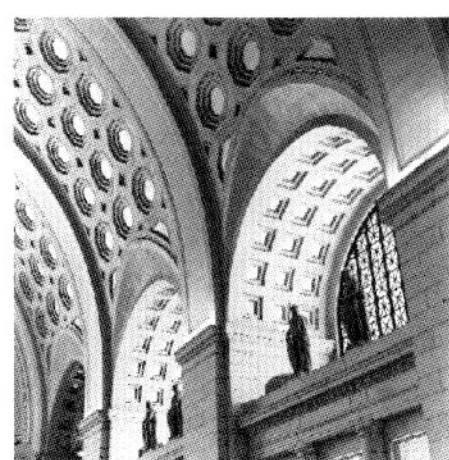

27 Union Station, Massachusetts and Louisiana Avenues. When completed in 1908 (Daniel H. Burnham, architect, and Lorado Taft, sculptor), this was the largest train station in the world. Its immense interior spaces—the main concourse stretches 760 feet long with 130-foot ceilings—evoke the coffered grandeur of Imperial Rome quite persuasively (and intentionally). Reopened in 1988 following a sorely needed $150-million renovation, Union Station is once again the gateway to the Capital City. See **30**, **31**, **92**, **94**

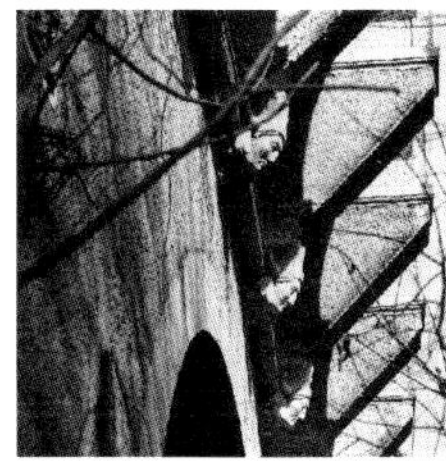

28 Q Street Bridge (correctly Dumbarton Bridge). One of the most endearing of Washington's many bridges, this span carries Q Street across Rock Creek Park to connect Georgetown and Kalorama. Completed in 1914, brothers Glen and Bedford Brown gave it massive battlements and dramatic arches. Sculptor A. P. Proctor added an American twist by decorating it with bronze bison and a series of sandstone heads modeled on Kicking Bear, chief of the Sioux.

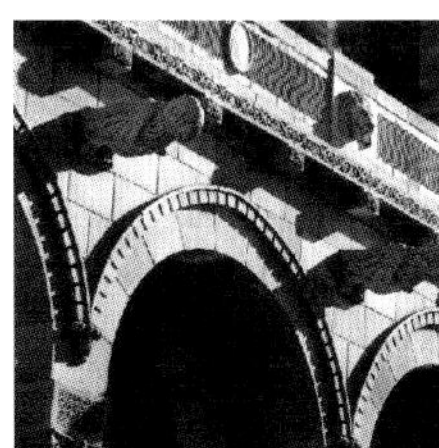

29 Limestone parrots decorate the façade of an apartment house at 2101 Connecticut Avenue, circa 1930. The 2000, 3000, and 4000 blocks of upper Connecticut Avenue gained their present character in the early decades of the twentieth century when dozens, if not scores, of well-designed apartment buildings and hotels began to line its sidewalks. See **74**

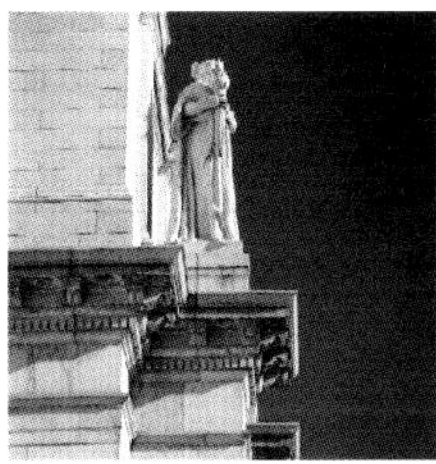

30 An allegorical sculpture on the main façade of Union Station. See **27**, **31**, **92**, **94**

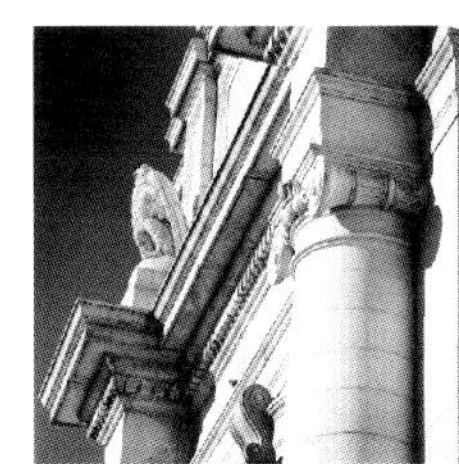

31 A fantastic heraldic bird perches itself on Union Station. See **27**, **30**, **92**, **94**

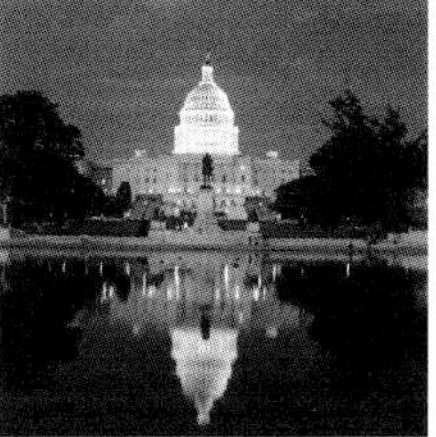

33 The Capitol. Begun in 1793 (William Thornton, architect) and still very much a work in progress. Two centuries of stop-and-go construction, changes, modifications, and often rancorous squabbling have made this magnificent building the perfect symbol of American democracy. See **19**, **20**, **21**

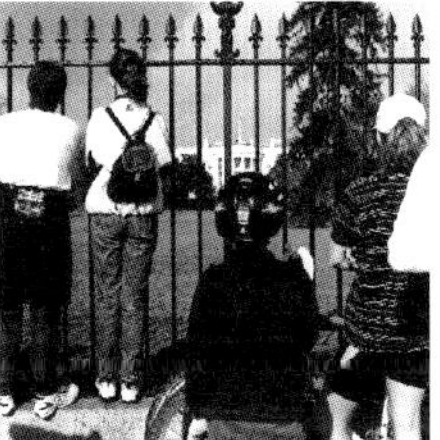

34 The White House, 1600 Pennsylvania Avenue. In 1792, Irish architect James Hoban won the design competition for the house and work began that year. President and Mrs. John Adams moved into the dwelling in 1800, and hated it. Thomas Jefferson, who took up residence here in 1801, didn't much care for the place, either; grumbling, he called it "big enough for two emperors, one Pope, and the grand Lama." In 1901, Theodore Roosevelt officially named it The White House.

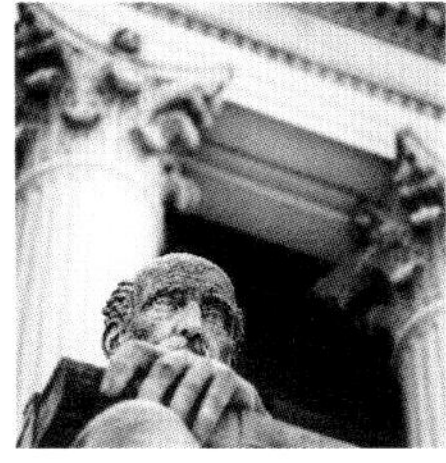

35 Detail, National Archives, Constitution Avenue between Seventh and Ninth Streets, 1935. Architect John Russell Pope treated the building as a large, limestone-sheathed mausoleum—the perfect repository for the tons of paper housed within. See **12**

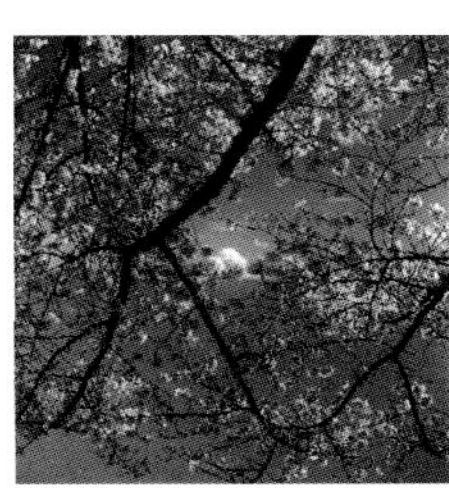

36 Jefferson Memorial. The Tidal Basin in front of the memorial is ringed with the city's famous cherry trees, presented in 1912 as a token of friendship from the Japanese government. See **37**, **146**

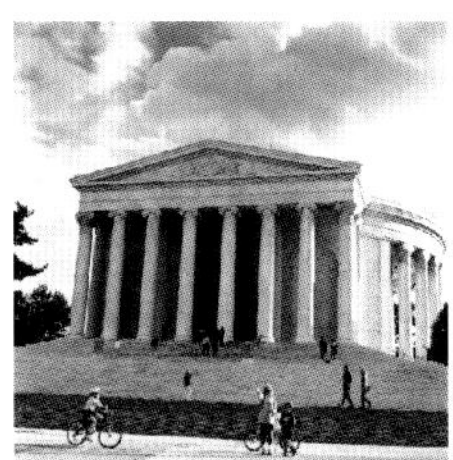

37 Jefferson Memorial. In the 1930s, with the Democratic party firmly in the saddle, Franklin Roosevelt, Squire of Hyde Park, decided it was time to honor the party's founder, Thomas Jefferson, Sage of Monticello. Architect John Russell Pope devised this somewhat tame version of one of Jefferson's favorite ancient buildings, the Pantheon in Rome. (Rudolph Evans sculpted the massive image of Jefferson for the interior.) F.D.R. dedicated the memorial on Jefferson's two-hundredth birthday in 1943. See **36**, **146**

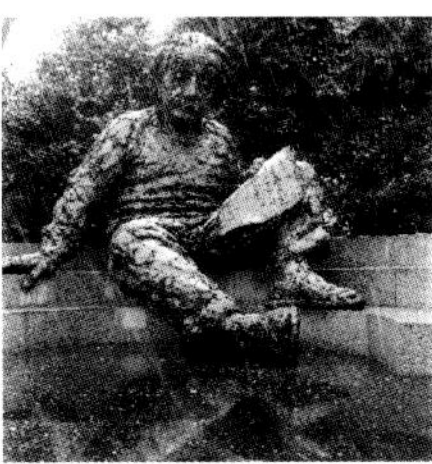

38 Albert Einstein Memorial, National Academy of Sciences, 2101 Constitution Avenue. This 1978 bronze by sculptor Robert Berks captures the humanism that characterized the great thinker.

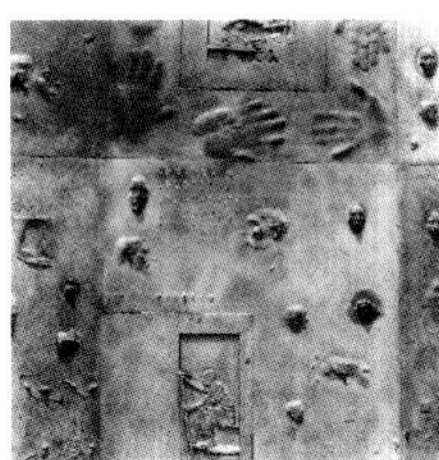

39 Detail, Franklin Delano Roosevelt Memorial. See **93**

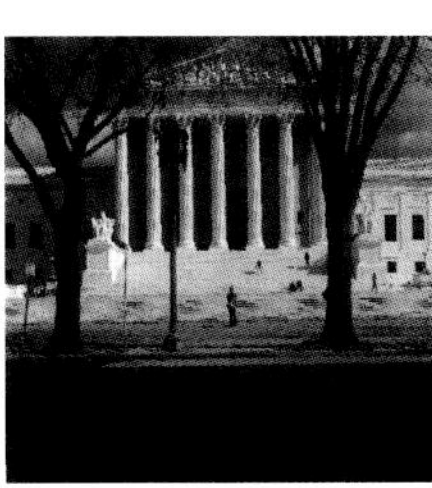

41 Supreme Court Building, First and East Capitol Streets. Cass Gilbert, Jr., architect. Wrapped in luminous Vermont marble and completed in 1935, this represents one of the city's latest, grandest—and most successful—ventures into Beaux-Arts classicism. Dean Acheson, however, complained that the building's immensity "seems to shrink the members of the Court." See **17**

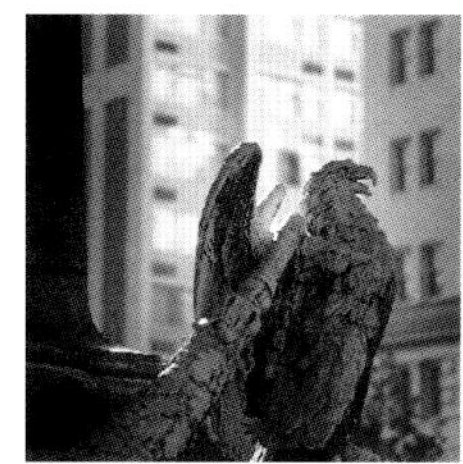

42 Pedestal detail of Major General George McClellan Statue, 1906. Located at Connecticut Avenue and Columbia Road, the nine-foot-tall bronze of one of Lincoln's generals has a richly decorated pedestal featuring eagles (one shown here) and eight escutcheons honoring McClellan's victories.

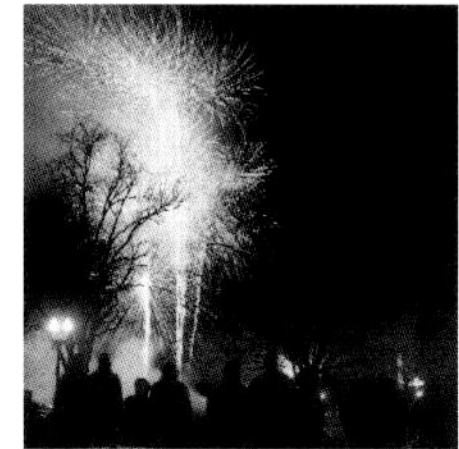

43 Inaugural fireworks, Capitol grounds.

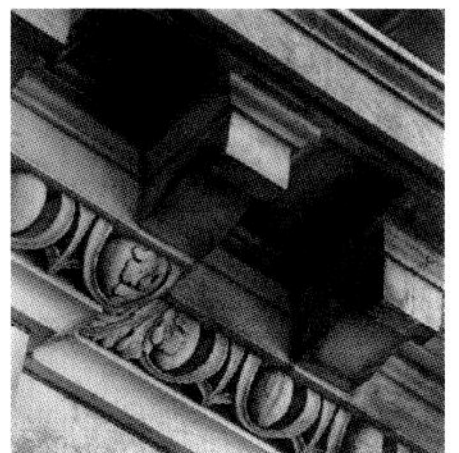

44 Detail of Anderson House, 2118 Massachusetts Avenue, 1905. Little and Browne, Boston-based architects. Now the headquarters for the Society of the Cincinnati (a benevolent organization George Washington established for his officers), this Italianate palace is now a museum.

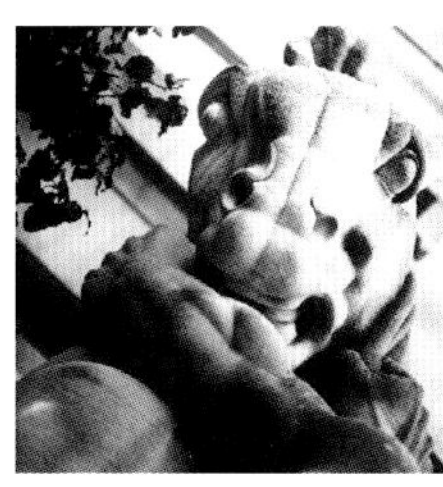

45 Detail of sculpture, *Man Controlling Trade*, 1942, Federal Trade Commission, Sixth Street and Constitution Avenue. Michael Lantz sculpted this Art-Deco symbol of the government restraining monopoly.

46 Cast-iron detail, Department of Commerce. When opened in 1932, the building's one-million-square-foot interior made it the largest office building in the country. It is part of the Federal Triangle, a collection of nine neoclassical office buildings. While the Triangle's components came from the drawing boards of different designers, they

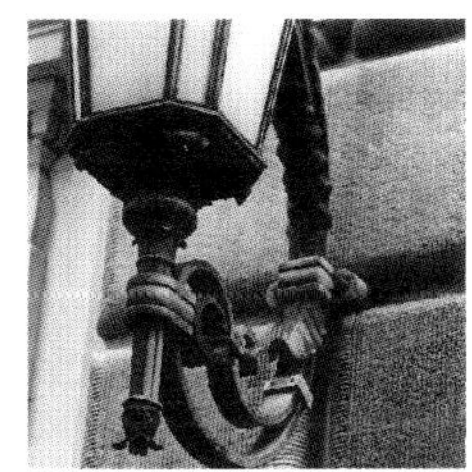

were conceived as a single monumental creation and guided to completion under the watchful eye of architect Edward Bennett. Much—perhaps too—pleased with his work, Bennett stated that the Triangle would stand as "a tribute to human order." See **10**

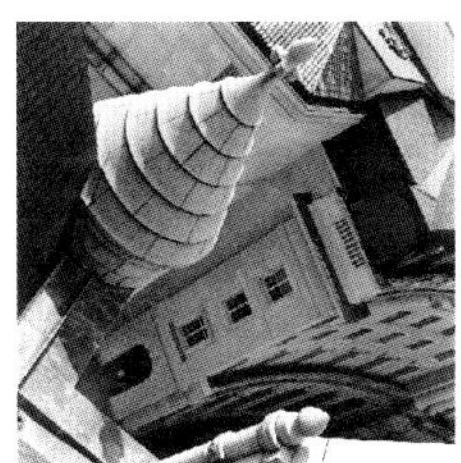

47 Old Post Office, Twelfth Street and Pennsylvania Avenue. Willoughby J. Edbrooke, architect. Controversy has swirled around this Romanesque building since it opened in 1890, when one critic dismissed it as "a cross between a cathedral and a cotton mill." By the 1930s, it sat abandoned and threatened with demolition. It was saved in the 1970s when architect Arthur Cotton Moore restored it and adapted it to new uses, most dramatically seen in the seven stories of shops and three of offices that line the 160-foot-tall atrium.

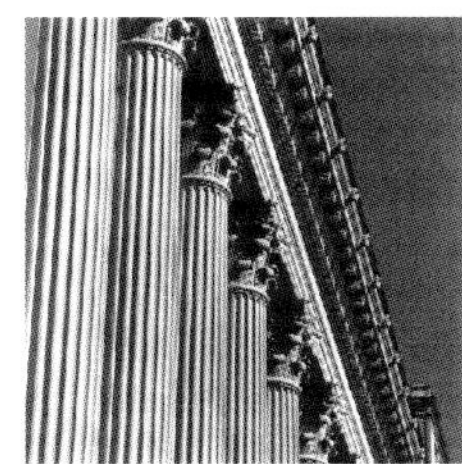

48 A detail of the Veteran Administration Building's Corinthian colonnade at Lafayette Square, 1918. James A. Wetmore, architect.

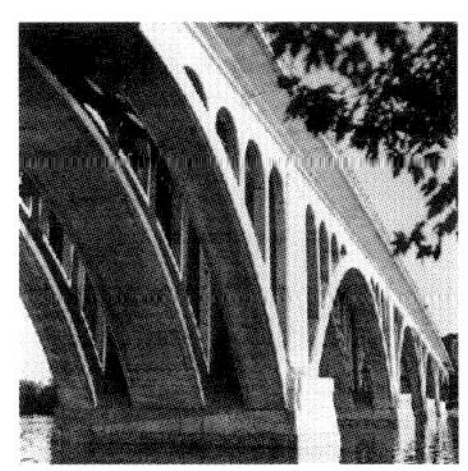

49 Key Bridge, an important span (at least for rush-hour commuters) that connects Georgetown and Arlington, Virginia. See **53**

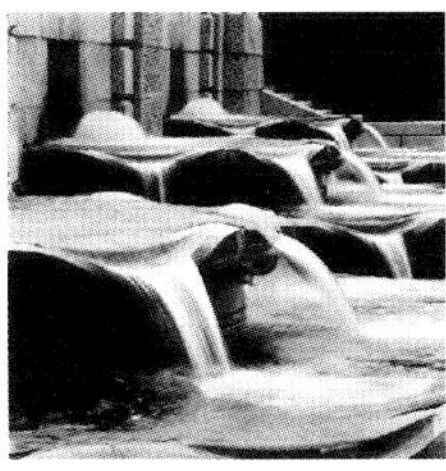

50 Fountain on Capitol grounds near Louisiana Avenue.

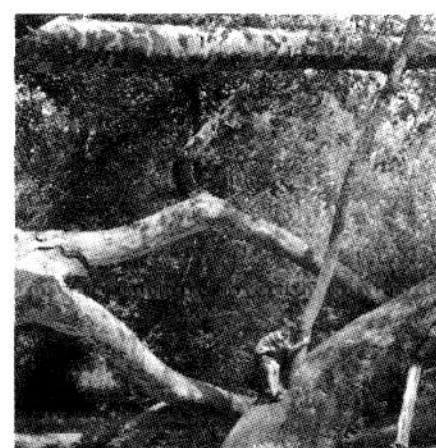

51 Chesapeake and Ohio Canal. Envisioned by George Washington as a commercial link with the fertile Ohio Valley, the canal actually only got as far as Cumberland, Maryland, 185 miles to the west. Closed to commerce in 1923, the canal and its towpath, all maintained by the National Park Service, now welcome bicyclists, hikers, fishermen, and canoeists. See **54**

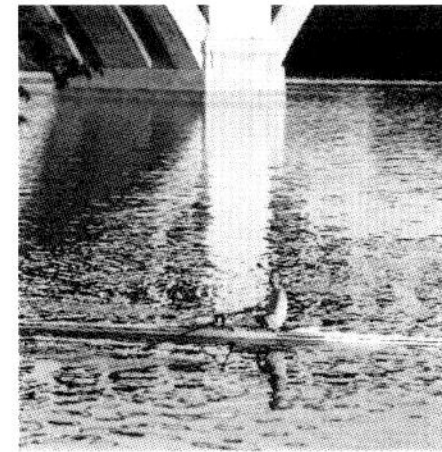

53 Rower and scull below Key Bridge, Georgetown. The Potomac's waters have been popular with generations of canoeists and crew teams. Many put in at the Washington Canoe Club, a shingley 1890s structure at K Street near the bridge. See **49**

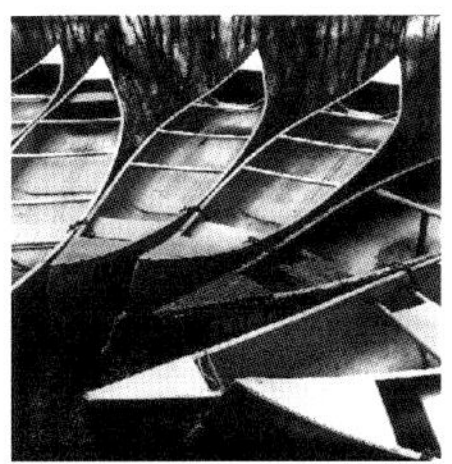

54 Canoes on the Chesapeake and Ohio Canal. See **51**

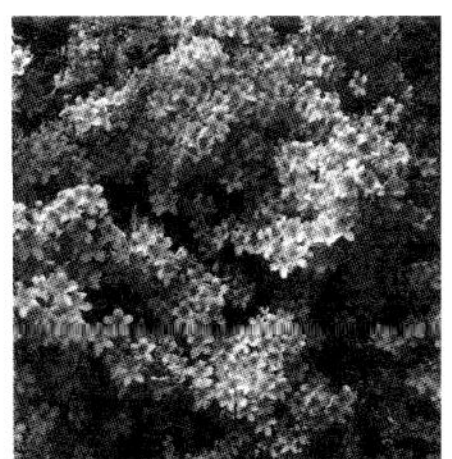

55 Millions of azaleas—Washington's unofficial official shrub—transform the city into a riot of color in late April and early May.

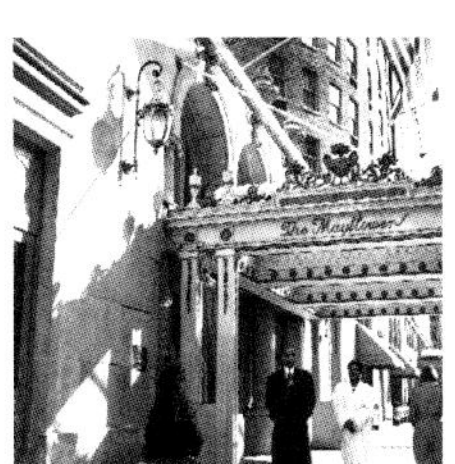

56 Mayflower Hotel, 1127 Connecticut Avenue. One of the grand dowagers among Washington's hotels, the Mayflower, designed by the firm Warren and Wetmore, opened its gilded doors in 1924—just in time to host Calvin Coolidge's inaugural ball. "Gilded" indeed: the hotel is said to contain more gold leaf than any building in the country except the Library of Congress.

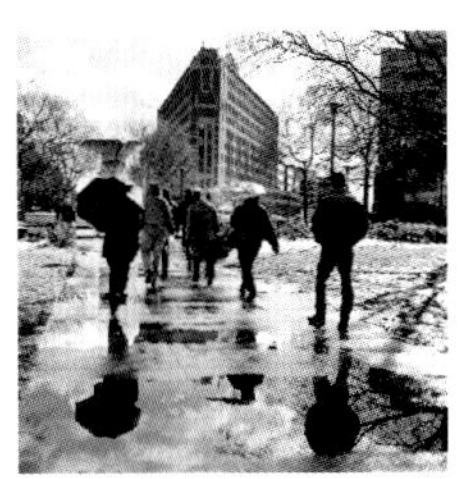

57 Dupont Circle. The Dupont Circle neighborhood has become a booming place, popular with locals and tourists alike who delight in the area's many shops, clubs, mansions, art galleries, and restaurants. See **58**, **61**, **130**

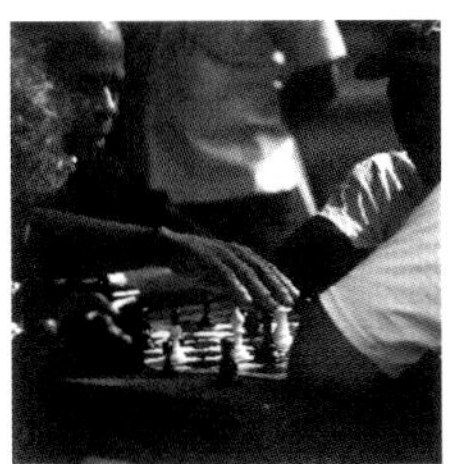

58 Chess is a venerable, and often spontaneous, tradition on Dupont Circle.

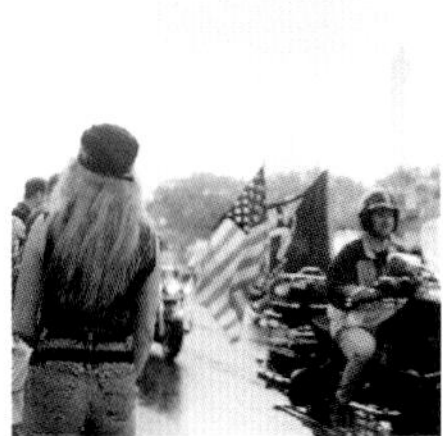

59 Memorial Day on Constitution Avenue: honoring Americans who died in war.

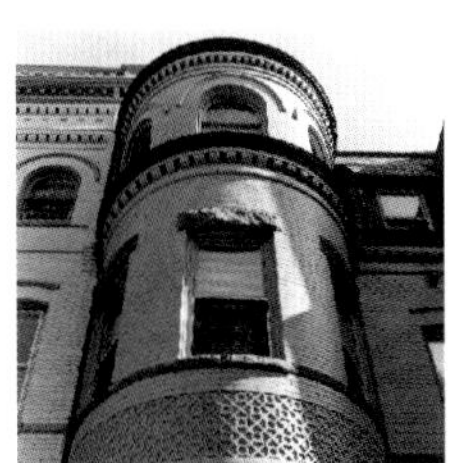

60 A late nineteenth-century rowhouse in Georgetown. Although Abigail Adams dismissed Georgetown, a community older than the capital city that surrounds it, as "a dirty little hole," since the Second World War it has become the most chic address in Washington. Thanks to strict historic preservation laws, most of Georgetown, with its brick houses, shady sidewalks, and romantic churches, manages to maintain its eighteenth and nineteenth-century feel. See **62**, **63**, **64**, **65**, **66**, **67**, **69**, **84**

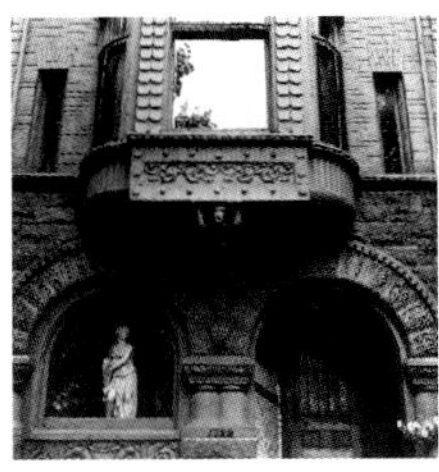

61 Some of Washington's most gracious old townhouses line the streets that radiate from Dupont Circle. See **130**

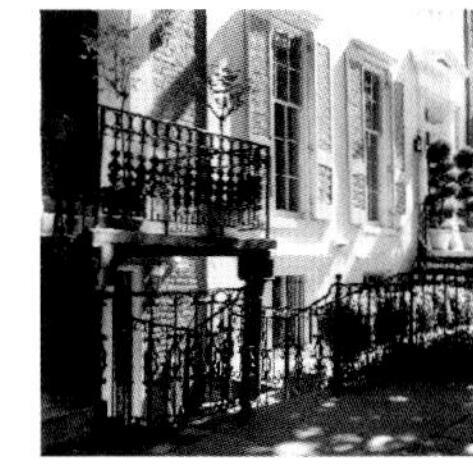

62 A townhouse on N Street in Georgetown. See **60**

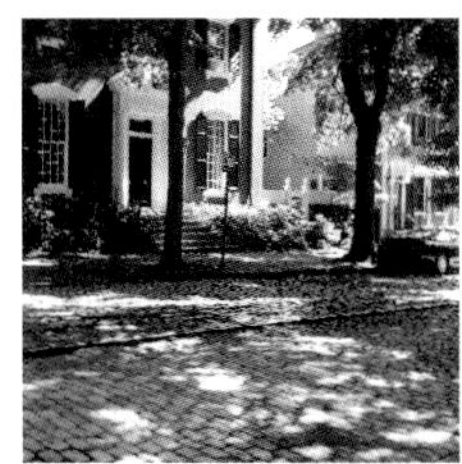

63 Houses on N Street, Georgetown. Georgetown can boast more Federal-period houses (most dating between 1780 and 1820) than any other section of the city. See **60**

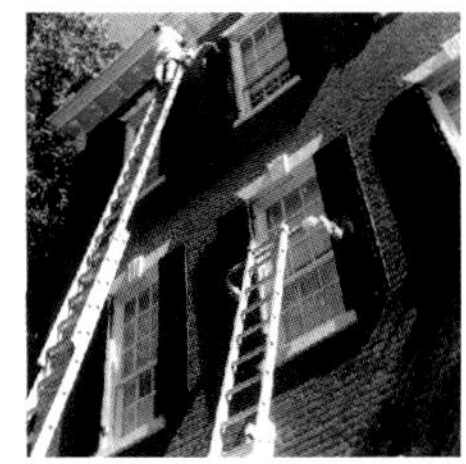

64 Maintaining a house in Georgetown. See **60**

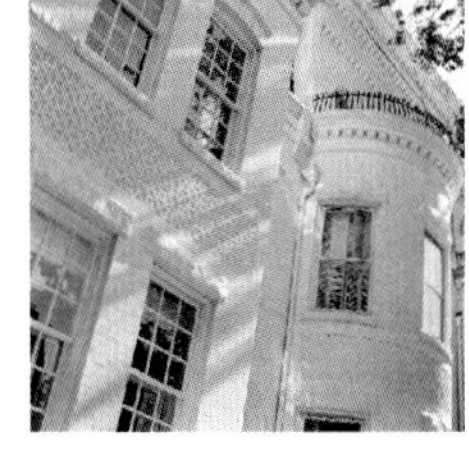

65 This 1880s rowhouse (like that shown on page **60**) was designed in the popular Queen-Anne style. Such residences, with their elegant bay windows, can be found throughout the city.

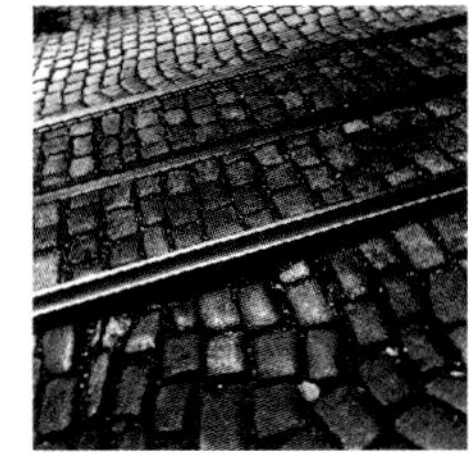

66 Cobblestone paving and trolley tracks on P Street. Tracks such as these were in service all through the city until the 1950s. See **60**

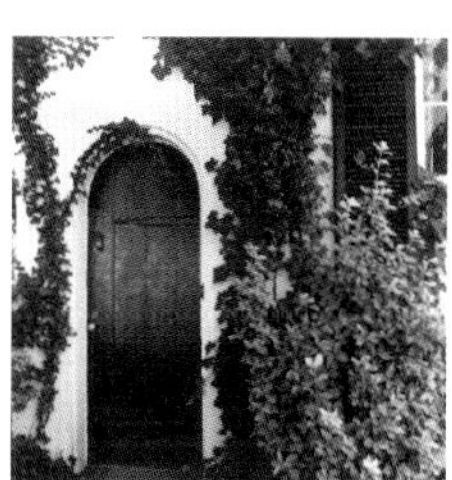

67 A Georgetown passageway. In the eighteenth and nineteenth centuries, horses were stabled behind houses and led through doors like these. See **60**

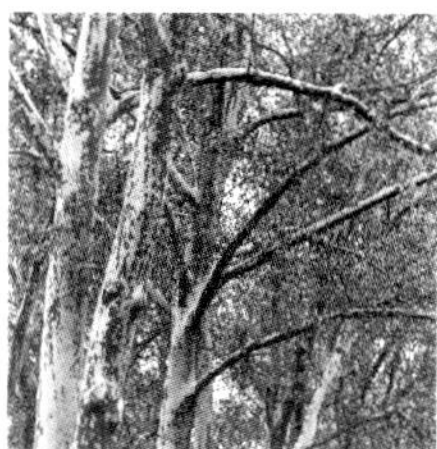

68 A stand of sycamores at Constitution Gardens, West Potomac Park, completed 1976. The architectural firm Skidmore, Owings, and Merrill designed these 52 acres, created from swampland reclaimed from the Potomac, to "establish the historic [Mall] buildings in a comprehensive landscape." While the gardens more than meet their serious purpose, they are also beloved of Washingtonians as a place to picnic, jog, feed birds, and just plain doze in the shade. See **76**

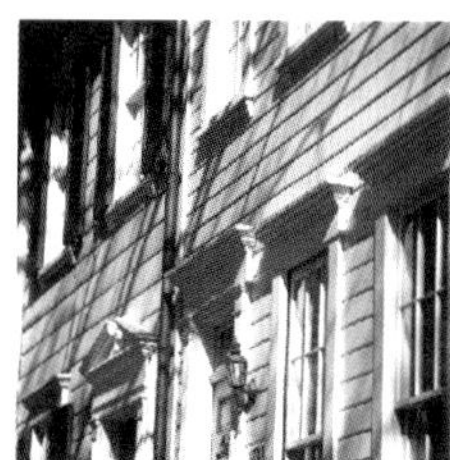

69 Federal rowhouses in Georgetown. See **60**

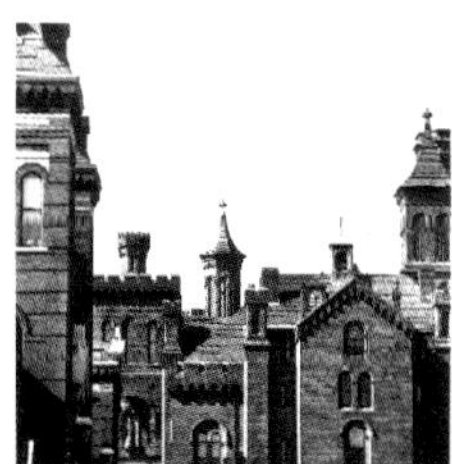

71 Affectionately nicknamed "The Castle," the red sandstone main building of the Smithsonian Institution on Jefferson Drive between Ninth and Twelfth Streets, opened in 1855. James Renwick served as architect. Named after the English chemist and mineralogist James Smithson, who was so contemptuous of the British monarchy that he left his entire fortune for the creation in Washington of "an establishment for the increase and diffusion of knowledge among men." See **22**

72 Luther Place Memorial Church, Vermont Avenue at Thomas Circle. Architect Judson York designed this landmark as a symbol of thanksgiving for the end of the Civil

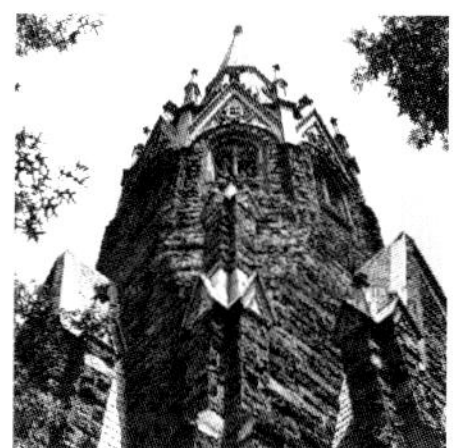

War. Completed in 1870, the church's craggy, neo-Gothic red sandstone is a dramatic contrast to the city's usual limestone-dressed neoclassical creations.

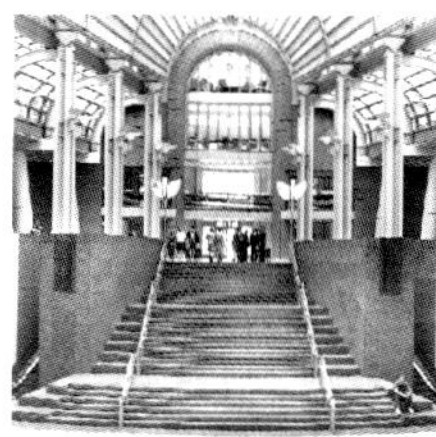

73 Ronald Reagan Building and International Trade Center, 1300 Pennsylvania Avenue, 1998, Pei, Cobb, and Freed, architects. A 3.1-million-square-foot colossus that cost some $800 million, this Indiana limestone structure imaginatively blends neoclassical and modern design. It certainly makes a welcome replacement for the site's previous occupant—a huge parking lot—and is the largest government-built structure in the area since the Pentagon.

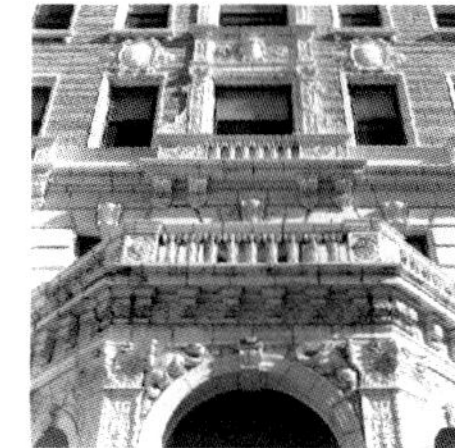

74 Many apartment buildings on Connecticut Avenue, such as this one at 2300, are festooned with exuberant, wedding-cake trim. See **29**

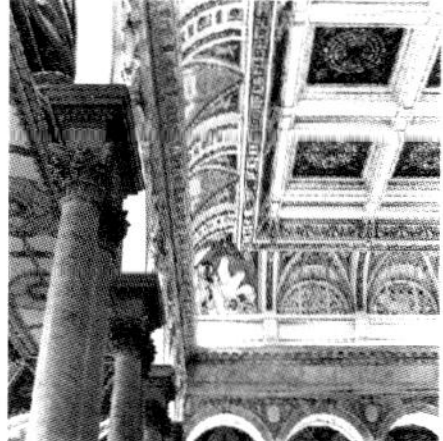

75 Great Hall, Library of Congress, First Street and Independence Avenue, 1892, Edward Pearce Casey, architect. The nation's library, begun with Thomas Jefferson's collection of some 6,500 books, has become the world's most comprehensive repository of knowledge: its 540 miles of shelves contain 110 million volumes, 48 million manuscripts, and the papers of everyone from Freud to Groucho Marx. Its main reading room, resplendent in carved marble and wood beneath 160-foot ceilings, is one of America's most breathtaking interior spaces. See **112**

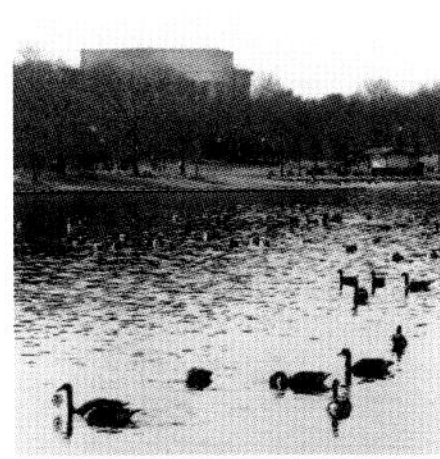

76 The pond at Constitution Gardens. See **68**

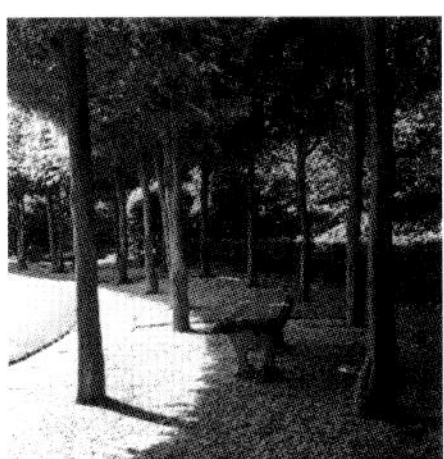

77 Garden at Dumbarton Oaks, 3101 R Street. The estate's mansion and ten acres of gardens, designed by Beatrix Farrand, took shape after Mr. and Mrs. Robert Bliss acquired the property in 1920. The Blisses left it to Harvard University, which has maintained the house as a museum and study center. Farrand hoped the gardens would be "the sort of place in which thrushes sing and … dreams are dreamt" and, thanks to Harvard's gentle care, they have remained just that. See **78**, **79**

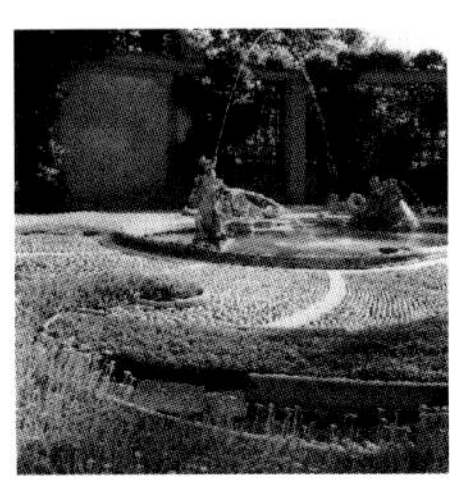

78 Dumbarton Oaks. Putti and seahorses frolick in the Pebble Garden Fountain sculpted by Vincent Benedetto. See **77**, **79**

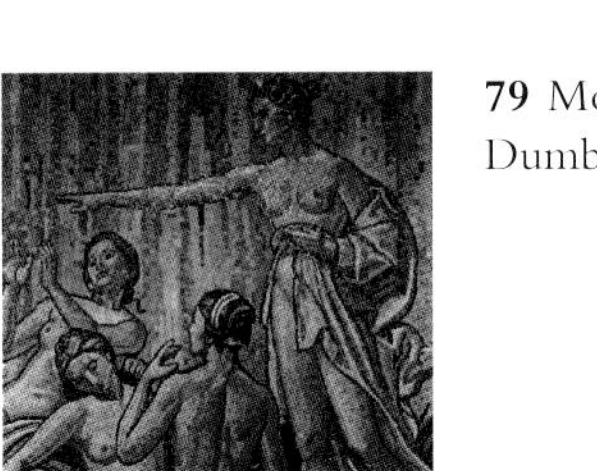

79 Mosaic at pool loggia, Dumbarton Oaks. See **77**, **78**

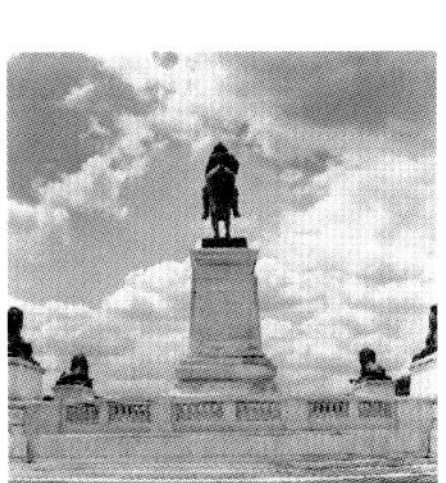

81 Ulysses S. Grant Memorial, First Street and East Mall, 1922. Edward Pearce Casey, architect, and Henry M. Shrady, sculptor. Prominently located at the base of the Capitol grounds, this statue, featuring Grant astride his horse Cincinnatus, is the world's second largest equestrian monument. Sculptor Shrady, who had meticulously dissected horses to learn their anatomy, died of exhaustion two weeks before the memorial was unveiled by Grant's granddaughter and great-granddaughter. See **89**

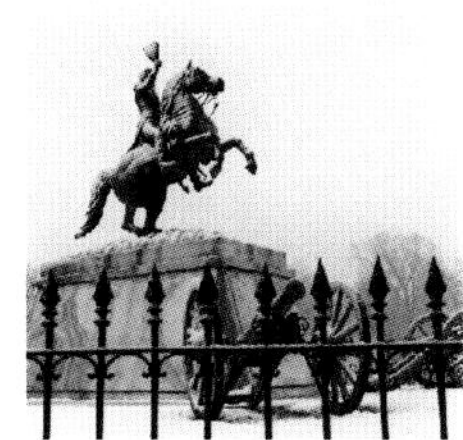

82 Lafayette Square is home to Clark Mills's energetic statue of Andrew Jackson of 1853, the first equestrian statue cast in America. Henry James deemed it "the most prodigious of all Presidential effigies…prancing and rocking through the ages."

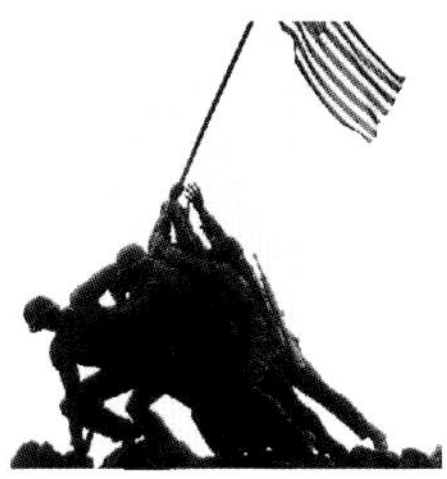

83 Marine Corps War Memorial (also known as the Iwo Jima Memorial), Arlington Boulevard and Ridge Road. Felix W. de Weldon, sculptor. Among the most recognizable of all statues, this powerful work of art has an almost baroque sense of tension and movement. This 78-foot-tall bronze, dedicated in 1954, symbolizes the indomitable courage of the American armed forces.

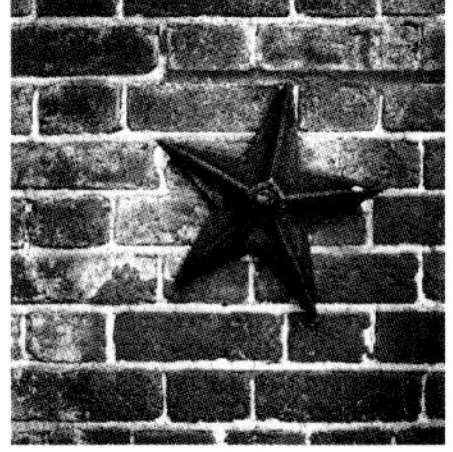

84 Cast-iron ties are a humble but time-honored means for preventing old brick walls from falling. This one secures an eighteenth-century building in Georgetown.

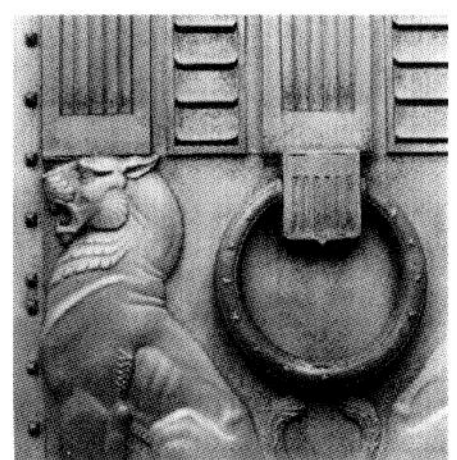

85 A detail of the massive metal doors at the Department of Justice, Constitution Avenue and Ninth Street, 1935, by sculptor Carl Paul Jennewein.

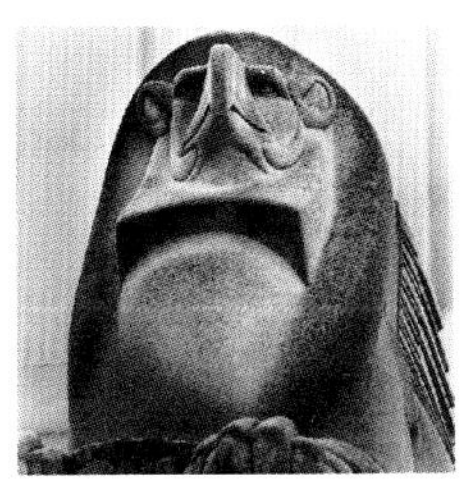

86 Acacia Griffin, Acacia Mutual Insurance Building, 51 Louisiana Avenue. Edmond Romulus, sculptor. The two Art-Deco limestone griffins that flank the entrance to this neoclassical building cut impressive figures. In ancient Greek mythology, griffins—beasts that are half lion, half eagle— watched over Scythian gold and became symbols of guardianship.

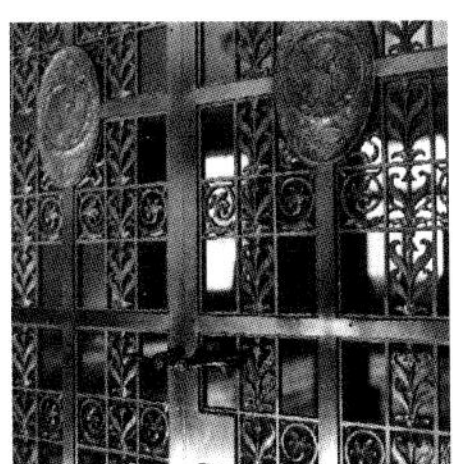

87 The bronze gates to the Cash Room, Treasury Building. See **18**

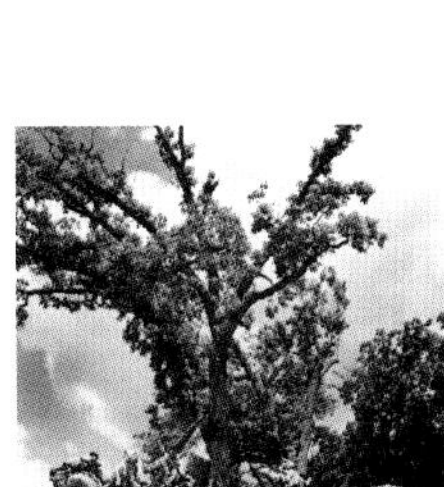

89 *Artillery Group*, 1912, an intense and dramatic scene of seven horsemen charging into battle, forms part of the Grant Memorial. Henry M. Shrady, sculptor. See **81**

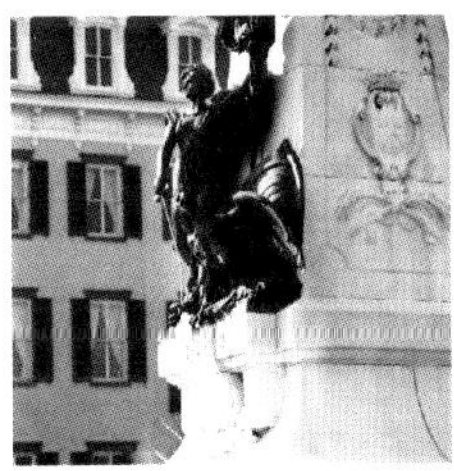

90 *Liberty* resides at the base of J. J. Fernand Hamar's exuberant statue of General Rochambeau (1902) in Lafayette Square.

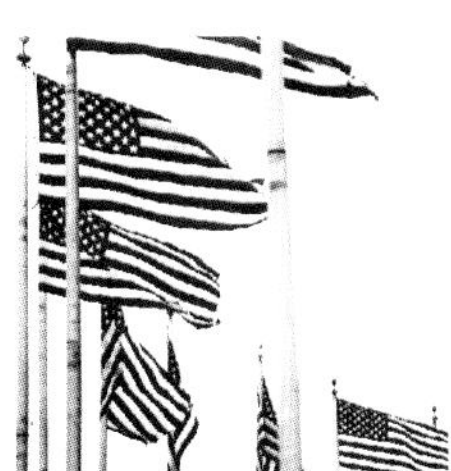

91 American flags, Washington Monument. See **123**

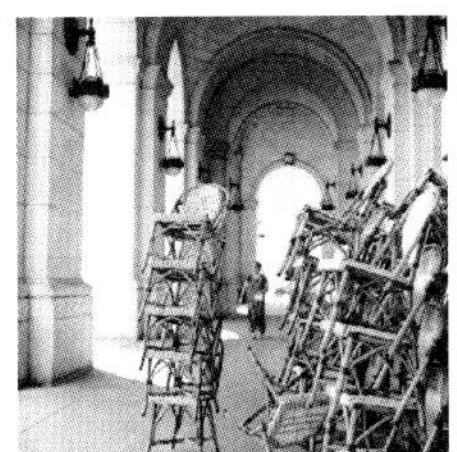

92 Union Station. See **27**, **30**, **31**, **94**

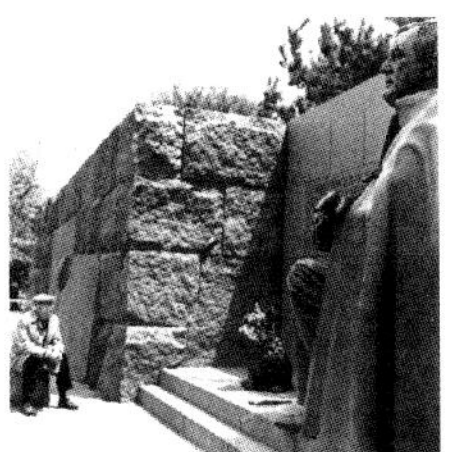

93 Franklin Delano Roosevelt Memorial, Tidal Basin, 1997. This meandering seven-acre tribute, designed by Lawrence Halprin, might be taken to symbolize the complex nature of our thirty-second president. Granite walls create four outdoor rooms, each dedicated to a different aspect of Roosevelt's twelve-year presidency. See **39**

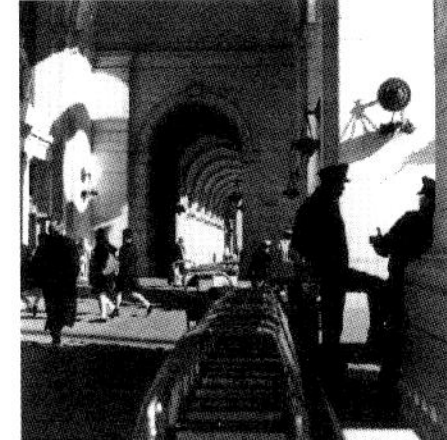

94 Union Station. See **27**, **30**, **31**, **92**

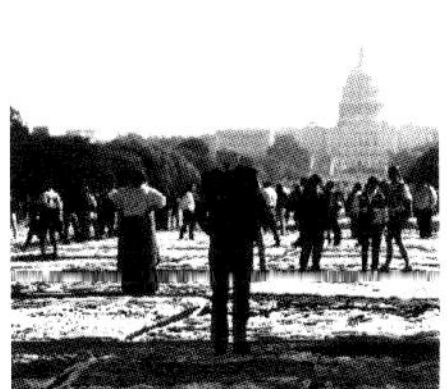

95 The annual summer exhibition of quilts in memory of those who died of AIDS is one of many events for which the Mall is ideally suited. Indeed, its creators envisioned it as a kind of three-mile long national park in the national Capital, a place, as L'Enfant wrote in 1791, that would "unite the useful with the commodious and agreeable." For most of the nineteenth century it was anything but: open sewers crisscrossed it, and railroad trains chugged across it to stations located at its center. Finally, in 1902, a Federal commission decided to turn the Mall from a national disgrace to the national treasure it was intended to be. Today the Mall, lined with some of the nation's most important museums and art galleries, has indeed become a kind of pilgrimage site for American and foreign visitors alike.

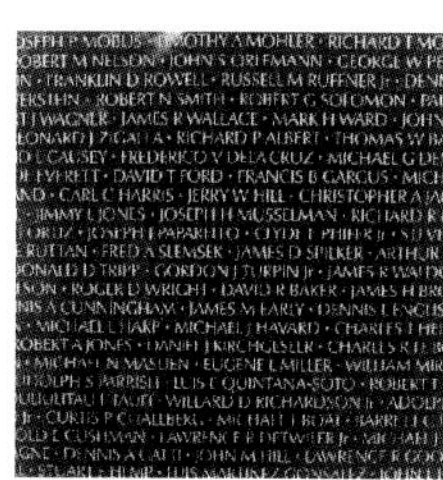

97 Vietnam Veterans Memorial, the Mall near Twenty-first Street, 1982. Maya Ying Lin, designer. Initially controversial for its unorthodox design, it has ultimately triumphed as one of the country's most eloquent and moving tributes to those who died in battle. Etched in black granite are the names of the 60,000 men and women who fell or are missing in the undeclared war in Southeast Asia. The victims' average age was 19.

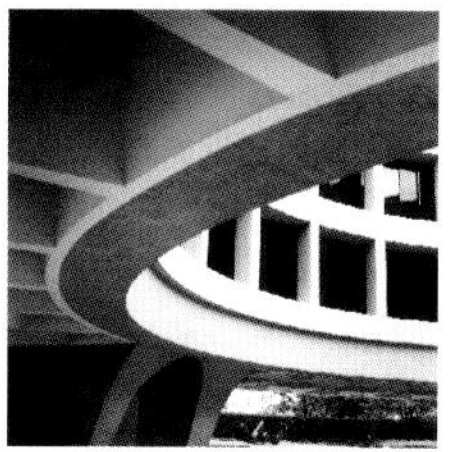

98 Joseph H. Hirshhorn Museum, Independence Avenue at Seventh Street, 1974. Skidmore, Owings, and Merrill, architects. When this "concrete doughnut" (as it's been called) was still in the talking stages, S. Dillon Ripley, secretary of the Smithsonian Institution from 1964 to 1984, commented that if the final building "were not controversial in almost every way, it would hardly qualify as a place to house contemporary art." The museum houses a collection of modernist masterpieces.

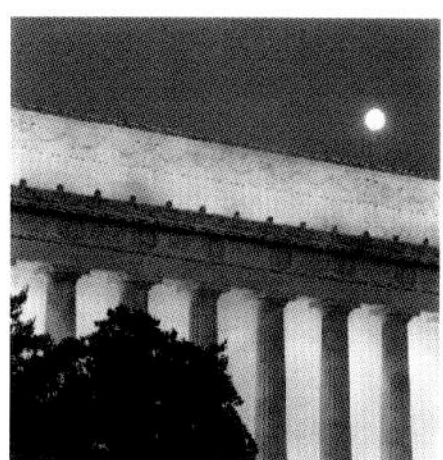

99 Lincoln Memorial. The top frieze contains the names of the forty-eight states in the Union when the memorial was dedicated in 1922. The thirty-eight state names engraved above the colonnade are those that were in the Union at the time of Lincoln's death in 1865. See **2**

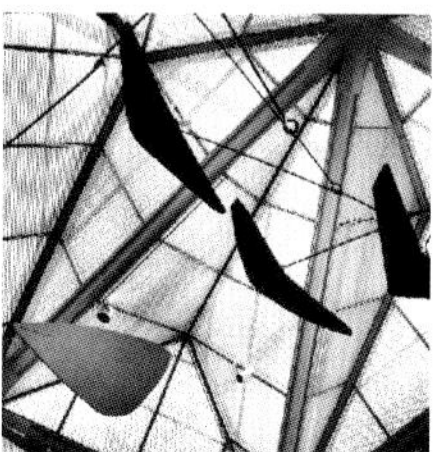

100 *Untitled*, 1976, a mobile by Alexander Calder, East Building, National Gallery of Art. See **8**

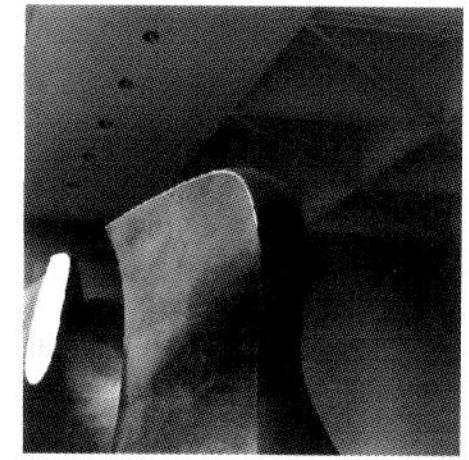

101 *Knife Edge Mirror Two Piece*, 1978, by Henry Moore, East Building, National Gallery of Art. See **8**

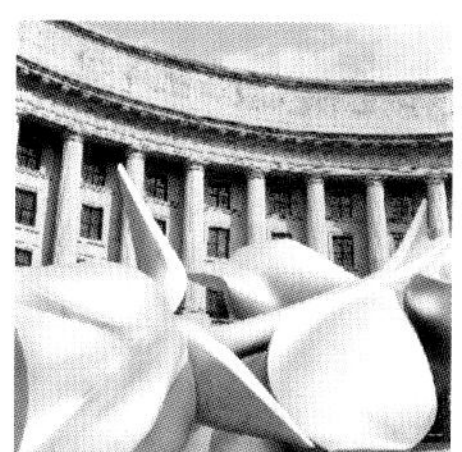

102 Sculptor Stephen Robin created these monumental rose petals for Woodrow Wilson Plaza and the embrace of the Ariel Rios Building's concave façade. See **10**

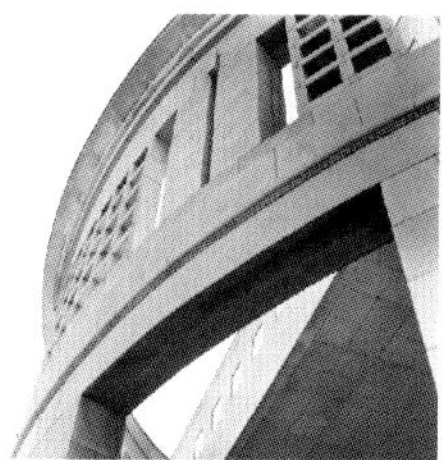

103 U.S. Holocaust Memorial Museum, Raoul Wallenberg Place and Fourteenth Street, 1993. James Ingo Freed, the architect of this passionately brutal structure, designed the building to shake visitors out of the complacency engendered by the city's safe, neoclassical monuments. "You cannot deal with the Holocaust as a reasonable thing," he explained.

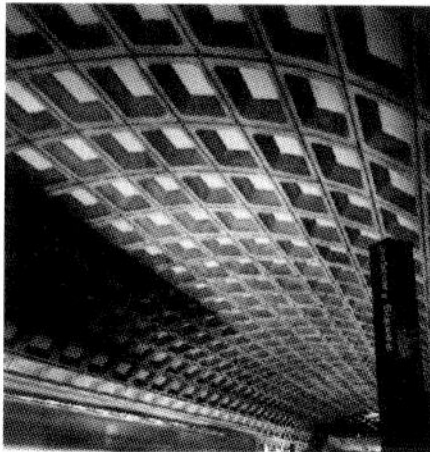

104 When the city's Metro system opened in 1975, *Fortune* magazine called it "a solid gold Cadillac for the masses." A good phrase, that, but it doesn't quite capture the aesthetic drama the system offers its riders: the experience of riding immense escalators deep into the ground and the interplay of light and shadow beneath the vast, coffered concrete vault ceilings. See **107**

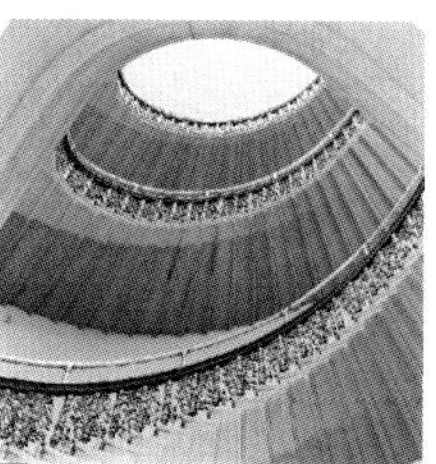

105 Staircase, Treasury Building. Is there a more graceful staircase in the city? See **18**

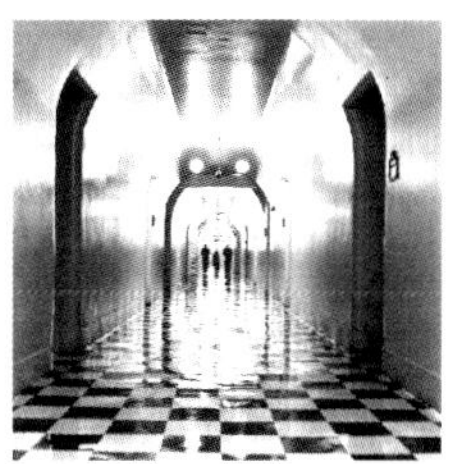

106 Treasury building basement. This subterranean hallway is but one link in a seemingly endless network. See **18**

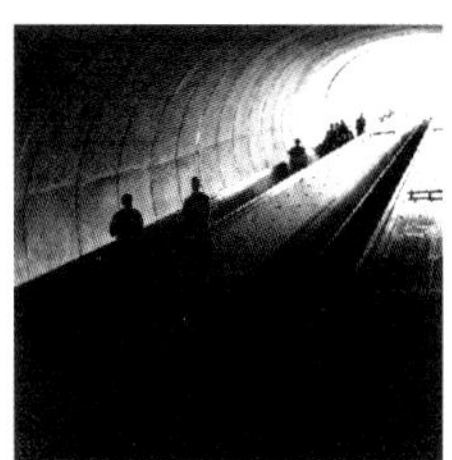

107 The Metro escalator at Dupont Circle. See **104**

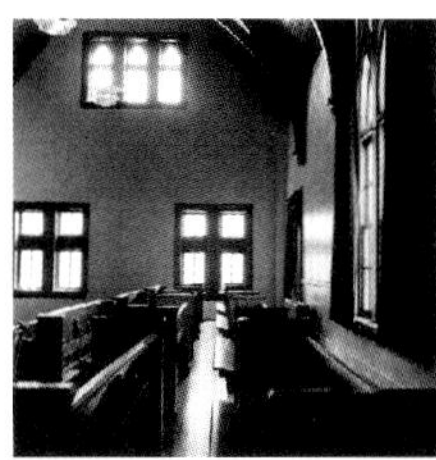

109 Chapel interior, Stanley Hall, U.S. Soldiers' and Airmen's Home, Rock Creek Church Road at Upshur Street, 1897, architect unknown. This fine neo-Gothic structure is part of the oldest veterans' home in the United States and is one of several handsome buildings on the extensive 300-acre grounds. The complex was underwritten with indemnity from Mexico following the 1846-48 Mexican War. See **11**, **26**, **148**

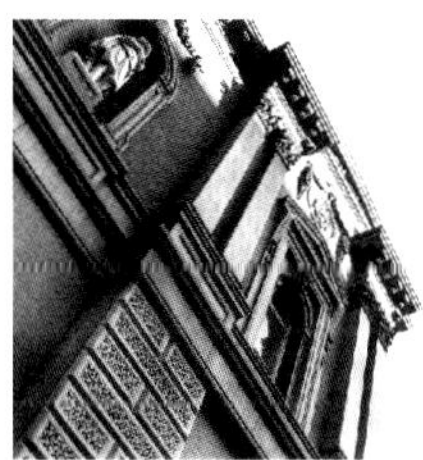

110 Detail of Renwick Gallery, Seventeenth Street and Pennsylvania Avenue, 1859. James Renwick, architect, and Moses Ezekiel, sculptor. This wonderful creation was built to house the art collection of financier William Wilson Corcoran, who opened it as the city's first public art gallery in 1870. After neglect and more than one demolition threat (in 1963, First Lady Jacqueline Kennedy intervened to save the building), the renamed gallery was restored in 1969-71. It now serves as a showcase for American crafts and decorative arts, a use that surely would have made Mrs. Kennedy smile approvingly.

111 Detail of Old Executive Office Building (former State, War, and Navy Building), Pennsylvania Avenue and Seventeenth Street. Designed by Alfred B. Mullett and built in various stages between 1875 and 1888, this is a

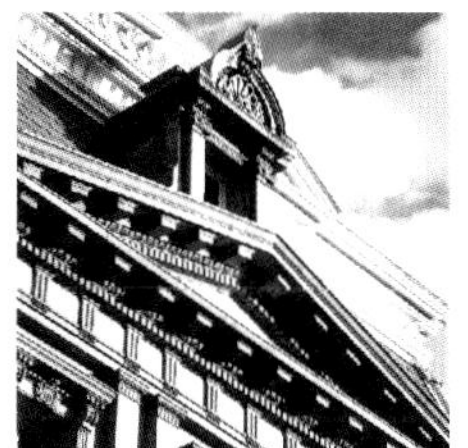

building one either loves or hates. The haters include Henry Adams, who fussed about "Mr. Mullett's architectural infant asylum"; Herbert Hoover, who deemed this "architectural orgy" the one building in town "we regret most"; and Harry Truman, who had no use at all for "the greatest monstrosity in America." (Architect Mullett committed suicide in 1890.) Douglas MacArthur was among those who were quietly happy here: he served as building superintendent and designed some of the extant street-level planters.

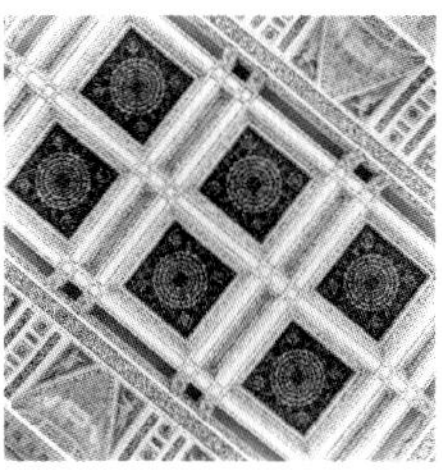

112 Ceiling detail, Library of Congress. See **75**

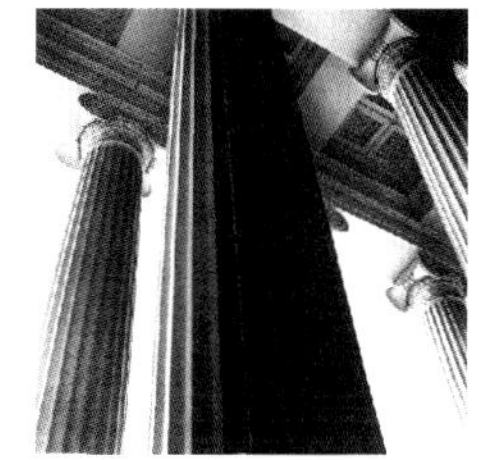

113 The Treasury Building's majestic Ionic columns. See **18**

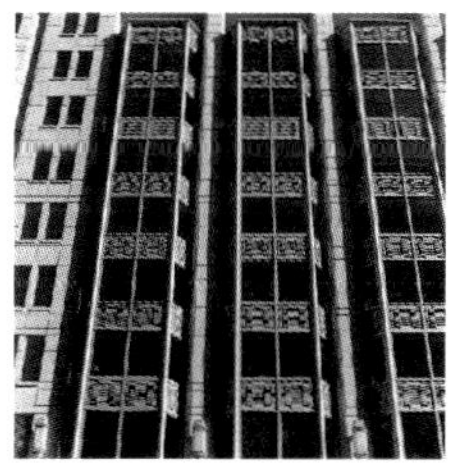

114 Office building at 555 Twelfth Street, 1994. Florance, Eichbaum, Esocoff, and King, architects. Metal panels on window bays evoke New York Art-Deco skyscrapers.

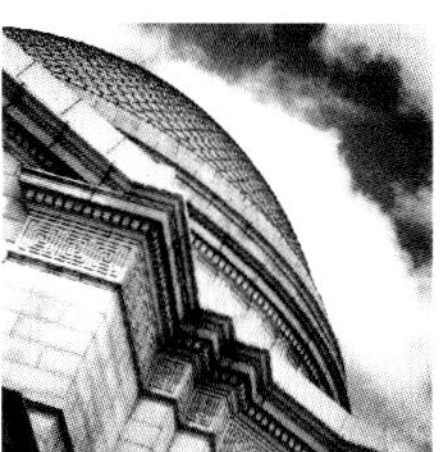

115 Detail of National Museum of Natural History, Constitution Avenue between Ninth and Twelfth Streets. Designed by the firm Hornblower and Marshall in 1911, this domed museum houses many of the nation's more esoteric natural treasures.

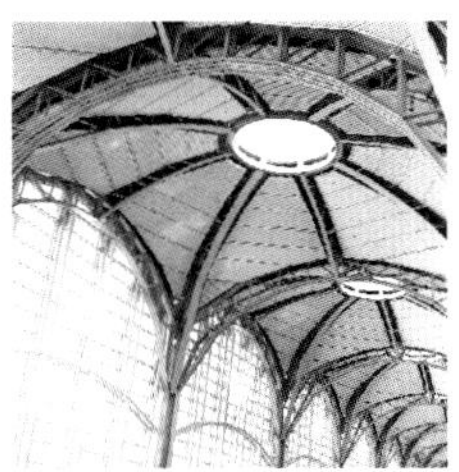

116 Ronald Reagan National Airport (formerly National Airport). Located just across the Potomac from Kennedy Center, the airport was more than large enough to serve the needs of the city when it opened in the 1930s. Despite expansion after expansion, one could hardly make that claim today. A 1996 addition by architect Cesar Pelli is shown here.

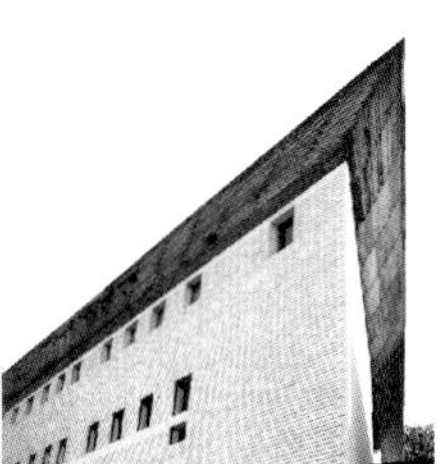

117 Italian Embassy, Whitehaven and Massachusetts Avenues. Opened in 2000, this nicely crafted addition to Embassy Row stands apart from its neighbors in at least two respects. First, it is avowedly modernist in style. And second, it was designed in two distinct sections to reflect, said architect Piero Sartogo, the ideological rivalry in contemporary Italy between conservatives and progressives.

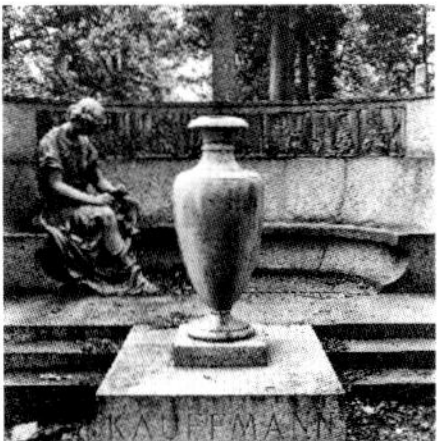

119 William Kauffman Monument, Rock Creek Cemetery, Rock Creek Church Road, 1906. William Ordway Partridge, sculptor. Rock Creek Cemetery, the oldest in the city, contains many exemplary monuments and memorials. Among the finest is this peaceful neoclassical creation featuring a bronze seated female figure in front of low-relief panels depicting the seven stages of life as portrayed in Shakespeare's *As You Like It*.

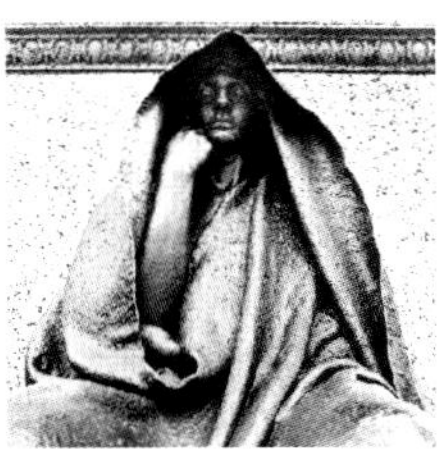

120 Adams Monument, Rock Creek Cemetery, 1890. This fine memorial was created by the masterful Augustus Saint-Gaudens (statue) and Stanford White (base). Titled *The Peace of God that Passeth Understanding*, it has drawn praise from the beginning. Lorado Taft, who sculpted Columbus Fountain at Union Station, said that to look at the shrouded figure's face is like "confronting eternity." See **119**

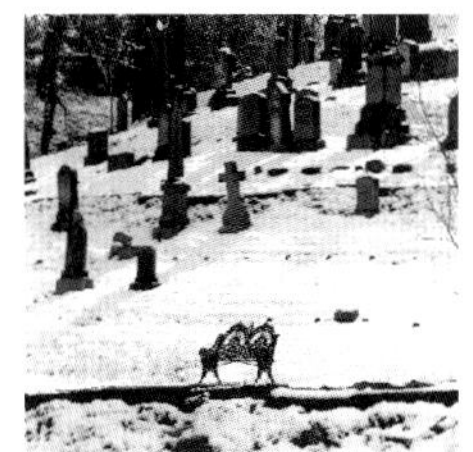

121 Mount Zion Cemetery, Thirtieth and Q Streets. In segregated nineteenth-century Georgetown, black Americans were buried on these rolling acres.

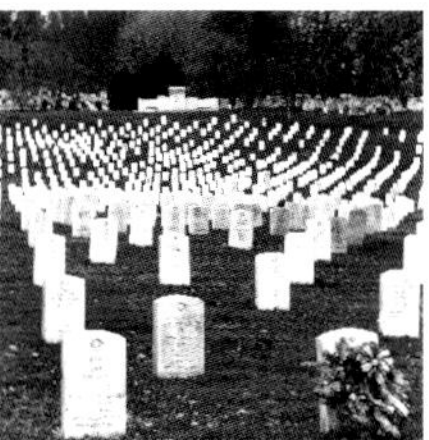

122 Arlington National Cemetery, Arlington, Virginia. A quiet, shady oasis in the midst of an ever-expanding suburbia, these 420 acres are held in reverence by all Americans. Since the first interment was made here during the Civil War, more than 200,000 war dead, medal-of-honor recipients, and high-ranking government officials have found their final resting place at Arlington.

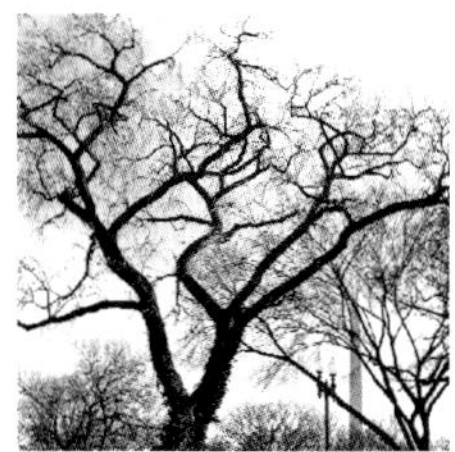

123 Washington Monument, the Mall. Soaring some 555 feet into the sky, this is the tallest masonry structure in the world. Planned as long ago as 1783 (when George Washington was still very much alive), actual work on the monument didn't start until July 4, 1848. Designed by architect Robert Mills, the monument suffered a chaotic and near-farcical construction history that belies its simple, elegant form. Today the monument, instantly recognizable by virtually anyone, anywhere, stands as a symbol for the city and an icon for the nation. See **91**

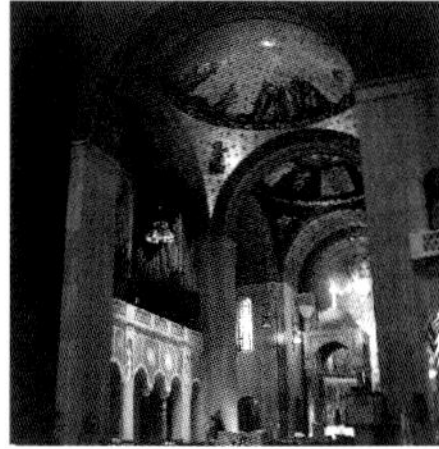

124 National Shrine of the Immaculate Conception, Fourth Street and Michigan Avenue, 1920. Many are surprised to learn that Washington ranks second only to Rome as a center of Catholicism. The District boasts two Catholic colleges, thirty-four seminaries, the seat of the Catholic Welfare League, and this, the largest Roman Catholic church in the country (it can seat 3,000). Architects Maginnis and Walsh melded Romanesque and Byzantine styles with what seem like acres of mosaics.

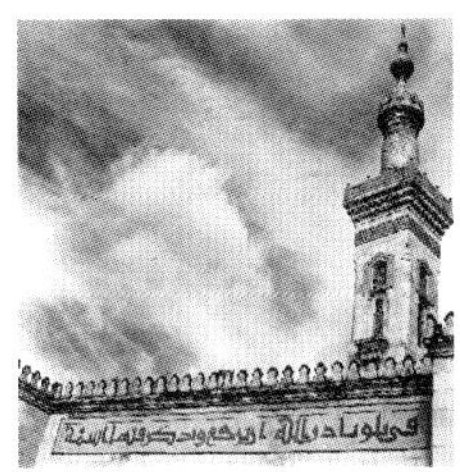

125 Islamic Center, 2551 Massachusetts Avenue. Completed in 1949 and designed by architects in the Egyptian Ministry of Works, this steel-framed mosque serves as the official religious center for all American Moslems. The building faces Mecca and its rich contents—magnificent carpets, ivory-inlaid furniture, and elaborate mosaics—make it a dazzling museum of Arabic art.

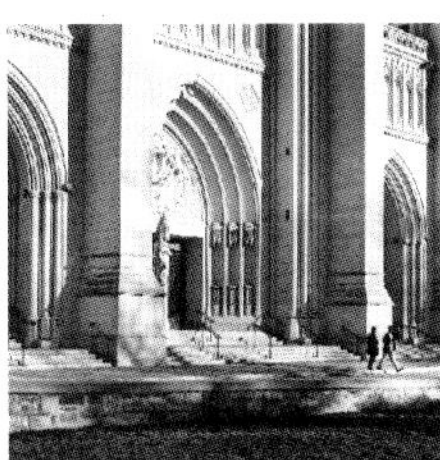

126 Washington National Cathedral. See **23**

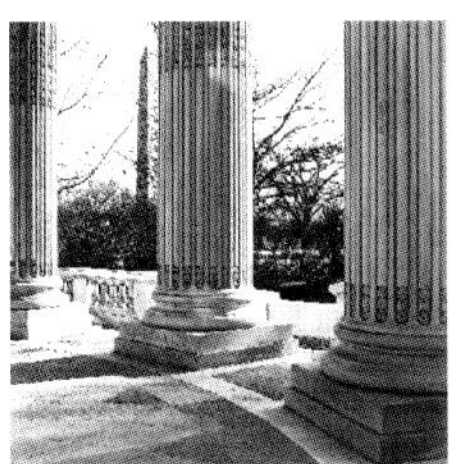

127 Continental Memorial Hall, Seventeenth and C Streets, 1910. Edward Pearce Casey, architect. This conservatively neoclassical, white-marble-sheathed auditorium and library was commissioned by the Daughters of the American Revolution.

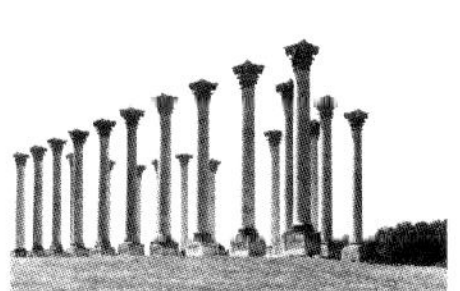

128 National Arboretum, Twenty-fourth and R Streets. Spread over 444 hilly acres, the arboretum is a favored picnic spot and a center of serious horticultural research, but the site's most visually striking feature doesn't grow at all. It is the group of twenty-two 34-foot-tall Corinthian columns removed from the Capitol during a 1950s remodeling, rescued and re-erected here in 1990.

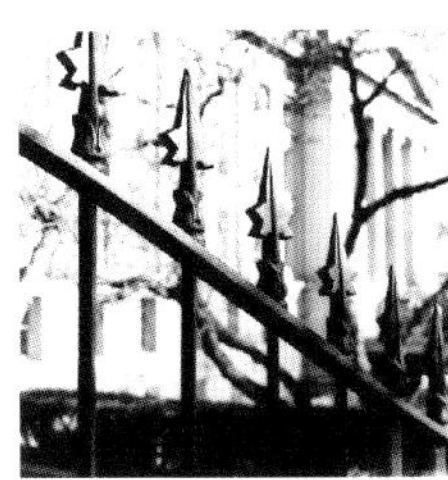

129 The spiky wrought-iron fence of the Treasury Building. See **18**

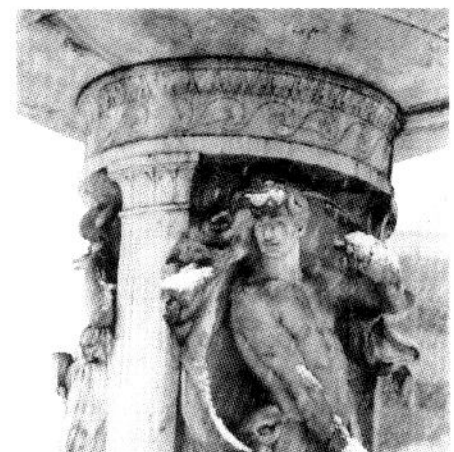

130 Dupont Circle. In 1882, Congress voted to commemorate Civil War hero Admiral Samuel Francis du Pont (1803-1865) by naming a circle for him and erecting a small bronze statue at its center. That didn't quite please du Pont's gunpowder-manufacturing relatives, who circumvented the federal government and paid to have the present (and far grander) statue-cum-fountain, by Daniel Chester French, erected instead. See **57**, **58**, **61**

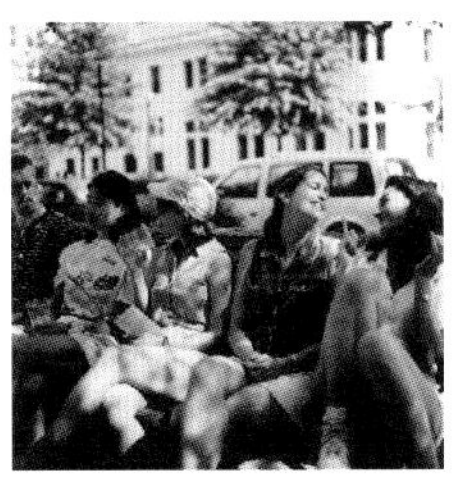

131 On Indiana Avenue, tourists and natives alike bask in the gentle sunshine that characterizes Washington's lengthy springs.

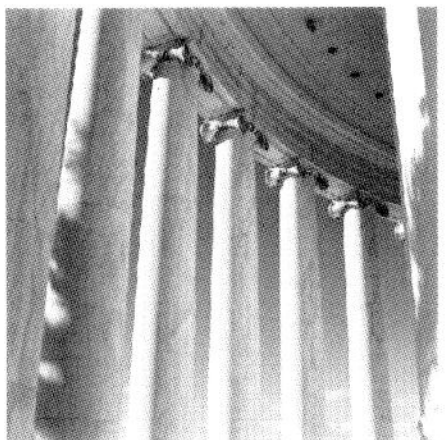

146 Detail of Jefferson Memorial. See **37**

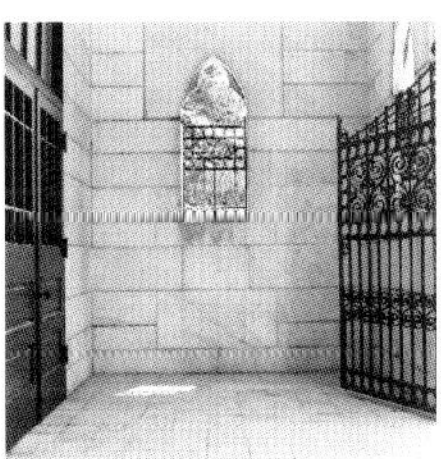

148 Entrance to the chapel at Stanley Hall, U.S. Soldiers' and Airmen's Home. See **109**

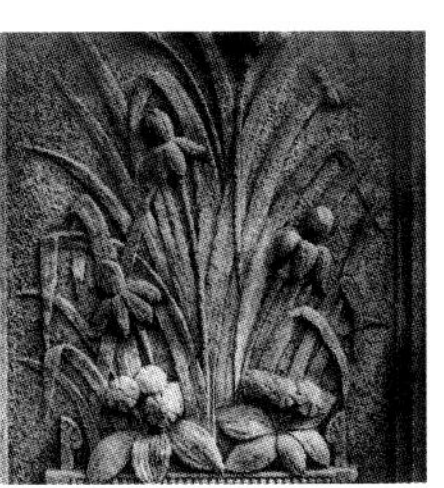

151 Sandstone relief panel, Capitol grounds.

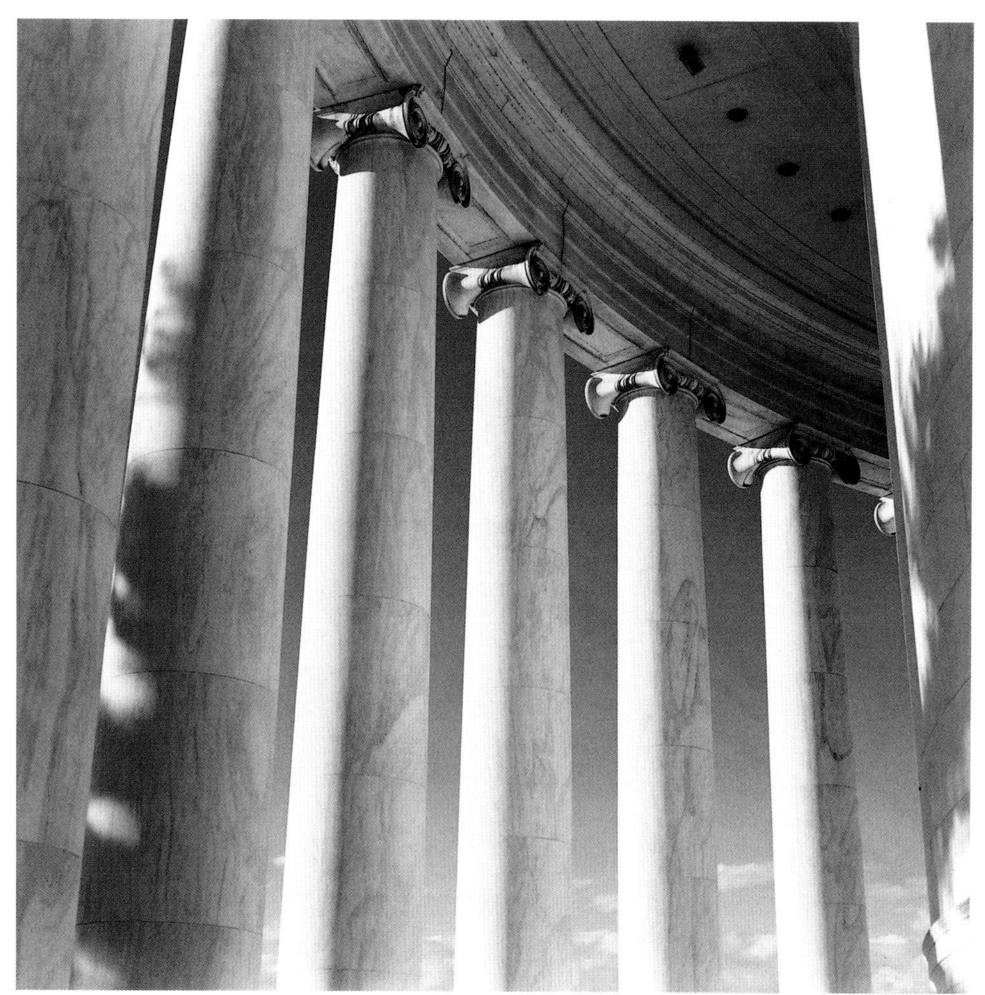

Jefferson Memorial

BIBLIOGRAPHY

Cox, Warren J., Hugh Newell Jacobsen, Francis D. Lethbridge, and David R. Rosenthal. *A Guide to the Architecture of Washington, D.C.* (New York: McGraw-Hill, 1974).

Goode, James M. *The Outdoor Sculpture of Washington, D.C.: A Comprehensive Historical Guide* (Washington, D.C.: Smithsonian Institution Press, 1974).

Goode, James, and Judith Waldrop Frank, with photographs by Volkmar Kurt Wentzel. *Washington by Night* (Washington, D.C.: Starwood, 1992).

Gutheim, Frederick, and William E. Washburn. *The Federal City, Plans & Realities* (Washington, D.C.: Smithsonian Institution Press, 1976).

Kousoulas, Claudia D., and George W. Kousoulas. *Contemporary Architecture in Washington, D.C.* (Washington, D.C.: The Preservation Press, 1995).

L'Enfant, Pierre Charles. Papers (Manuscript Division, Library of Congress).

Lowry, Bates. *Building a National Image: Architectural Drawings for the American Democracy, 1789-1912* (Washington, D.C.: National Building Museum, 1985).

Reps, John W. *Washington on View: The Nation's Capital Since 1790* (Chapel Hill: University of North Carolina Press, 1991).

Scott, Pamela, and Antoinette J. Lee. *Buildings of the District of Columbia* (New York: Oxford University Press, 1993).

Weeks, Christopher. *AIA Guide to the Architecture of Washington, D.C.*, Third Edition (Baltimore: The Johns Hopkins University Press, 1994).

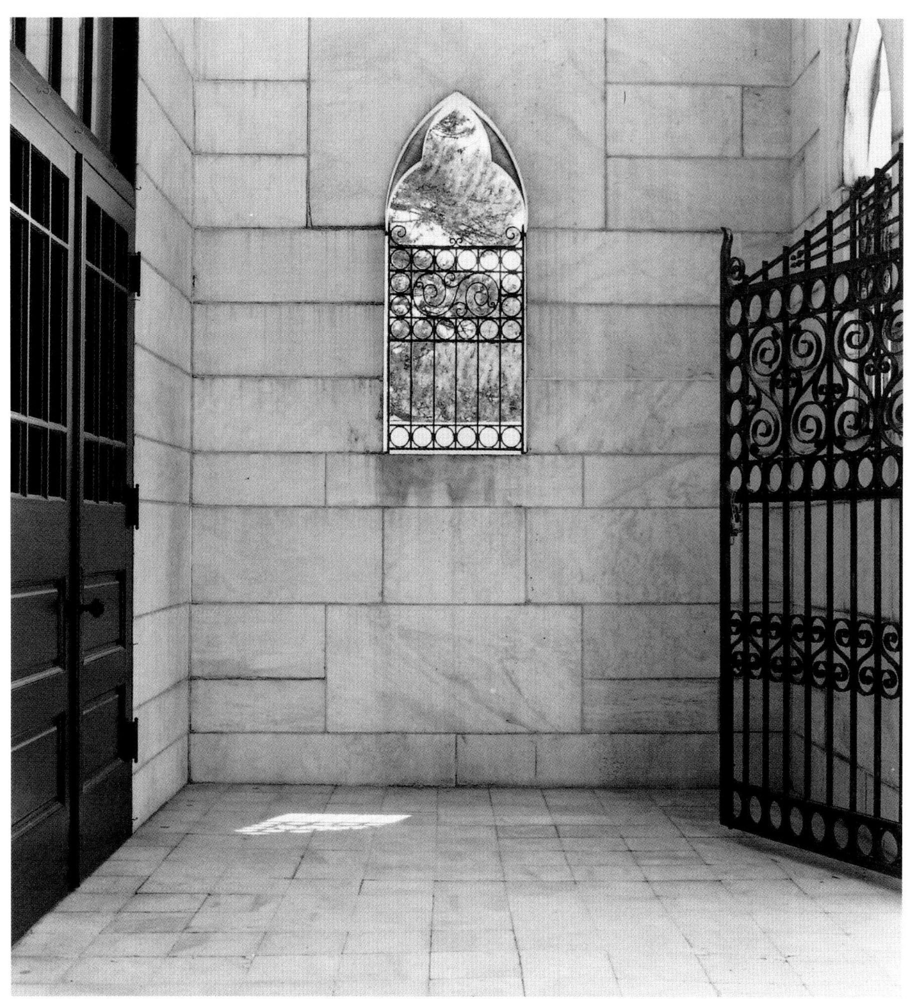

U.S. Soldiers' and Airmen's Home

ACKNOWLEDGMENTS

This portfolio of Washington was inspired by the belief that most photographs of the city's buildings and monuments have depicted their monumentality but few have captured their richness of form and detail. My goal in these pages was to bring this richness to light.

Serendipity played an important role. Often, the image that appears in this book is not what I expected to shoot but was the shot over my shoulder, or across the street. And, as in all worthwhile endeavors, there were frustrations. There were many repeat visits to capture a building under just the right conditions, and it sometimes seemed that just when the season was right for a particular shot, construction cranes or scaffolding would appear overnight. So I am quite thankful to the many people who made the effort a little easier.

First, I thank Buckley Jeppson, who worked with me on my previous book and recommended me for this one. I also thank David L. Boren, who provided gracious introduction to his friend, and former colleague, Daniel Patrick Moynihan. I would also like to thank Helen Dalrymple of the Library of Congress and Kerri Childress of the U.S. Soldiers' and Airmen's Home, both of whom gave unstintingly of their time. Paula Mohr, curator of the U.S. Treasury, was especially helpful in guiding me through one of the oldest public buildings in Washington.

There were many others who provided valuable expertise and guidance in the creation of the book itself. They include Christopher Weeks, a consultant on this project and an exemplary writer on American architecture; Bruce Campbell, this book's masterful designer; and Maya Khazarian Lea, its patient yet rigorous copy editor. A special acknowledgment must go to John Graham Tucker, publisher of Norfleet Press, whose editorial skills kept pushing and honing the collection of images that became this book. Others who gave generously of their time or talent were Matthew Cloud, Barry Lewis, James Owen Mathews, David Rippey, Alan Kaufman, Carmen Tucker, Gladys Tucker, Nancy Freeman, and Joan Farrell.

Finally, I thank my wife Claudia, who indulged hundreds of hours in the darkroom refining the prints, and my son Matthew, who was a welcome companion on my many weekend shoots.

George Kousoulas
Bethesda, Maryland

The text for this book was composed in Bembo,
a typeface based on the Roman type originally cut for
Aldus Manutius by Francisco Griffo in 1495.
Typesetting by Aardvark Editorial, New Haven, Connecticut.
Duotone separations, printing, and binding by
Mondadori Printing, S.p.A., Verona, Italy.
Text paper and endleaves are archival quality.

Book design by Bruce Campbell

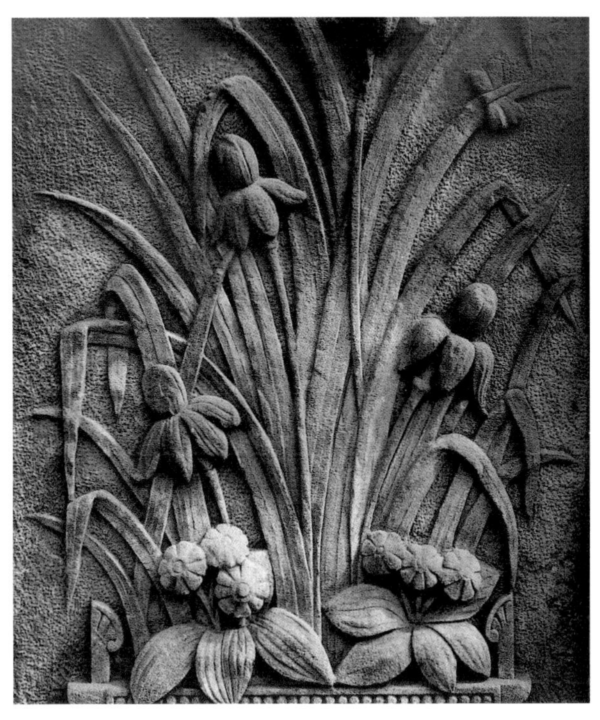